TH. A. FISCHER

THE SCOTS IN EASTERN

AND

WESTERN PRUSSIA

A SEQUEL TO

"THE SCOTS IN GERMANY,

A CONTRIBUTION TOWARDS THE HISTORY

OF THE SCOT ABROAD"

Elibron Classics
www.elibron.com

Elibron Classics series.

© 2005 Adamant Media Corporation.

ISBN 1-4021-9250-9 (paperback)
ISBN 1-4021-1771-X (hardcover)

This Elibron Classics Replica Edition is an unabridged facsimile
of the edition published in 1903 by Otto Schulze & Co.,
Edinburgh.

THE SCOTS IN EASTERN AND WESTERN PRUSSIA.

FELDMARSCHALL KEITH

THE SCOTS IN EASTERN

AND

WESTERN PRUSSIA

A SEQUEL TO

"THE SCOTS IN GERMANY

A CONTRIBUTION TOWARDS THE HISTORY

OF THE SCOT ABROAD"

BY

TH. A. FISCHER

TRANSLATOR OF "SARTOR RESARTUS"

AUTHOR OF

"DAS LEBEN CARLYLE'S;" "LEBEN UND WERKE ALFRED LORD TENNYSON'S;"
"DREI STUDIEN ZUR ENGLISCHEN LITERATURGESCHICHTE;"
"THE SCOTS IN GERMANY," ETC.

WITH SEVEN PORTRAITS AND A MAP

OTTO SCHULZE & CO.

20 SOUTH FREDERICK STREET, EDINBURGH

1903

Dedicated

TO THE

SENATUS ACADEMICUS

OF

ABERDEEN

PREFACE.

To a conscientious author the writing of a Preface never will be an agreeable task. Now that the work is finished, and no change of style or any additional subject matter can be introduced, all the shortcomings of his book arise before him enlarged and made painfully visible to the critical reader as if through Röntgen rays.

Whilst this is an experience common to all authors in a world where everything goes by approximation only, my present case is worse. I have not only to acknowledge the general human frailty, but to begin with special apologies. First, concerning the title. I am aware that the title of this volume is too narrow, but it could not very well be made longer, knowing that long titles, once essential to a book, are now a fatal dowry on its way. I have therefore availed myself of the very modern and highly diplomatic method of making excursions into the "Hinterland," that is, to Poland proper, to Pomerania and Mecklenburg. A second apology is due to the reader on account of the portraits, which, with one or two exceptions, ought to have had their places in the *Scots in Germany*. The difficulty of procuring them, and the fact that both my volumes are really one, may serve as an excuse.

A much more grateful task remains: that of placing on record the very kind help received in Germany and elsewhere during the time of collecting materials for this volume. My best thanks are due to the Rev. *J. Milne*, M.A., minister of Newlands Parish, Peeblesshire, who not only granted me the free use of his excellent polyglot library, but also looked over my proofs; to Archivrath *Dr Joachim* and staff at the Royal Archives, Königsberg, in Prussia; to Archivrath *Dr Bär* and staff at the Royal

Archives, Danzig; to the *Director* of the Episcopal
Archives at Frauenburg; to Archivrath *Dr Warschauer*
at Posen; to Geheimrath *John Gibsone*, and the elders of
the Presbyterian Church at Danzig; to the Rev. *Ladislas
Sarna*, Szebnie near Moderowka in Galicia;—for the
kind assistance given me in my researches; to the *Director*
of the Hohenzollern Museum at *Berlin*, to the *Provost and
Bailies* of *Stonehaven*, to the *Historical Society* at Würzburg,
to the *Lord Abbot* of *Fort Augustus*, to the *Directors* of
the Picture Gallery at *Danzig*, and of the Royal Bavarian
Observatory at *Bogenhausen* near Munich;—for their kind
permission to reproduce paintings or sketches in their
possession.

The original of Field-marshal Keith, painted by Ramsay,
adorns the walls of Town-hall at Stonehaven; the small
sketch of his aged brother, the last Earl Marischal, is
taken from the original in possession of Prince Eulenburg
at Berlin.   Abbot Arbuthnot's portrait is in the library of
the Abbey at Fort Augustus, Abbot Asloan's in Würzburg.   The portraits of the two Danzig celebrities are
gratefully preserved in the museum of their adopted home,
whilst the Observatory at Bogenhausen harbours the
original likeness of its famous astronomer Lamont.

I have also to thank Herrn Eugen Jantzen at Stettin, who
has made most diligent researches into the genealogy of
the families of foreign settlers at Danzig, for the permission of using his sketches of Scottish coats-of-arms.

The map, I hope, will be useful not only as proving the
decreasing density of Scottish emigration as it advanced
towards the West, but also as a companion and guide for
those Scottish travellers who may wish to visit these far-off
scenes of the labours and sufferings of their countrymen.

THE AUTHOR.

EDINBURGH, *April* 21, 1903.

CONTENTS.

INTRODUCTORY.

NOTABLE PERIODS IN THE HISTORY OF DANZIG
AND KÖNIGSBERG.

DANZIG, now the Capital of the Province of Western Prussia, was, in the years

1200-1310 capital of Pomerellen.

During 1310-1454 it was ruled by the Teutonic Order of Knights;

Since 1360 it joined the Hanseatic League.

From 1454-1793 it belonged to Poland, though retaining many privileges.

In 1793 it was ceded to Prussia.

1807-1814 French Government.

1814 Finally ceded to Prussia.

DANZIG's internal affairs were ruled over by the so-called three Orders besides the "Burggraf" as representative of the King of Poland; four burgomasters and councillors; bailies elected by the council from the citizens; and the so-called "Hundertmannen" = hundred men, representing *the trades.*

Königsberg, now the capital of Eastern Prussia, consists of the three old towns of Altstadt, Kneiphof and Löbenicht. It owes its existence to the Teutonic Order. This famous and valiant body of knights erected a castle on the river Pregel in 1255, which was called in honour perhaps of Ottokar II., King of Bohemia, who had supported the cause of the knights in one of their crusades, Königsburg or -berg. Soon after the Altstadt arose round the castle (1256). The so-called Löbenicht, or New Town, was founded as a separate township about 1300, and the town of Kneiphof on an island of the river Pregel about the same time. Hence the denomination of the "three towned" Königsberg. After the fall of the Marienburg, the old residence of the Hochmeister of the Teutonic Knights during a disastrous war with Poland in 1457, Königsberg became the seat of the Grand Master of the Order. The last of them was Markgraf Albrecht of Brandenburg, a scion of the House of Hohenzollern, who resided here as Duke of Prussia. He converted the possessions of the Order into a hereditary secular Protestant Duchy. After the demise of the ducal line, the Duchy passed to the Kurbrandenburg line of Hohenzollern, and the famous "Great Elector" received homage at the Castle of Königsberg as Sovereign Duke of Prussia in 1663. Here also Frederick III., Elector of Brandenburg, crowned himself with the royal crown, and raised Brandenburg-Prussia to a kingdom (1701). During the Napoleonic tyranny, King Frederick William III. and his Queen Luise resided in Königsberg in 1807-8. Königsberg has a university. It is the native place of the great philosopher Kant, whose grandfather was of humble Scotch origin.[1]

[1] See *Scots in Germany*, pp. 231 ff., 317.

PART I.

THE SCOTTISH TRADER.

THE SCOTS IN EASTERN AND WESTERN
PRUSSIA.

THE fact of a large emigration of Scotsmen to Prussia
and Poland during the XVIth and XVIIth centuries has
hitherto either escaped the notice of the Scottish historian
altogether, or been deemed by him too unimportant an
item to be registered in his pages. He has not forgotten
the fame of the Scottish warriors in the armies of France
or Sweden, whose heroic deeds commanded the admiration
of the world; but where the Scot lived out a quiet life of
suffering, hardships, countless struggles bravely met, and
final successes tenaciously secured, his claim to be remembered by the future historian has been brushed aside; his
tombstone and his name have been forgotten.

This neglect would have been, and would be, excusable
if the Scot abroad, rapidly and entirely losing his in-
dividuality, had at once become amalgamated with the
new hosts among whom he lived. But so little has this
been the case, that a learned German writer of to-day
says: "A very characteristic element of the population
of German towns in Eastern and Western Prussia is
formed by the descendants of former Scotsmen. They
being exposed to many dangers and persecutions as pedlars,
gradually settled in the towns and married daughters of
the citizens. The increase in strength and industrial
capacity which this Scottish admixture instilled into the
German was of the very highest importance, and it can

scarcely be doubted that the peculiar compound of stubbornness and shrewdness which characterises the inhabitants of
the small towns of Eastern Prussia has its root in the
natural disposition of the Scot." [1]

The proof of this assertion can be found in innumerable
instances, which, though not written largely in the annals
of political history, nor proclaimed loudly by the blare of
military trumpets, are still interesting and dear to those
students of history that see in it more than an illimitable
ghastly stretch of battlefields or the hopelessly tangled
web of political intrigue.

It is this "vie intime" of the Scot in Germany that is
to form the main substance of the present volume. The
facts of the Scottish settlements have been stated; it now
remains to fill up the sketch and to present to the reader
as complete a picture as possible of how the Scot lived in
those remote regions that they had chosen as the scene
of their enterprise.

Before entering upon our task let us clear up two mis-
conceptions that might arise out of our former statements.
We have almost exclusively spoken of the Scottish
immigration of the XVIth and XVIIth Centuries. We
are now compelled to admit the existence of the Scottish
pedlar, in German called "Schotte," in the XIVth Century,
though not without hesitation. The word "Schotte"
unmistakably occurs in this sense in the Krämerrolle of
Anclam, i.e. the constitution of the guild of grocers or
small merchants in the Pomeranian town of Anclam, dating
as far back as 1330.[2]

---

[1] Dr F. Schmidt, Geschichte des Deutsch Kroner Kreises, *History of
the district of Deutsch Krone* (Western Prussia), p. 145.

[2] The original document has since been lost; it was first printed by
Stavenhagen in 1773. The passage itself runs: "Tho deme so scholen

Now as it is difficult from Scotch sources to prove an emigration of Scotsmen to Germany at that early date sufficiently large to warrant the expression "Schotte" for the swarms of vagrant pedlars all over Germany, one is almost tempted to inquire whether this name at the period we speak of might not have a derivation altogether independent of nationality. But no other derivation has been put forward, and all our lexicographers headed by the successors of Grimm in the recent volume of the great German Dictionary adhere to the old meaning. There are, moreover, other laws and constitutions nearly as old as that of Anclam, which leave no doubt as to the meaning of "Schotte."

Among the oldest rules of the cloth merchants at Stralsund, and dating back to about 1370, we find this: "Vortmer so schal nen Schotte *edder Engelsman* varen in de lant, he sy we he sy";[1] and a little later, about the year 1412: "Nyn borger de nicht hefft de werdicheit der cumpanien des wantsnedes, Schotten *edder Engelsman* schal nicht varen yn de landen edder hyr bynnen der stadt sniden he sy we he sy ane he hebbe de werdicheit der kumpanien des wantsnedes," *i.e.* No citizen who has not obtained the dignity of a guild - brother of the cloth merchant's guild, no Scot or Englishman shall travel about the country or cut (cloth) within this town, let him be who he may be, without his being a member of the guild.[2] Both these passages prove by the addition of "edder Engelsman" that "Schotte" cannot be taken in any

---

hir keine Schotten edder andere tafelichskremer . . . lynewandt edder andere kramware van huse to huse dragen " ; *i.e.* Moreover no Scots or other dealers in linen ware shall in this place carry linen or other retail goods from house to house. Cp. Fock, *Rügen Pommersche Geschichte*, iii. 250.

[1] Cp. *Scots in Germany.*   [2] Fock, *l.c.* iv. 214, 216.

other sense than that of Scotsman, a native of Scotland. We must therefore assume a much earlier date for the itinerant Scot in Germany, unless we suppose that the word Schotte, Scotus, in those earlier centuries referred to the Irish. There seems to be some show of reason in this, as the expression "Schotte" for a vagrant pedlar is also common in Bavaria and the south of Germany, where the Irish had established the so-called "Schotten-klöster."[1] We are told as early as the VIIIth Century that vagrant priests, called Scotti, passed themselves off as bishops. Be this as it may, of wide-spread Scotch settlements properly so-called we hear nothing till eight or nine centuries later.

A second misconception may arise from passages[2] where it was stated that the situation of the Scot in Germany was tolerable, that his lot was not worse than that of the pedlar at home, that he suffered no religious persecution and obtained many privileges. These state-ments are rather too favourable. The obstacles put in the way of the Scot, particularly of the travelling trades-man, were innumerable. Only when he had succeeded in obtaining the rights of citizenship in the smaller or larger towns of Prussia did his difficulties diminish; and to obtain these rights was for many a hopeless task. Religious persecutions in the old cruel sense, it is true, did not obtain, but nevertheless, the Calvinistic Scot was not looked upon with favour by his proud Lutheran brother of Germany; in his eye he was an Arian, worse than an unbeliever and an anabaptist. This was a weapon

---

[1] See Schmeller, *Bairisches Wörterbuch*. The Police Regulations of Nürnberg prohibit the harbouring or housing of any vagrant Scotsman or Scotswoman in the town or within a mile around it without permission of the magistrates (XVth Century). [2] *The Scots in Germany*, p. 50.

that was used with virulence and success by the hostile trades. Only the unwearied and indomitable energy of the Scot, combined with physical endurance as great as his skill and his shrewdness as merchant and banker, made him succeed in many cases and obtain the highest honours in the country of his adoption.

SCOTLAND AND PRUSSIA IN THE XVTH CENTURY.

Whilst we hear but little of Scottish settlements in Germany at this time, notices are not wanting of the brisk commercial intercourse between Scotland and Danzig and between Scotland and the Teutonic Order, which from a religious Society of Knights for the defence and the spreading of Christianity had rapidly grown not only into a territorial Power, but also into a huge commercial trading society. Thus King Henry IV. of England requests the Hochmeister von Jungingen to grant the Scottish shipmasters who were then sailing to Prussia in order to bring home cargoes of food-stuffs, neither favour nor protection (Dec. 7, 1401). Königsberg writes to the Gubernator of Scotland, Rupert, " duci Albaniae et comiti de Fiff," with the request to order the restoration of goods confiscated from some Königsberg merchants (July 23, 1418) ; whilst the magistrates of Edinburgh petition the Hochmeister to make the city of Danzig raise the arrest put upon the goods of various Scottish merchants in Danske, notably of James Lawdre, Jacob King and Robert Young, " for Scotland had been altogether innocent of the alleged spoliation of Danzig merchants."[1] In a similar case King James I.

[1] The undated letter is to be found in the Königlichen Staats Archiv at Königsberg.   On account of Jac. Lawdre Queen Mary also writes to the Hochmeister in 1448.

writes two letters to the Hochmeister blaming a Prussian merchant called Claus Zarn or Czarn for the arrestment of Scottish goods (10th of March and 26th of March 142?).

The dreaded Earl of March appears again in the records of Danzig writing about the liberation of a Danzig citizen called Johann Lange, and charging a Scot, Ricardus de Camera, with the conclusion of a commercial treaty.[1]

Under the date of April 13th, 1438, there exists the rough draught of a letter of the Hochmeister to the King of Scotland and the Guild of Merchants in Edinburgh, praying them to hand over the goods which the merchant Heinrich Holthusen left behind him at his death in Leith, to the Danzig merchant Johann Fischmeister.[2]

Mayor and Bailies of "St Johann" in Scocia (Perth) announce in a letter that by a decision of the law-courts the claim of the Danzig skipper, Hanneke How, must be disallowed (Jan. 20, 1439). Somewhat later King James recommends the Edinburgh merchant, John Foulis, who with some business friends is travelling to Danzig, to the notice of the magistrates there (March 28, 1475); "quatenus auxilio Dei et vestro salve redeant." A letter of recommendation is also given by the magistrates of Edinburgh to Jacob Crag, who is going to Danzig on law business (1480). Similarly, Queen Margaret and King James intercede on behalf of the Scottish merchants, Thomas Halkerston, Thomas Lewis, and Robert Paisley (April 8, 1482). In every way the interest of the

[1] Letter written "apud castrum nostrum de Dunbar," 26th of Aug., N.D., in the *Kgl. Staats Archiv*, Danzig.

[2] *Kgl. St. Archiv*, Königsberg.

Scottish trader seems to have been well taken care of. Instances of this are found in two other letters addressed to Danzig. In one of them Edinburgh declares that Stephen Lawson, a citizen of Haddington, had honestly paid for all goods which he had brought from Danzig to Leith about four years ago (June 5, 1483). Interesting is a letter from the magistrates of Aberdeen to Danzig in which they express themselves grieved at the fact that ships from that city for some time past sail to more remote ports of Scotland instead of to Aberdeen; and they declare themselves willing to indemnify the cloth merchant of Danzig who had suffered loss at Aberdeen on account of spurious money being given to him in payment, if he would personally appear before them. They pray that the old commercial intercourse should be restored.[1] About the same time Aberdeen further proves her goodwill by explaining to the Danzig magistrates that all assistance would be given to the Danzig citizens, Vasolt and Conrad (or Connert), on their arrival in Scotland, to obtain payment for goods sold; and in a later letter she explains to Danzig the measures taken for this purpose, adding the testimony of merchants from Stralsund, Greipwald and Stettin.[2]

The brothers John and Francis Tulane are appointed to take care of the commissioner sent by Conrad to Aberdeen.

Besides Aberdeen and Leith, Dundee is again mentioned in 1492 as trading with Danzig, and the name of Thomas Spalding occurs in this connection.

How important the trade between the Baltic ports and Scotland was, is also seen from a notice in *Weinreich's*

---

[1] Letter dated Aberdeen, May 1st, 1487, *Kl. Staats Archiv.*, Danzig.
[2] Letters dated Aug. 6, 1487, and July 18th, 1489, *Kgl. Staats Archiv*, Danzig.

Prussian Chronicle, where it is stated that between the years 1474 and 1476 twenty-four Scottish ships entered the harbour of Danzig.[1]

Thus the names of the great Baltic ports were well known to the trading communities of Scotland, and the way was prepared for the Scottish emigrant.

What attracted them to Danzig besides the shipping facilities was a tradition that there they would be the recipients of numerous privileges granted—perhaps in grateful recollection of military assistance—by the Hoch-meister to the English and Scots. Frequently they refer to these privileges in their petitions—chiefly to a free retail trade throughout the country—but, as their adversaries tauntingly said, they " could never produce them." They remained merely traditional, though the names of the Hochmeisters, Paul von Russdorf—about 1426—is mentioned in connection with the matter. At any rate, if they ever possessed these privileges, every trace of them was lost in the XVIth Century, as indeed it was much more in the spirit of the times to disfranchise people than to grant them trading liberties.

However this may be, the Scots are present in Danzig, though not in great numbers, early in the XVth Century.[2]

They are not unfrequently met with in the minutes of the courts of justice (Schöppenbücher) there. Walter, a Scot and a dyer by trade, owns to certain debts in 1447 ; in 1453, on the 23rd of march, the Magistrates compose a quarrel between a citizen and a Scottish merchant ; another Scot, called Thomas, sues a citizen for the debt of twenty-six marks in 1469. More serious is the following entry : " A settlement has been arranged between

---

[1] Dr Theod. Hirsch, *Weinreich's Chronik.*, p. xi.
[2] English cloth is mentioned in Danzig in 1388.

Claus Wugerson, on the one part, and Peter Black, a Scot, on the other, on account of manslaughter committed by the aforesaid Peter Black against Reemer Wugerson, brother of the aforesaid Claus." Peter consents to pay certain sums of money, and to undertake a " Sühn-reise," *i.e.* a journey of expiation " to the holy Blood at Aken (Aix la Chapelle), to Einsiedelen, a famous place of pilgrimage in Switzerland, to St Jacob of Compostella, and to St Adrian, and to bring good proofs of his having visited these places " (1471).[1]

A similar compromise is entered upon four years later in 1475 between Wylm (William) Watson and Zander (Alexander) Gustis (?) "on account of a wound given by Zander to the aforesaid Wylm."[2] They decided that the culprit should bear all expenses, and undertake a pilgrimage to the Holy Blood, and, moreover, give to the Altar of the Scots in the Church of the Black Monks at Danzig two marks, and likewise two marks to Our Lady's Church at Dundee in Scotland. Therewith all dispute should be ended for ever (" geendet unde gelendet ").[3]

That the Scots had their own Altar at the Schwarz-mönchenkirche, as it is called, is an additional proof of

[1] " Eene Berichtunge is gescheen tuschen Claus Wugerson (Wugersyn?) vun eyne und tuschen Peter Black, eyne Schotten, van dem andern deele als van eynes dodslages wegen den de vorben. Peter Black an Reemer Wugerson des vorges Claus broder begangen hefft." . . . *Kgl. St. Archiv*, Danzig.

[2] " Eene Berichtunge is gescheen tuschen . . . van eyner wunde wegen de . . . Zander an dem vorbem. Wylm gewracht hefft . . . also dat Zander up sik genamen hefft alle ungelt . . . unde sal ok gan eyne hillige blodes reyse unde ok geven to den Schotten Altar hir to den swarten moneken 2 mark unde sal ok II. mark geven to unser leiwen vronwen kerke to Dondyn yn Schottlande gelegen . . ." *Kgl. St. Archiv*, Danzig.

[3] *Kgl. St. Archiv*, Danzig.

the importance of their commercial intercourse with Danzig.

The names of other Scotsmen, together with their debts, are entered in the Schöppenbuch; *e.g.*, John Wylinck, curiously enough called "de swartte Schotte," the black Scotsman; William Simpson, Robert Lofftus and Richard, in 1427; also Will. Patrick in 1429, and Fenton and Grant in 1430.

In consequence of the many acts of piracy in Scottish waters Heinrick Vorrath, the Burgomaster of Danzig, advises the Prussian and German ships to carry arms and ammunition (March 12th, 1437).[1]

Another curious light is shed on the political state of Great Britain and the neutral attitude of the Teutonic Order, by a complaint of the English merchants in the year 1439. They tell the woeful tale of a ship from Hull to Prussia called Peter and carrying a rich cargo. "When we came to the Baltic, we came upon three ships from Scotland by which we were in warlike manner attacked during the night. But by the Grace of God the English held their own, and took the Scottish ships together with their goods. Then the Scottish said to the English: "We know that we have done you great harm; therefore we ask you from a full heart to make known to us the estimate of the damage." And it was estimated then at two hundred and forty pounds sterling. And the Scottish placed five of their number as hostages on board of the English ship whilst the others were allowed to sail away unhurt. Now when the English brought these five with them into Prussia, they were compelled by the Hochmeister to set them free and release their goods, and it was done. After this the

---

[1] *Hanserecesse*, 2nd Series, ii. 49.

Komptur of Danczke sent for the skippers and the merchants of the said ship, and ordered thirteen of them to be cast into prison, where they were nearly suffocated and scarcely got out alive. Still they had to pay to the Komptur twenty-four mark in Prussian coin, and a piece of cloth to the value of twenty mark in order to be liberated."[1]

On the whole, the information to be gathered regarding the Scots in Prussia during this century is but small. It is only in the next century that light is thrown upon the difficulties and hardships of their life.

THE SCOTTISH PEDLAR AND SETTLER IN PRUSSIA IN THE XVITH AND XVIITH CENTURIES.

It is well to remember that a distinction has always to be made between the itinerant trader, the "institor circumforaneus," as the Latin documents call him, or the "umbfahrende Schotte" of the German, and between those of his countrymen, who had settled in the towns as "foreign guests," as smaller or larger tradesmen, some

[1] " Item clagen die Engelischen koufflewte das im jar 1439 eyn schiff von Hull geheyssen Peter mit mancherhande Kouffenschatcz geladen ken Prussen zegelte und do sie quomen in die Osterzee do quomen sie by anderen dreyen schiffen us Schotlande van welchen das vorbenante enge-lische Schiff in Krieges weise by nachtes czeiten hertlichen und geweldig-lichen angefochten wart; und die Schotten eynfielen und eynbrochen in das Engelische schiff also dach das van den gnaden Gotes die vorbenanten Engelischen die oberwyndinge davon behilden und nemen die Schotten mit eren gutteren. Und is geschach, das die Schotten zu den Enge-lischen sprochen, wir wissen, das wir euch grossen schaden getan haben, hierumme bitten wir euch us ganczem herczen das ir us solchen schaden taxiren wellet und wart getaxiret uf 240 pfund Sterling. Und die Schotten satczten den Engelischen vumff Schotten zu güsel und die Engelischen liessen die andern frey wegsegelen. Und do die Engelischen

of them having even succeeded in obtaining civil rights. The life of the latter was much less burdensome; nay, their hardihood and energy often gained for them the highest distinctions, both in the governing body of the city, and within the sacred precincts of the guilds.

The itinerant trader was the successor and companion of the Jew, the true Ishmael whose hands were against everybody while everybody's hands were against him. He was greeted by the jealous tradesmen with a general howl of execration; he was driven from village to village, the gates of the towns were closed against him except on fair-days; laws and edicts innumerable were issued against him; he was accused of being a spy, a cheat, an Arian; even his own countrymen disdained him. His life was so fenced in with prohibitions that he could hardly take a step without coming into conflict with the authorities.

His difficulties commenced with his arrival in the foreign port. We have a very eloquent proof of this in a Petition addressed to the Magistrates of Danzig by some Scotch merchants in the year 1597. It runs:

"Edle, ehrenfeste, hoch achtbare und wohlweise Herren![1] We, the undersigned strangers offer you our willing services after wishing you the strength of God's spirit to rule for the welfare of all, and we notify to you, the

---

die vumff Schotten mit en in Prussen brochten, do wurden sie vam Homeister getwungen, dieselben mit eren gutteren qwit zu geben und das geschach. Dornoch sante der Komptur van Danczke noch den schipperen und koufflewten des vorbenanten Schiffes und lies ir 13 in eynen kerker setczen, dorinne sie viel noch verstigkten und kume lebending herus herquomen und musten gleichewol dem komptur geben 24 mark Preusch und ½ laken van 20 mark das sie gefreyet wurden." *Hanserecesse*, ii. 2, 73.

[1] Modes of addressing; literally: noble, honorable, highly estimable and wise gentlemen.

ruling authority of this famous seaport of Danzig, that we have arrived here with our ship and goods through God's grace for the coming Dominik's Fair, like other strangers to attend to our trade and gain our modest profit. But as soon as we left our ship we encountered the difficulty of finding suitable lodgings, we having first sent to the honorable John Kilfauns, one of our own nation, who has been here for some years, but he excused himself as being a widower. After that Hans Gelletlie did the same on the plea of the pressure of business. Others to whom we had introductions explained that they had no citizen's rights and were therefore prohibited from taking us in; so that we wonder how different we find everything in this famous city from what we were told by our countrymen in our own country. Now we know indeed that we must comply with the customs and rules of every place, nevertheless we think that the Magistrates of Danzig in their free-trading port should meet the arriving tradesman and sailor according to their well known friendliness with humanity and good favour just as it is done in other countries.

"We understand that those indwellers belonging to foreign nations have been forbidden the other day to receive lodgers, whereby we feel aggrieved on this account, that whilst other strangers from the Netherlands or other places can use their own language with the German citizen, we that come from Scotland cannot talk German and find very few here of our own nation who are citizens, whilst those that enjoy this privilege partly excuse themselves, partly have no accommodation. Nor is it convenient for everybody to accommodate strangers not of their own race and tongue, especially when these must take their crew without distinction with them for their meals, that they also may enjoy a fresh morsel sometimes, our meals being very uncertain indeed. Some of us do our own ship's cooking in the houses of the innkeepers where we can find lodgings ; others ordering sometimes breakfast, dinner and supper at our own expense, returning on board ship again after meal-time, so that very few sleep away from their ship.

"Now, as every stranger likes best to stay with his countrymen if possible, and as experience taught us that the Germans don't like to take so much trouble with us, therefore we must humbly pray and look to the magistrates of this goodly town that they would grant us during the little time of the fair until we sail away again, the liberty of lodging with our fellow-countrymen. We also promise, as honest people, that we do not want to carry on forbidden trade—for we hear that the new ordinance arose out of this—but that we will behave orderly and duly like strangers and guests. We hope that the authorities of this town will grant us our request for the sake of our most gracious Lord, the King His Majesty of Scotland, and that they will likewise grant citizens' rights to some of our countrymen who have been dwelling here for long years past, so that they might have the right to harbour us, and that the difficulties some of our nation suffer under when they sail to this town might be removed, certain lodgings being provided for them and their necessities. This will not only add to the praise and honor of you, wise and noble sirs, but we shall also duly proclaim it before our most gracious master, the King's Majesty, and throughout the whole of our native country. Ever ready to deserve well of this glorious town, we sign in the expectation of a favourable answer :—

John Trotter	David Carnegie
Gilbert Dick	Thos. Greiff.
Robt. Traquair	Robt. Luikup

Gilbert Dickson	Robt. Broun
Adam Lindsay	Will. Weir
Robt. Stark	David Gilbert
Alex. Ramsay	James Hamilton

from Scotland, traders, skippers, for themselves and crew, and others of their countrymen arriving after them."[1]

Now this law, according to which no Scotsman was allowed to harbour a Scotsman, issued for fear of illicit trading, was one of the chief complaints of the Scottish settler and trader and remained so for long years afterwards. The city of Danzig, however, more liberal in her treatment of strangers, especially of the Scots to whom she owed much in times of war, and remembering that the present case was one of occasional visitors only, resolved to investigate the matter. The Scotch interpreter, one Michael Kock, was commissioned to inquire who among the Scots at Danzig were willing to take lodgers. He draws up the following list, headed by the remark: "The following are the names of those who got the freedom of the city but are not willing to keep lodgers ("gest zu halten"), as much as I have been able to gather: Hans Kilfauns, Jürgen Patherson, Hans Gelletlie, Jacob Gelletlie, William Roan, Hans Wolson, Andreas Hardy, Jacob Broun, Andreas Liddell, Jürgen Kittrigk and Andreas Thomson. Four other citizens: Hillebrant Shorbrand, Jacob Konningk (King or Cumming?), Andreas Teller and William Shorbrant keep lodgers and are still willing to do so, as far as I could ascertain, but they only take merchants."

He then continues: "The following are those that possess no citizens' rights, but are willing to take honest lodgers if the magistrates would only relent: Thomas

---

[1] *Kgl. St. Archiv*, Danzig. *Handschriften* (MSS.) I. Bb, 32.

Griffith's widow,[1] who has kept a house here for over thirty years, is an old woman, has nothing else to live upon, and is well suited for it; Jacob Griffith, who married her daughter; Andreas Harvie, David Ardus (Allardyce), Thomas Carstairs and Jacob Schmert (Smart)."

The list concludes with the names of William Duncken and Alexander Ramisa (Ramsay), "who do not care much for lodgers, but take in their friends from Scotland as they arrive during the year."

Prejudice, however, proved too strong even for Danzig, the petition was refused, and the Scots were referred to German citizens.

The Scotch Pedlar was well received by the country folk, who, living many miles away from any town, were glad to have the shop brought to their doors. The "Schotte" on his yearly rounds became quite a familiar figure with them and entered into their proverbial speech. A proverb in East Prussia in days not long gone by, said, "Warte bis der Schotte kommt," *i.e.* wait till the Scot comes, as a term of encouragement or maybe a threat for naughty children.[2]

Yet his life was full of danger. Countless numbers of these poor travellers must have succumbed to the rigour of an almost Russian winter. Dense forests covered the land, few and bad were the roads and wolves abounded. Thus a Scot is "miserably murdered on the open road" in the district of Tapiau with the Scotsman's own knife, by a peasant who afterwards perished by the hand of the executioner, 1609; the widow of Thomas Eland (Allan), a tailor by trade, declared before the court, in a case of succession, that Hans Eland was dead, "being miserably

---

[1] "Die Griffitsche." In the German of the day the ending "sche" signified woman.   [2] Frischbier, *Sprüchwörter.*

slain on the road when he travelled in foreign parts"
(1612); thus a fine Scottish lad, Hans Rylands, was
murdered at Rummelsburg, a small place in Pomerania,
"by a wicked citizen" (1626); thus William Kyth
(Keith), perished on his road to Jaroslaw (1636); and
young Alec Forbes was killed on his journey in Poland
in 1644.

Or take the case of Gottfried Burnet, son of Jacob
Burnet, who, according to the testimony of two Scottish
merchants at Danzig, was sent by his master, Robert
Brown, a citizen of Zamosc in Poland, to Lemberg on
business. On the road, near a small town, he was shot
in a wood, and miserably killed together with his servant.
The next day his body was brought to Janowitz and
buried at a small village about sixteen miles off Lemberg
(1692).[1]

Another very serious grievance of these Pedlars was the
frequent abuse of power on the part of the over zealous
bailiffs or other authorities in the country districts. The
Burggraf (governor) of Rossitten, for instance, confiscates
the goods of one Daniel Henderson of Memel. They are,
however, released by the Duke's order because Henderson not only proves that he did not want to hawk them
about, but also that the Governor himself owes him the
price of goods bought for the last four years (1589).

Particularly severe was the so-called "Strandknecht,"
i.e. the official whose duty it was to watch the strand of
Samland, the peninsula north of Königsberg, on account
of its amber. Jacob Stien, a Scotsman and burgess of
Fischhausen complains of one of them, who confiscated
his wares at Lockstedt "under the lime-trees in front of
the Castle whilst I had gone inside to report myself to the
Governor." The Duke commands the bailiff to restore his

---

[1] *Kgl. St. Archiv,* Danzig.

goods at once to the plaintiff if found innocent (1592). A similar complaint is addressed to Albrecht the Elder, Duke of Prussia, in 1557 by a Scotsman with the name of Thomas Gepson (Gibson?) He writes: "When I, last Christmas, like other small merchants went to the Fair at the small town of Rastenburg and spread my wares there, as in a free and public fair, and when I had already taken some money, there comes the Governor together with some of the magistrates, in order to examine my yard-measure and my weights, according to an old custom. After he had found everything right he turns to me, and asks: 'What are you doing here?' to which I replied, that I should like to make some money. Then he commenced: 'You know very well that this Duchy is closed and forbidden to you; because you have acted against this decree all your goods are forfeited.' When I answered, I knew well that it was forbidden to travel about from village to village and to sell my goods to the peasant, but that we should be prohibited from going to the free Fairs in the towns, of that I knew nothing, he flew at me in a rage, took everything I possessed to the value of four hundred marks from me, struck me, and cast me into a loathsome prison, where I was kept a fortnight in durance and almost on the point of starvation. At last I had to stretch out my fingers through a hole in the tower-wall and swear an oath before the bailies, whom he had ordered to be present, that I would straightways leave the country and never come back to it. How unwillingly I consented to do this everybody will understand. The Governor kept my goods and my money, and I was obliged to leave the land begging my bread in the most miserable and pitiful manner. Moreover, I am owing both in Danzig and in Königsberg for my confiscated wares. . . Now since it has come to my knowledge that the above-named Governor lives at the present moment at Marienwerder under the immediate rule of your Serene Highness, I pray you, my most gracious sovereign, for the sake of eternal justice, to listen to my grievance and to order a restitution of my goods and due compensation for this uncalled for violence." [1]

The Duke wrote to one of his most trusted servants, the Bishop Paulus Speratus, asking him for a written report on this incident. At the same time, he expressed astonishment that so young a Scotsman should possess so costly a stall. He also appointed a commission to look into the matter, and it is to be hoped that poor Gibson was indemnified for the harsh treatment he underwent.

Another very serious complaint of the Scots was touched upon in a petition drawn up by Thomas Stien, Zander Donasson, William Lockerbie, Hans Rains (?), Hans Nemen (Newman?), Hans Hunter and Hans Morray, in the year 1581, for the magistrates of Danzig. It arose from the fact that these men having visited the fair at Elbing, had been asked to pay taxes there, a demand which was accentuated by the arrest of their goods. Now, it was obviously and grossly unjust to make those pay over again that had already satisfied their duties as citizens in Danzig. Petitioners also lay stress on the fact that they were not pedlars (Paudelkrämer) but given to honourable trade and dealing. [2]

The worst enemy, however, of the Scot was the German tradesman and guild brother. Fair competition in business being then unknown he was eaten up with jealousy and envy, [3] and ousted by the superior skill and

---

[1] *Kgl. St. Archiv*, Königsberg.

[2] " Sich eines aufrichtigen Handels und Wandels beflissen." (*Kgl. St. A. D.*). The same combination of names occurs later on. William Lockerbie hailed from Dumfries.

[3] Cp. Dr Fr. Schulz, *Chronik der Stadt Jastrow*, 1896.

the shrewd and very likely not always scrupulous activity of the stranger. He was at the bottom of the number-less edicts and decrees that for more than two hundred years by every king, prince, bishop, and magistrates were hurled against the Scot. It would obviously be impossible to cite all these letters of complaint or even to enumerate them all. They were issued by the guilds of merchants, of clothmakers, of small traders, of tailors in nearly all the important towns of Prussia at that time. We can only mention some of them as specimens of the rest.

The clothiers of Marienburg in 1531 write to the Duke complaining of the "vagrant Scots" (die losen Schotten), who are of no fixed abode nor pay the taxes or dues of any town, are getting so common with their cloths in the country that they are to be found and their presence felt in all the fairs in great numbers, carrying their cloth to the villages and into houses and selling it to the great detriment of the King's resident subjects.[1]

The retail merchants of Thorn address a petition to the members of the governing Board of Prussia in 1556. They remind the crown of former prohibitions against Jews, Scots and pedlars who roam about the country to the ruin of the whole country, and they continue : "These prohibitions are not obeyed. Much adulterated mer-chandise both in cloths and in silks and groceries is being carried into this land by the Jews and the Scots. They are also objectionable on account of their obstinacy, and their ways of selling. When they travel about the country and perchance arrive at a gentleman's estate, they sell to the steward or his wife not only pepper and saffron, and especially cloth, linen and macheier,[1] but

---

[1] G. Lengenich, *Geschichte Preussens*, ii. 97.

[2] A kind of coarse woollen stuff. Cp. Schiller and Lübben, *Mittel Niederdeutsches Wörterbuch*.

talk them into buying all sorts of groceries. Now when it so happens, and it does happen frequently, that the steward or the stewardess have no money, they accept not only whey-cheese[1] and butter and especially oats and barley, but all sorts of skins and furs which are secretly purloined from the owner of the estate and given to the Scots for their spurious goods, their false weight and measures. Everybody knows, moreover, how much of what has been spun by our honest womenfolk is pawned to the Scot."

Finally, the letter complains that the Scots have more than one booth at the Fair and always in the best place, and that they are masters in hiding their fraud.[2]

Here we have not only the deceitful dealing of the Scots attacked, but also their mode of dealing, their giving and taking in exchange, perhaps even on credit.

The grievances of the Krämers of Königsberg are dealt with at the Prussian Diet of 1566. They draw attention to the fact that the Scots, because they know all the passes and roads in the country, might do great harm to the country in times of war.[3]

Similarly the whole guild of retail merchants of Prussia in a petition dated November 16th, 1569, complain of the laws against the Scots not being obeyed. " There is, for instance," the document continues, " a Scot at Fischhausen[4] who maintains that he has the privilege of hawking about in every corner of the sea coast. The country folk no longer want to make their purchases in the towns.

---

[1] The word is "twarge Käse " = Quark = whey.

[2] Original in the Episcopal Archives at Frauenburg.   (See of Ermeland.)   [3] *Kgl. St. Archiv*, Königsberg.

[4] A small place to the West of Königsberg. Samland was and is the name of the country round Königsberg bordered in the N. and W. by the Baltic Sea, in the S. by the river Pregel and in the E. by the Dieme river. There are famous amber pits on its coast.

Another Scot lives at Zinten[1] who says he is a citizen of that place, but he does not live as such, but keeps a number of unmarried young fellows, who in his name travel up and down the whole of Samlandt. And as if this were not enough, he himself hawks his goods about. And withal these Scots are obstinate and arrogant, not friendly spoken to anybody, not performing any civil duties, but buying beaver-skins and marten-skins and amber at Pillau, selling it afterwards at Lublin or Thorn.[2] They betray the country."[3]

To understand the above properly we must bear in mind that it went against the laws of the guilds to sell from house to house or to sell on commission. The trade in amber was a Government monopoly as it is now; it was the same with the trade in furs. To this long list of crimes, we have to add the buying up of old silver and copper, whereby the trade privileges of the silver and coppersmiths were infringed.[4]

Very frequently in this connection the buying up of grain on the part of the Scottish trader forestalling is mentioned and in consequence of it the artificial rise in the price of corn. Thus in 1596 in a letter of the citizens and bailies of Marienwerder.[5] The clothmakers blame the Scots for buying the wool on the back of the sheep cheaply, "so that in course of time nobody will be safe against their tricks, since they seek everywhere their own profit and the discomfiture of the native trader. To those that cannot work the wool up the buying of wool is forbidden by law; let them be lords or commons, priests or peasants, Jews or Scots, Poles or Masures.[6] Moreover the interloper's hands are strengthened by the Scots, to whom

[1] A small place to the South of Königsberg.
[2] That is to say smuggling it out of Prussia into Poland.
[3] *Kgl. St. Archiv*, Königsberg.   [4] *Ibidem.*
[5] *Ibidem.*   [6] *Ibidem.*

they sell for a trifle their false cloths only to be sold again to the ignorant peasant on public fairs (1612)."[1]

When all these reasons for resenting the intrusion of the Scot had been exhausted others presented themselves, some of a very amusing character. Thus in a petition of the guild of merchants at Königsberg towards the close of the XVIIth Century it is said that the Scots skim the cream off the milk of the country, usurp the whole trade and are so bold and so smart withal that nothing can happen in a nobleman's or a common citizen's house, be it even a case of death, without the Scot being there at the very moment offering to supply his goods.

The same petition contains the following list of Scotsmen who carry on illegal traffic at Königsberg, or travel all over the country " fairs or no fairs."

IN THE OLD TOWN.

Collins, an Englishman, lives on the Market Square, takes in lodgers, " raises his own smoke,"[2] lets his rooms and sends out his "bad servants during the summer to sell stockings publicly."

2

Robert Walker, a Scot, dwelling near the Market Place, has likewise his own house, keeps lodgers, lets rooms, has his store and an open shop near the castle as well, buys all his goods from strangers and nothing from citizens.

3

Robert Schwentor (?) is an unmarried fellow, lives at the wig-maker's house near the castle, travels about the country to Memel, Tilsit, Insterburg, and to other places.

[1] *Kgl. St. Archiv*, Königsberg.
[2] " Seinen eigenen Rauch halten " for to own a house is one of the many picturesque legal expressions in old German documents; derived from the immemorial custom of lighting a fire on the hearth as a symbolic token of taking possession.

4

Gilbert Morra (Murray), an unmarried fellow, lives also at the wig-maker's, has an open shop between the castle gates, buys all his goods from strangers, and boldly fetches the buyers away from the towns and the bridges and leads them to his shop.

5

The whole of the horse-market near the Steinthor is full of Scottish people, among them is one Morrisson, who keeps four carts and sends them up and down the country continually carrying cloth, smallwares, etc.

6

One with the name of Walker has one store at Fischhausen and another at Pillau, and visits all the estates and villages in the Samland district.

KNEIPHOF.

Robert Mill, a Scot, not only keeps lodgers, but as soon as any English or Scotch arrive, he takes their goods and divides them again among his countrymen; visits the country, fair or no fair, and is guilty of all kinds of embezzlement.

2

Fullert, a Scot, has two fellows to scour the small towns.

3

Andreas Marshall, a Scot, has many young fellows who travel for him throughout the country.

4

Jacob Wass (?), from Elbing, is a Scot, lives in Prusitzki's house, deals as much with strangers as with natives.

5

The Ramit'sche,[1] a Scottish widow, has two shops with cloth and other wares.

6

John Krehe[2] is well known for his knavery, having a store in his house and an open shop near the castle; he sells by the piece and by the yard cloth, silk, buttons and other things, he also trades with scythes and never neglects an opportunity where he can injure the town.

7

John Malkan (Malcolm), an unmarried fellow, and a Scot, keeps an open shop near the castle with cloth and dry goods, is now in the camp before Stettin,[3] but left a boy behind to look after his goods.

8

Peter Bewy, a Scot, dwells in Löbenicht,[4] has an open shop near the mill with various goods.

9

Robert Marshall, a Scot, lives near the mill gate, keeps a store as well as a shop, travels about, buys and orders all his goods from strangers, and not "one thread" from the citizens.

10

Thomas Hervie, has no less than three shops, and wherever he espies an opportunity for doing business, he buys everything from and through strangers lest the citizens should get a chance, and so noblemen are obliged to buy of him, as happened the other day when the Governor died and he bought up all the black cloth in the

---

[1] See note to page 18.   [3] Serving in the war against the Swedes.
[2] See about him further down.   [4] See Introduction.

face of his fellow-citizens.[1] He also in the summer time buys up the wool.

Another amusing addition occurs in a similar petition of the end of the XVIth Century. " The wily Scots," the petitioners say, " have hit upon a new trick Whenever there is a Fair in sight in a town, they scour the whole country for miles around, about a week previous, selling their goods. So that we, when we arrive in due time to turn an honest penny, find that the Scot has ' bagged ' everything before us. Our dear wives often come home weeping." No less amusing is the charge preferred by the municipal authorities of Bartenstein against the vagrant Scots, that they "aspire to barons' and earls' estates and to high offices in the State " (1590).

Looking over these long and formidable charges, it would be unfair to deny that in some cases there may have been good reasons for them. Even now, to the moral sense of the uneducated Scot, it seems manifestly unjust that what he calls fishing should be spelt poaching by the judge ; and as to smuggling, a hundred or two hundred years ago, every reader of Sir Walter will know what the prevalent Scottish ideas were. In the letters of Francis Craw,[2] the youth of sixteen, who emigrated to Prussia in 1671, he carefully inquires after the price of amber at home and the fashion of wearing the beads. Moreover, it was natural, that when the emigration was at its height, that is, from about 1590 to 1630, a great many undesirable elements must have crossed the Baltic. Of this there is no better proof than the petition of the Scots at Danzig, addressed to the magistrates, against their own countrymen in 1592 ; a most remarkable document, which we here give in its entirety :—

[1] " Vor der Nase weg."
[2] See *Scots in Germany*, pp. 250-255.

" Herr Bürgermeister, Gestrenge, Ehrenfeste, Ehrbare, etc. etc.[1]

" Whilst offering to you our ever-ready services, we cannot refrain from bringing to your notice, that among other evils from without and within, this also must be numbered, that many of our nation now arrived in this city sit with their baskets on the bridges among the warehouses, or go to the strangers in the public-houses, and, if they do not find them there, into the court-yards of the Langemarkt,[2] or into the very houses of citizens, up one lane down the other; but they especially crowd the bridges exhibiting and selling their wares, not being satisfied with the space before their houses. They have not obtained any privileges. Their interloping and forestalling trade is now carried on not by the fellows themselves or their young assistants, but by lazy women and loose servants, who, whilst they refuse to serve honest people or to do well, allow themselves to be used for such unlawful trade. And yet did we formerly assist them with our alms, because they pretended to be crooked or lame. Such a state of things must, as we now see with our own eyes, of necessity be very detrimental to the citizens and to other small merchants, who gained their citizenship through the favour of the magistrates, owing them not only the greatest gratitude, but having also taken all sorts of burdensome duties upon them as citizens; to say nothing of the disgrace to our nation when such people, lazy and unwilling to work as they are, crowd the streets. This is the reason why we see, with a sorrow past telling, how every year many an honest citizen gets into debt, whilst we must be told that we

[1] Modes of addressing the mayor and bailies.
[2] Not a market-place properly speaking, but the widening of the chief street of Danzig, the Langgasse, in the centre of the town.

ourselves are to blame for it. And although the aid
of the police and the night watches has often been
called in, no energetic steps have hitherto been taken.
Numbers of citizens have approached us concerning this
matter, and begged of us to declare ourselves openly
against such a prevalent abuse.

"We consider further that not only single citizens,
but the whole of this city suffers great injury from this
state of affairs, especially since great numbers are required for the common statute-labour in the fortifications,[1]
and yet this loose servant-pack[2] refuse to work. We
therefore approve of the proposal of some good citizens
to appoint men among ourselves—being most willing to
mend matters according to our simple minds—who are
to work together with the already appointed public
servants, keeping an eye on these traders, reporting to
the magistrates, and making daily seizures, the profit
of which is to go to poor churches, schools, or the
fortification works.[3]

"This we thought fit to bring before you. Hoping
you will not blame us for it, and expecting a favourable
answer in this case of urgent necessity, we remain,

"HANS KILFAUNS, HANS GELLETLIE,
"GEO. PATTERSON, THOS. STEEN,
"GEO. MAGOTTRY (?), ANDR. EDDEL (LIDDEL),
"ANDR. HARDY, HANS BROWN,
"JACOB GELLETLIE, H. VORBRANT (SHORBRANT).

"*Citizens of Danzig, for themselves and in the
name of the whole Scottish nation dwelling
there.*"

The decision of the magistrates was to take down the

---

[1] "Scharwerk." [2] "Das leichtfertige Gesindtlin."
[3] "Wallgebände," *i.e.* the office for the fortification-works of the city.

names of the transgressors; whereupon an order to seize the goods would be given if necessary, and the seizures brought to the police offices (April 15th, 1592).[1]

A similar case happened in Königsberg in the year 1620. There some small Scottish traders had received the privilege of living upon the so-called Ducal "Freiheiten," i.e. "liberties," or the ground surrounding the Castle, where most of the Duke's retainers had their dwellings. They were under the immediate jurisdiction of the Duke and the proud citizen of Königsberg despised them. Four Scotsmen, Jacob From, Andreas and Heinrich Wricht (Wright), and Jacob Koch, write to the magistrates as follows: "We cannot hide from you that from time immemorial, when the Fairs in the small towns occurred, we have been in the habit of drawing lots about our stands with those Scots who have settled in those towns. We have also been permitted hitherto to visit the weekly markets unhindered by them, and the magistrates have willingly conceded us these rights, as we always bring good, fresh goods to the market of every description so as to please everybody, which goods cannot easily be procured from the Scottish inhabitants. But now we are to be deprived of this privilege, not, indeed, by the authorities of the small towns, but by our own countrymen who dwell in them. They call us and our gracious master names, maintaining that we were but 'Gärtner,'[2] and refusing not only to draw lots, but to admit us to the markets, whilst they suffer those of the Scots who hawk their goods about from house to house; a thing which we would not do. We are indeed not 'Gärtner,' but settled inhabitants here at

---

[1] *Kgl. St. Archiv*, Danzig.

[2] Gärtner is a peasant without a field, a word denoting the lowest member of a community. It occurs in this sense in Luther.

Königsberg, paying taxes and dues to our sovereign and sharing in all other burdens that have to be borne by all the dwellers on the Liberties, as pay for the watch service, for fortification work, and assisting at the harvest time. We therefore pray you to let us have an open letter, so that we, being settled inhabitants, may earn our living as well as those vagrant traders."

The same grievances against their own countrymen are presented to the Markgraf of Brandenburg by the Scots dwelling in the small town of Margrabova in the year 1624.

In short, the Scots themselves, as soon as they settled down, seem to have succumbed to the same infectious trade jealousy and narrow-minded trading principles that actuated their German brethren; only they did not go to the same extremes of inventing charges where there was no other foundation to go upon.

Moved by these petitions, pouring in from all sides and quarters, the rulers of the whole north-east of Germany [1] issued, as we have seen, quite a number of edicts, laws and prohibitions against the Scots. So frequent did they become that we fancy we detect a slight indication of annoyance in many of them. "We cannot for ever be bothered with the Scot; let our former mandates suffice."

Most of these royal decrees date from the XVIth Century; but some were issued in Prussia much earlier. Fundamental for Poland was the so-called "Royal Universale" against the Scots of the year 1566. It is of a very sweeping character, forbidding the Scottish

---

[1] Indeed they were not behind-hand in the south. In Regensburg a decree is issued in 1501 against the peddling Scots. Those, however, who with "good merchandise, such as gold, silver, velvet and silk," visit the monasteries and noblemen's seats, are excepted in 1553 from a similar prohibition. See Supplement and Schmeller, l.c.

pedlars to roam about the country, and even going so far as to declare any letters issuing at any future time from the Royal Secretary's Office and purporting to convey different opinions to be null and void.[1]

Other prohibitions of later kings repeat the same reasons and restrictions. Thus Sigismund III. issues a mandate against Jews, Scots and other vagabonds in 1594 at the request of the town of Kcyna. The Scots are chiefly forbidden to make large purchases of grain.[2] About a hundred years later King Augustus II., in a privilege granted to the town of Kosten, refers to the old laws against the Scots. He forbids that they should acquire any landed or town property with the significant addition that they were "a religione Romana Catholica dissidentes" (1699).

The dukes of Pomerania issued similar mandates in 1585 from Wolgast, also in 1594. Philipp Julius, Duke of Stettin, on the usual plea of "false goods" and detrimental competition, commands his governors to prevent the Scottish pedlar from hawking about in the country; "those, however, who live at Stettin, sharing the common burdens of a citizen, shall be free to exhibit their goods and sell them at the usual fairs and during one week annually like the other merchants."[3]

In the Duchy of Prussia we have the edicts of 1525 (7th of May), according to which, not only vagabondage of the Scots is forbidden, but also the drawing of lots for the position of stalls at the fairs. This edict of Albrecht the Elder was confirmed in 1530, 1542, 1545 and in 1558, expressing at the same time astonishment that former Ducal laws had been evaded, and displeasure at

---

[1] One is tempted to pronounce the last clauses interpolated.

[2] *Kgl. St. Archiv*, Posen, Dep. Exin., N. 1.

[3] Stettin, *Wolgast Archiv*, Tit. 36, No. 14.

those of the nobility who harbour the Scots for any length
of time (1549). On the whole, however, the rulers of
Prussia showed a most remarkable sense of justice and
fair play; they never granted all the requests of the irate
guilds, and, as we shall see by and by, often put themselves in distinct opposition to the narrow-mindedness of
the city magistrates. It was this same Albrecht, a man
of great uprightness and a strong desire to rule well, who
in 1549 on the 9th of September writes to his minister
Nostiz: "Before us appeared the bearer of this letter,
Wilhelmus Scotus, and told us how he for the sake of
the gospel had been driven out of Scotland, at the same
time asking us in our mercy for a contribution towards
his sustenance. We have therefore promised him a plain
suit of clothes as well as four Gulden for his food, and
request of you to let him have it out of our Exchequer." [1]

There are later edicts in the Lithuanian language
(1589) [2] and in German, printed and unprinted. In some
of them a certain district is assigned to the Scot for free
trading, notably in the so-called Prussische Landesedict of
1551.

In Mecklenburg also, where large numbers of Scottish
Tabuletkrämer [3] went about the country in the XVIth
and XVIIth Centuries, we have the sketch of a mandate
from the hand of Duke Johann Albrecht, and dated Feb.
25th, 1554. [4]

Even the bishops joined. The Bishop of Ermeland,
whose territory cleaves the Prussian possessions like a
wedge, draws special attention to the Scotsman's unlawful

---

[1] The charming naïveté of this Ducal note is quite lost in the translation. We give the original in Part III.

[2] Printed in the *Altpreuss Monatsschrift*, 1878, pp. 119 f.

[3] So called from "*tabulet*" = the pedlar's box.

[4] *Gr. St. Archiv*, Schwerin.

dealing in furs and skins, which trade was a monopoly, and to the corruption of the magistrates and bailiffs in the country "who are not above receiving bribes." The goods of any hawking Jew or Scot in any part of his dominions are to be confiscated and sold, one half of the proceeds to go to the bishop, the other to the village. There is to be a fine of forty marks besides [1] (1551 and 1579).

In short there seems to have been a general consent to stamp out the Scottish pedlars as a nuisance. Not only was their trade hampered, but they were heavily taxed. This tax varied somewhat in the different countries; for Poland it amounted to two florins for a man on horseback, one florin for a pedestrian; in Prussia the amount was fixed at two thalers. Besides this they had to pay for their stands at the fairs. The accurate amount of this rent is handed down to us in the account books of Marienwerder, a small town in Eastern Prussia. There we read (1606-7): "Received forty marks 'marktgeld' from four Scotsmen who are allowed to sell their goods in the lower parts of this district. Formerly there used to be eight of them paying for their privilege at the rate of eight marks annually; but four of them either died or moved elsewhere. The remaining four: Thomas Stehler (?) David Feller, Andres Morgiss and George Allan have paid at this time of Michaelmas their ten marks and are bound to do so annually."

Two remedies were open to the much harassed Scottish itinerant trader: he could lay his complaints before the sovereign of his country, or he could remove to the towns and acquire a fixed abode. He tried both, and in Prussia

[1] Cp. *Acta Curiæ Episcop. Warm.* (1539-1572) at Frauenburg. There is an edict also of the bishops of Posen issued for the benefit of the merchant guild of the town of Buk (1595) which was confirmed in 1619. *Pos. St. Archiv*, A. 8, 25, No. 5.

at least, he tried effectually. We have given some of his supplications before,[1] showing how the Scots themselves proposed a tax and a central receiver and certain articles for their organisation. The Duke, partly influenced by the intercession of the King of Great Britain, to whom the Scots in their distress had appealed a few years previously, appointed several influential men to investigate the matter. One was a certain Dr Mirander, a famous legal luminary of the day, who proceeded with prudence and energy, arguing with some of the more obstinate ones, and reminding them of the fact that not for their "yellow hair" but for the "prince's liberality" they could earn so much in the country; that they were very well off indeed, and so forth. Finally he succeeded in making them agree to a self-imposed tax.

Together with Mirander, Koch or Kook, a Scotsman, was appointed to make a census of the Krämers in 1615.[2] For this trouble he received an annual emolument of fifty thalers in gold, half a last of corn, half a last of malt and a last of oats.

His report is still extant. The Scots are willing, he says, to pay four Thalers annually for horse and cart, two Thalers when on foot; he moreover recalls to the Duke's memory the fact that many Scots died in his country without heirs, in which case their property fell to the Crown, that their ships were bringing goods into his dominions for which duty was being paid. Finally, he proposes to collect the above tax against 1000 marks (1615). He encloses certain rules ("Rolle") which the Scots had agreed upon, and adds the following introduction: "As many of the Scottish nation in this Duchy of Prussia seek their living up and down the country, most

---

[1] See *Scots in Germany*, p. 265. See also pp. 37-38. Important was the Scottish petition of 1612.   [2] *Ibid.*, p. 258.

of them without a fixed abode and under no jurisdiction, and as frequently transgressions of the law have taken place amongst them, the Governor of this country has granted them leave, some years ago, to draw up their own rules so as to remove the unjust stigma of vagabonds, and to found 'unanimo consensu' a fixed Brotherhood. They are to meet four times a year . . . the whole guild is responsible for the payment of the tax; the elders of each district forming a commission with their head committee in Königsberg." Then follow the articles which we have given elsewhere.[1]

Now at this time Patrick Gordon, of whom we have spoken,[2] was still British Consul or factor at Danzig. Meddlesome and officious character as he was, he felt aggrieved that somebody else should take the credit of this transaction. He objected to the articles in their present form, promised the Scots to intercede for them with His British Majesty, so that they should not have to pay *any* taxes, and blamed Koch for having taken upon him to act in an official capacity. A breach occurred. Some of the Scots, aggrieved at Koch having laid bare some of their unlawful trade practices, adhered to Gordon, whereupon Koch wrote pitiful letters to the Churfürst on his own behalf, quoting Gordon's threat, that his fate should be worse than that of Stercovius who had suffered the death penalty at Rastenburg,[3] but in the end the "mandatarius regis" won. He relies on his dignity and refuses to be a procurator causæ. Koch was guilty of a "crimen falsi," he maintained, having deported himself as a regularly paid official of the Duke, which he was not, and he had no "causam litigandi." The Court declared in Gordon's favour; Koch was dismissed with

[1] See *Scots in Germany*.   [2] *Ibid.*, p. 255.
[3] *The Scots in Germany*, p. 255.

his complaint, and the Scottish nation received a copy of the judgment (19th Sept. 1616).

The new articles, eighty in number, which Gordon now published, or rather submitted to the government of the Duchy of Prussia, were based upon the original rules given by us previously.[1] The first article deals with the constitution of the fraternity, and with the election of elders who are to officiate for one year only. They are to have jurisdiction in minor matters, and are to meet in proper places and at proper times, and not during " dinner and talking hours." The second article bears the heading : "On the worship of God " (De Divino Cultu), and enjoins regular attendance at church and at the communion, besides the closing of the doors and windows of the shops on Sundays and the avoidance of religious controversies. The third article deals with the relations of master and servant. Every servant is to have a certificate of good conduct ; the master is responsible for his servant ; a servant (or journeyman), not knowing German, must bind himself to serve four years. Fines are fixed for various transgressions on the part of master or boy ; e.g., if the servant calls his master out to a duel or lays violent hands on him, he shall be deprived of the benefit of the Brotherhood. The fourth article deals with vagabonds, drunkards, gamblers and others. Nobody shall be allowed to hawk his despicable wares about unless they be worth fifty Gulden. Riotous living is to be fined. In the fifth article, treating of public moneys, provision is made for the maintenance of the poor, the care for the sick, and the burial of the dead. Guild brothers must make an inventory of a deceased brother's property. Debts and the stands or booths on the fairs are dealt with in the sixth and seventh articles ; whilst the eighth provides against adulterated goods and false measure.

[1] *Scots in Germany*, p. 42, ff.

The ninth article is an enlargement of articles thirteen and fourteen of the original draft,[1] the tenth of the eleventh ; the eleventh, on the dangers of travelling, of the original fifteenth. The twelfth article settles the contributions of the brethren, whilst the last two deal with appeals to a higher court and the carrying out of the sentence; the whole constitution ends with these words: " Should any articles of a similar description be deemed necessary by common consent, which are not expressly stated in the foregoing rules, the same shall be observed as if they were expressed" (1616).

As will be seen, the constitution is well drawn up, and Gordon, if he did nothing else, deserved well of the Scottish nation on account of its composition. Curiously enough, a confirmation of these statutes from the hand of the Duke or the magistrates could not be discovered; all that remains is a short draft of marginal notes and annotations, probably drawn up by one of the members of the government.[2] The immediate effect, however, was the same.

The advantages of the letters of protection, and the self-imposed tax, were eagerly embraced, and the lot of the Scottish itinerant trader considerably improved. Königsberg became the centre of the Scottish settlements and of the Brotherhood in Prussia. In a census of Scotsmen in the small town of Welau, only two, Jacob Ertzbell (Archibald?) and William Schott were found that had no Schutzzeddel, both giving a reasonable excuse. Others were of the opinion that as citizens of smaller towns they did not require them.

---

[1] *Scots in Germany*, p. 44.

[2] The articles were written in English, it appears, and then translated by Gordon. The corrections and annotations date from the year 1624. Various petitions for the confirmation of the rules date from 1617 and 1622.—*Kgl. St. Archiv*, Königsberg.

The original of one of these letters of protection is preserved in the case of Alexander Murray, a citizen of Memel, who is permitted to trade in Ermeland for a year with two horses and his pack. "The bearer," the document continues, "in the name of His Grace the Duke, is to be protected by the magistrates of each place against all violence and oppression at the hands of soldiers and recruiting officers. And because Alexander Murray has paid as protection-tax the sum of two ducats this will serve as a receipt. He is, however, not to use false weight, measure, or merchandise under pain of confiscation, and to pay other taxes imposed by the diet of the country willingly " (July 3, 1656).

As to the protection duty to be paid, the question arose whether the servants who went with their master's goods about the country were also liable. A number of Scots in Königsberg petition the Duke in this matter, complaining, at the same time, that the present representative of the fiscal had exacted the tax without distinction, and, being a slave of drink and lazy in the performance of his duty, had molested the Scots greatly in the fairs, when they had not yet earned a penny, " flying at them with slanderous speech in his drunken state,[1] so that manslaughter and murder might have been the consequence." They pray the duke to rid them of this fellow, and rather to appoint a place at Königsberg, either an office in the town hall or the governor's office, for the payment of their "protection-money" (Schutzpfennig), and, as a term, the annual great fair.[2]

In the neighbouring state of Pomerania the case of the Scottish pedlar was not settled satisfactorily. Here also

---

[1] "Uns trunckenerweise mit ehrenrührigen worten anfährt."

[2] *Kgl. St. Archiv*, Königsberg, N.D., but apparently not long after agreeing to the tax.

we have the proposal of appointing a captain or spokesman. A certain Colonel Getberg writes to the Duke asking to be given the mill at Lauenburg in reward for faithful services during twenty-six years. He then continues his letter in these terms : " Because a week ago a handsome Scotch lad, Hans Rylands, a pedlar, was murderously slain with an axe by a wicked citizen at Rummelsburg, the Scots again urge me, praying me for God's sake to be their captain, patron, and advocate, and to appoint a learned man of the law in each principality who would attend to their business. They offer to pay one Thaler each to the local treasurer in each place at Michaelmas. Now because His Majesty of Poland, my most gracious sovereign, ten years ago, appointed a captain called Adam Young [1] (Junge) for the purpose of advocating the cause of this foreign nation at court and of protecting them against uncalled for violence, Your Majesty might also grant such a privilege for thirty years to me and my successors, this being my first prayer, and it would in no way be derogatory to your own prerogatives. Therefore I trust your Serene Highness will arrange matters so that each treasurer at Michaelmas, when he hands in his accounts, shall also pay me a Thaler on the part of the Scots. For this service I shall give to each of these collectors, as an annual recompense, a handsome young horse in token of gratitude. Not doubting the granting of my petition.

" PETER GETBERGK, Colonel."

(Jan. 1626).[2]

Unfortunately the Duke was of a different opinion. He feared that if those traders, who were already taxpayers, had an additional tax laid upon them, they would raise the price of their goods, which would be a hardship

---

[1] Also called Abraham Young, see *Scots in Germany*, p. 38.

[2] *Kgl. St. Archiv*, Stettin, Pars. II., Tit. 28, No. 41.

to other inhabitants and to his "poor subjects." The petition was therefore refused, and the bailies had to go without their beautiful young horses.

In Prussia, however, we hear much less of the grievances of the Scottish pedlar. Altogether he seems to have drifted little by little into the towns where the chances of earning an honest and less dangerous livelihood seemed certainly better. From about the middle of the XVIIth Century we notice a large and steadily increasing influx of Scotsmen into the smaller and larger towns of Prussia and Poland. In many cases these men's hopes of finding at last a haven of rest were disappointed; for here also the trade hostilities were great, more bitter, perhaps, in close proximity than at a distance. Here also the magistrates showed little inclination to grant any freedom of movement, though, it must be said, the towns varied greatly in this respect; Danzig, for instance, distinguishing herself by a certain amount of liberal treatment of the foreign merchant. In most other places, especially in Prussia, the Scots and other strangers—notably the Dutch, of whom there was at this time a large immigration [1]—had to submit to a number of irritating restrictions. They had to report themselves at their arrival, and tell the value of their goods and the character of their trading; they were not allowed to sell to strangers; they were not allowed to have more than one shop; they could not lodge or board their own countrymen, or sell any new clothes; [2] they could not acquire any house property; [3] the retail trade by the ell and the pound was closed to them

[1] *Kgl. St. Archiv*, Königsberg.

[2] Decree from 1580 at Danzig. See *Libri Memorand.* xxxiii., D. 12. In Königsberg an exception was made in favour of married men with a family.

[3] "Seinen eigenen Rauch zu halten" = to raise his own smoke. See above, p. 25 n.

as well as the traffic on the river.[1] They could not, as a rule, become burgesses, though they paid the taxes of such. It was this last restriction which caused most dissatisfaction.

In Poland, King Vladislaus among others, had sanctioned the principle in 1635, and in Prussia a decree of the Churfürst of Brandenburg, in 1613 (Feb. 3rd), in its fourth paragraph restated the former law that no Dutchmen, Scot, or Englishman could acquire civil rights. Sixteen of the smaller Prussian towns had also proclaimed this restriction which, so far from being an innovation, had already been imposed by the Hanseatic League more than a century ago. For a very long time the war between these German towns and the Scottish petitioners was waged with great bitterness, and, at first sight, we do not expect ever to hear of any Scottish-German citizens within the length and breadth of Prussia.

The law, however, was more severe in its letter than in its administration. There were various ways of bringing a certain amount of pressure to bear upon the city fathers, and it goes without saying that in availing themselves of these the Scots had no equals. First of all, there was the intercession of the sovereign and other men of influence, and secondly—a more pleasant way—the fact of having married a German lady, the daughter of a native of the place.

In Danzig we find after the year 1577, in which the Scots together with the other citizens so valiantly helped to drive off the King of Poland, a number of applications for the freedom of the city at the intercession of the Scottish Colonel; thus Andreas Moncreiff in 1577, Osias Kilfauns

---

[1] This was considered a monopoly of the townspeople. They complain most bitterly against " the cunning Scots who use the calmest, nay the ' holiest' nights to put whole bales of their goods into boats, sail up the river, and smuggle great quantities of merchandise " (1678 Jan. 18th), *Kgl. St. Archiv*, Königsberg.

in 1578,[1] and in the same year George Patterson. In 1580 or 1581, to keep the ball rolling, eight Scotsmen apply for the burgess-ship on the same grounds. Their names are Steen, Donaldson, Lockerbie, Simpson, Newman, Henton, More (or Murray). This William Lockerbie from Domfries (!) writes again in 1609, after wishing a blissful rule to the magistrates: " I, poor man that I am, will not withhold from you, that I have been at Danzig for the last thirty-six years, having served in the wars as a soldier, married and reared children, and lived for twenty years on the Vendeten.[2] I have dragged myself to the fairs of the small towns back and forward and thus kept myself, my wife, and my children alive with sorrow. Now the Almighty has taken my children and left me lonely together with my decrepit, sick old woman. Moreover, I am getting old, and being loth to travel, I should like to earn my bread honourably and with the help of God, as long as it pleases Him to prolong my life. But, because I need to be enrolled as a burgess for that, and having served this town in time of need and being still willing to serve it faithfully as long as I live, my prayer is, that you would grant my humble request and endow me with the citizens' rights as a Vendeter, for which I am ready to pay the necessary sum."[3]

Thomas Gregor in 1589 and 1592, and Thomas Griffin or Grieff in 1583 adopt the same course, the latter adding "that he had been sworn in as a soldier in the defence of the city and did not spare his gray hair." In a similar strain Jacob Brown (Brunaeus), addresses the Danzig Courts in

[1] "Auf Forpitt (intercession) des Schottischen Herrn Obersten." Compare List of Scottish Citizens at Danzig, in Part III.

[2] A Vendeter or Venteter was an old-clothes man, also a pedlar, small trader. The Ventete was the place or street where this trade was carried on.

[3] *Kgl. St. Archiv.*, Danzig.

1592. He writes: "I beg to state that I have lived in this good town more than twenty years, and have by the grace of God and my own activity earned my living, and although in the last war I, being under no obligation, might with others have sought my advantage elsewhere, yet have I, without any pay, from sheer good nature and special affection, taken part in all the skirmishes under Captain Gourlay, and, after he was drowned, under Captain Trotter, having been shot through the leg in consequence of my willingness on one of the bastions. Now, having served this good town in times of need to the risk of my life, I did so in the hope, that in the future, when I should be wishing to settle in this place, you would grant my request and enroll me on the list of your burgesses."[1] Indeed it is stated in the petition of Gregor that civil rights were promised to all Scots at the Colonel's intercession in or about 1577, "provided they be faithful and of honest birth."[2]

At other times we read of the intercession of Kings and Queens. One Jacob Hill and his friend John Tamson, towards the end of the XVIth Century, depend upon the recommendation of the King and Queen of Poland. Sophia Charlotte, wife of the Markgraf of Brandenburg, intercedes for Andrew Marshall, a Scottish merchant, who desires to settle at Königsberg. "His character is known to us, his conduct is irreproachable," she writes (April 29, 1690). Prince Radziwill intercedes for William Buchan; and the good services of His Majesty the King of Great Britain are on several occasions appealed to and obtained.

The King of Poland pleads for several Scotsmen, candidates for the citizenship of Danzig, at the request of Andrew Keith, Baron of Dingwall. But the third Order

---

[1] *Kgl. St. Archiv*, Danzig.

[2] Gabriel Foster obtains civil rights at Bartenstein at the intercession of Captain Caspar Sack in 1588.

objects, because the city was overrun with strangers, and their own daily business interfered with by them (1588).

With the nobility of the country, as well as with the ruling powers, the Scots had managed to live on terms of friendly intercourse. They had lent them money; they were raised to the high position of royal merchants in Poland; they procured among other things the cloth for the uniforms of the soldiery in Prussia and had ingratiated themselves with the rulers by many other friendly services, such as offering to procure dogs for them from England,[1] or silks and velvets from other countries.

Numberless, in consequence, were the appeals to the different Dukes of Prussia from Scotsmen wishing to be enrolled as citizens of any of the towns of their Duchy. Indeed, these poor Dukes must have led a miserable life between the complaints of the guilds of merchants, clothiers, tailors, shoemakers and furriers against the Scots, and of the " afflicted " Scots against these, and, finally, having to listen to their recalcitrant and obstinate magistrates, especially those of Königsberg, their capital, whose views did not coincide with the more liberal and broad-minded treatment of strangers inhabiting their towns proposed by the Head of the State. Already, in 1589, in the case of the Scottish pedlars, whose trade had been so seriously crippled by the

---

[1] William Watson writes to the Duke Albrecht of Prussia in 1544 from Danzig: " My brother Richard asked me in a letter to send some English dogs to Your Grace. I have ordered some, and they have been put on board a vessel. Of these three one jumped overboard; the other two can be fetched from Jürgen Rudloff, the skipper. In case Your Grace wanted more, it would be well to let me know if You want them young or old. I shall then willingly order them." He also offers to procure court dresses or dress material for the Duke.—*Kgl. St. Archiv*, Königsberg (Herzogliches Brief Archiv). Jacob Ramsay, asking for a passport for his servant, offers to bring fine cloth and silks to the Duke (1590)—*Ibid.* Already a century previous Jacob Wricht had made purchases of cloth, velvet and damask for the Grand Master of the Teutonic Order (1475).

Ducal decrees forbidding their hawking about the country
except on settled fair days, George Frederick the then
Markgraf of Brandenburg or Duke of Prussia, had proved
his humane inclinations. It is true, neither he nor his
successors could put themselves in opposition to the trades
or emancipate themselves from the trading principles then
adopted, so far as to give the pedlar free trade, or throw
open the gates of the cities to the merchant-stranger. By
doing so they would have had to override trade and city
privileges sanctioned ages ago. But they could mitigate
harsh laws as far as possible, and by an occasional "*sic
volo sic jubeo*" assert their own royal prerogatives against
those of the cities.

The case of 1589 was this. Hans Drum and his son,
Scotsmen, had appeared before him protesting, that they,
though acknowledging their duty to abstain from hawking,
had given goods on credit and lent money up and down
the country *previous* to the promulgation of the Duke's
decrees, and that he could not recover these debts now,
when the "Scots on the highways were seized and over-
powered whether they carried their merchandise about
them or no," without a letter of protection. This letter
the Duke granted for the said purpose, and promised him
protection throughout the whole extent of his dominions,
with the exception only of the sea-board, where he was
not allowed to set foot. From January till the next Easter
the letter was to be in force, and its protection was
extended to fifteen or sixteen other Scotsmen, and in the
following year (1590) to two more: Hans Adie and
Andrew Park.[1]

The same desire of mitigating the rigour of the law
and of stemming the tide of petty persecution that had set
in against the Scot in the towns was shown by the rulers

[1] *Kgl. St. Archiv*, Königsberg.

of Prussia on many occasions, giving rise to much angry correspondence between the civil rulers of the towns and their Sovereign.

In Rastenburg, in 1570, the magistrates return a petition of Zander Wilson, praying the Duke not to interfere with their ancient rights; "Let him settle elsewhere." And when, in 1594, a Scot named Andrew Schott asks to be enrolled as burgess, the magistrates immediately write to the Duke stating that they had never conferred civil rights on any but Germans, least of all on the Scots, who were given to all sorts of "cunning devices" and cheating practices, enriching themselves and impoverishing the native trader. They go on quoting the case of a Scot at Bartenstein who, even although he married a citizen's daughter, was not admitted as a burgess and had to remove elsewhere. Moreover, the candidate was said to deal in amber "secretly on the sea coast." In 1627, Rastenburg again refuses to admit a Scot with the name of David Hunter, for the same reasons. "Such a thing never happened before," the letter of the magistrates says, "except once in the case of Andrew Ruperten Sohn (Robertson), at the intercession of the most gracious Lady the Duchess, who was then staying in the town during the time of the plague (at Königsberg?)."

Many complaints reach the Prince from Riesenburg, another small town. Andrew Rutherford had acquired civil rights there on account of the Prince's intercession about 1560; [1] but when his widow had married another

---

[1] "Because Andrew Rutherford (Rudersfurt) has performed all the duties of a citizen, paying taxes, working at the fortifications, and so forth, and has also proved his honest birth by birth briefs, His Grace wishes him to be admitted as a citizen, and like his neighbours in their town of Riesenburg, to earn his bread by brewing, distilling and the sale of small merchandise. This is granted to him provided no deceit or false dealing be proved against him " (1561).—*Kgl. St. Archiv*, Königsberg.

Scotsman and complained that the town did not give him these rights as well, the magistrates' reply was that in the meantime the rule had been adopted only to receive Germans as citizens (1565).

In Memel the magistrates, in a letter to the Duke, assert their right to refuse any but German burgesses, according to the statute-law of Cologne, which had been adopted by them. Theirs being a border town one Scot would draw many other Scots after him, and the consequence would be "that if the Lord gave them daughters, their countrymen would conclude marriages and settle there, whereby we Germans would be oppressed. Moreover, no trust could be placed in a Scotsman in times of need." This was their argument, and the Duke's reply and decision ran: "If you can show real privileges and have not given citizens' rights to other strangers already, your supplication shall be granted"; thus leaving a door open to the petitioner, one Hans Mancke (Mackey?), whose condition was rendered all the more pitiful, since the validity of his promise of marriage had been made conditional upon his acquiring civil rights (2nd of May 1606).[1]

Another petition, signed by William Turner, Hans Bessett and Zander Bisset, Scotsmen of Memel, refers to former decrees in favour of the admission of the Scots granted by Markgraf Joachim Friedrich in 1606, May 2nd, and in 1608, July 5th; also by the father of the present Duke, Markgraf Johann Sigismund, in 1611, Jan. 10th, and complains of the dilatoriness of the magistates who had postponed the final meeting in this matter of civil rights till October on account of the great fair; though this fair was no business of theirs, and their purpose no other but to humble the Scottish nation and

---

[1] *Kgl. St. Archiv*, Königsberg.

make it lose all patience.[1]   They wanted to elude the
term, for in the end of October the ice was just beginning
to bear on the Haff, rendering all travelling most difficult ;
the delay was indeed rooted only in the unwillingness of
the authorities to show reason why the Scots should not
enjoy the privileges of citizens when they did bear a
citizen's burdens.   Petitioners therefore pray to fix upon
the earlier date of the 1st of September for their meeting.

In 1627 and again in 1636, by decree[2] of the Duke,
the town of Memel was permitted until further notice to
exact from the Scots who were admitted to the privileges
of burgess "the sum of one hundred thaler, in consideration of the great hardships it had to endure during the
Swedish occupation in 1629-1635, and of the exhausted
state of its treasury."   If the Scots were admitted indiscriminately they would deprive the inhabitants of their
living, the decree says.   In consequence of this high
fee difficulties arose ; a Scotsman with the name of
Gilbert refusing to pay more than 100 mark, although
he neither served the town in times of war, nor had he
stayed in it for a considerable length of time.   As he was,
moreover, a man of means, it was hoped that the Duke
would not listen to his representations.   Thus the Mayor
and Town Councillors of Memel wrote in 1642, April 10th,
and the Duke saw no reason for changing his mind.

Of all the cities in his realm, it was his own capital,
however, that gave him most trouble.   Fierce and long
were the conflicts between the Dukes and the magistrates of Königsberg on account of the Scots.   Let us
take a few typical instances.

Already in 1624 a Scotsman with the name of Dick
tried hard to obtain civil rights there, and was finally

---

[1] " Matt und mürbe machen."
[2] Dated Jan. 27, 1636. *Kgl. St. Archiv*, Königsberg.

successful. But only after a most determined resistance on the part of the city authorities. The latter wrote to the Duke complaining that Dick attempted to wrest the civil rights from them with his "cunning practices;"[1] that he had certain friends among the councillors of the township of Kneiphof, and that he had approached the Duke in order to gain his intercession *per importunas preces*. Dick, it appears, relied on the fact of his having married the daughter of a famous Prussian legal adviser to the Crown, one Johannes Mirander. King Sigismund III. of Poland also supported his claim in a Latin letter to the magistrates, dated Warsaw, May 3rd, 1624, in which the merits of Mirander are extolled; nor did the Churfürst George Wilhelm hesitate to join issue with his royal cousin. He insisted on this candidature being an exceptional one, and pleaded with the town council not to consider Dick as a Scotsman, but as the husband of his wife.[2] Kneiphof, however, not only refused to enroll him but distrained his goods. Again it required the severe reproof of their sovereign, and even threats, to make the magistrates relent, restore the property to its owner (1626), and grant his request.

Churfürst (Elector) Frederick William in 1642 had yielded to the request of Hans Dennis, who had produced letters of recommendation from the Kings of England and of Poland, and granted him liberty of trading not only "throughout our duchy by land and water, but chiefly also in and around our town of Königsberg; by which he may trade in cloth, woollen stuffs, silks and other goods with the strangers and inhabitants at the annual fairs, especially those at Candlemas and Michael-

---

[1] "Mit List und Practiken."

[2] Letter dated Dec. 4, 1624. *Kgl. St. Archiv*, Königsberg. About Mirander see also p. 36.

mas, freely and unrestrictedly. In this we will protect him against the magistrates of any place." Soon this ominous addition was to be put to the test. In the year 1644 Dennis's goods are distrained in the town on the pretence that he secretly carried his wares about by night; that he had hired a house; that he had made purchases outside the city boundaries; and that he had defrauded the customs. The Churfürst, on hearing of the matter, ordered his goods to be released, and sent for Dennis. He proposed to him to move his quarters to the Liberties and to restrict his trading to cloths. He might freely visit Memel and Tilsit and the rent of his house would not be required of him.

Now the guild of merchants as the defendant showed itself at first very hard and not at all inclined to desist from its suit; it had also made such proposals of settlement as could not be accepted by Dennis. They complain that Dennis had bought a house in the Kneiphöfische Langgasse, where he carried on business with strangers and natives alike for mere " bravado " and against former orders of the Duke, and they actually propose to force not only Dennis but all other Scots that dwelt in the suburb of Kneiphof, occupying houses in the best situations with their families and receiving their countrymen as guests from abroad and from the country districts, to leave the town as quickly as possible. Finally, however, the guild gave in, and from the law courts of Königsberg the case was transferred to the Duke for his arbitration. The following conditions were proposed by the town: 1, Dennis resigns his privileges; 2, he settles on the Ducal liberties; 3, he may buy his goods from the citizens and sell them either to strangers or to natives by the ell; 4, the defendants have to be compensated for their expenses; 5, insulting words or writings have to be retracted by Dennis. These conditions were considered too hard ; Dennis is however willing to concede 1 and 2 if he had liberty to bring his goods from Elbing and Danzig and Thorn and sell them to strangers or natives alike by the piece and by the ell the whole year through. The Duke holds out the possibility that Dennis would restrict his commercial transactions to the trade in cloth and expects that an arrangement could be made with the widow from whom Dennis had hired the house for a term of six years, three of them having yet to run, so that he would not be pressed for the rent. As to law expenses he proposes share and share alike. To this the deputies of the town reply, that if Dennis was to restrict his trading to cloth only, they would try to persuade the Guild to grant him one of the Königsberg fairs where he could then make purchases sufficient for his living. They also agree after some more parley to allow him the great Dominic fair at Danzig as well as the fairs of Elbing and Thorn. Finally an arrangement is arrived at, according to which the Duke recedes from his privilege, Dennis settles on the Liberties, trades in cloth only, promises to pay an instalment on his rent and to revoke his insults as spoken and written " *nullo injuriandi animo.* " On the other hand he is free to buy his goods at the towns and times mentioned (but not from ships on the river and not dearer than at 6 gulden the yard), and to sell them here at Königsberg and in the country towns to anyone by the piece or by the ell not only at the fairs but at all times unrestrictedly. In this way a reconciliation was effected in 1645 on the 22nd of November.[1]

---

[1] The magistrates were unwilling also to enroll Dennis because of his religion. He had stoutly declared that he belonged neither to the Roman Catholic nor to the Lutheran, but to the Presbyterian Church, in which he had been born and brought up and in which he intended to remain (April 1642). *Kgl. St. Archiv,* Königsberg.

Some time later, about the year 1657, another exchange of strongly worded letters took place between the Duke and the magistrates. "Next to the loss of our means of subsistence," the latter say, "the impairment of our privileges and customs must be our most anxious consideration. We therefore pray You not to receive our petition ungraciously since we have sworn solemnly to defend our civil liberties. As great difficulties are raised in these days about the conferring of civil rights upon strangers, we must insist on the fact that as long as our town of Königsberg is in existence this has not been done indiscriminately, but only after due consideration of the petitioner's birth-place, his married state, etc. Above all, foreign nations, especially the Scots and the Dutch, have been refused admission to our rolls of burgesses. For this law, not unknown to Your Grace, there have been very weighty reasons, among others the fear of introducing foreign manners and customs. Nor do our own people in England or Scotland enjoy civil rights and unrestricted trading liberties. In spite of all this, two Scotsmen, Gilbert Ramsay, Andrew Ritch [1] and others by their importunate prayers have obtained intercessions from Your Highness and the privilege of free-trade and civil rights, though hitherto this concession has belonged to the magistrates only and has always been left undisturbed ; whilst the principle has been confirmed by Markgraf Johann Sigismund in his decree of 1613, paragraph 4." Then the letter reminds the Prince of former decrees against the Scots issued by his forefathers, and of the fact that in the case of Dennis he had promised not to create a precedent, and concludes with the old assertion that their trade would be ruined by the influx of the Scots. In conclusion they maintain their ancient

[1] The Churfürst had interceded for these two men in 1656.

privileges and mention incidentally that the Scots, so far from having enjoyed equal rights with the citizens, had only been tolerated in their city, and that only during a certain time of the year, whilst they had had to leave in winter. To admit one or two Scots as burgesses would mean to admit many, on account of their extraordinary clannishness.[1]

In spite of all this opposition, guilds and civil authorities had to yield to the Duke's pressure and after having used their last resource, that of distraining these Scotsmen's goods, they had to admit Ramsay and Ritch among the number of their citizens.

Other instances presented the same difficulty owing to the obstinacy of the town guild and magistrates. Take the case of Johann Krehl (Crail) who had applied for admission to the roll of citizens in Königsberg. As usual the magistrates refuse on the ground of his being a stranger. Krehl appeals to the Duke.

In his petition, dated 1676, he stated that his goods, though properly registered at the Custom House, had been twice distrained and his offer to find security been rejected; nay, the magistrates of the three towns apparently "tried to ruin me by appealing from one court to another, under the pretext that I, not being a citizen, had no right to trade at all. And yet," he continues, "I have carried on my business unmolested on the Castle Liberties and under protection of the Duke for nearly sixteen years, having previously served my time with Gilbert Ramsay, now a citizen and a merchant in the town of Kneiphof, for which I again beg to thank Your Grace most humbly. To supply this want I am most ready to acquire citizens' rights ; but here again they refuse to admit me "*propter Nationem.*" Now, as I have

---

[1] " Sie kleben an einander."

no other profession nor have learned any other trade by which I could earn bread for my wife and children . . . I should be compelled, if I be not allowed to trade here, to remove with my poor family to another place, and because others of my nation who live on the Liberties [1] would for the like reasons be forced to do what I did, Your Grace's customs would be deprived annually of a considerable sum. But because Your Grace's whole and well-known intention has always been to let everybody carry on his business securely in your domains, I pray to have my goods restored and my application for the citizenship granted."

Thereupon the Duke, in 1677, issues the following letter: " John Krehl, a merchant in the Castle Liberties, has approached us and informed us how he had lived in Königsberg almost from his boyhood up, and how after having attained ripe years, he had for more than sixteen years carried on his business there. He also complains that he has not been able, in spite of all his efforts, to obtain the rights of a burgess, on account of his being of Scottish extraction. He begs of us to intercede on his behalf. Now we are fully aware of the decrees issued by our diets in this matter, and we have no intention to annoy you, but you will easily see for yourselves how ungracious a thing it would be on your part to let Krehl, a man who has dwelt among you so long and has been carrying on a large trade, the benefits of which in taxes and duties you also reap, come under the common rule of the exclusion of Scotsmen, and to put him on a level with a stranger who only recently put foot in your town and as to whose intentions you are utterly ignorant. Such harsh treatment would be a discredit and a detri-

[1] The inhabitants of the Liberties were not counted for full by the inhabitants of the towns of Königsberg.

ment to you and yours. It would be a disgrace in the
eyes of the strangers and above all of the English nation,
between which and the Scottish there is such excellent
understanding (!) and with which you carry on so much
commerce. We do not doubt, therefore, that you will
take everything into due consideration, and that you will
not refuse to admit Krehl as a burgess; especially since
this case shall not establish any precedent.

Given in the camp before Stettin, July 10th, 1677."[1]

Still the magistrates remained obstinate, and the dispute
grew in bitterness, especially when the Duke Frederick
William had granted Krehl's son, a lad of sixteen, the
veniam ætatis or majority, ostensibly because he had
done well in business, and could manage for himself, in
reality only to invalidate the objection of being a stranger
in the boy's case, who, being a German by birth, now
had a right to claim citizenship (1682). It was a
clever stroke, but the civil authorities were still masters
of the situation. They reply by another move. On
the 30th of November the Duke writes to them: "We
let you know that John Krehl complained that you
refused his son civil rights under the pretext that he was
not married yet, and that you also wrongfully seized five
pieces of his cloth. Now, as there are no other valid
reasons to be brought against this son, to whom we have
granted the *veniam ætatis* in order to let him continue his
father's business, surely his being not married would
make no difficulty. For although you may have in your
laws certain passages to that effect, yet is it known that
you yourselves have often made a change and have given
to those who applied for civil rights, being bachelors, a
certain time within which they might marry. This course
would be the one to adopt in young Krehl's case until

[1] *Kgl. St. Archiv*, Königsberg.

his years permit him to take a wife. We therefore
order you to restore the five pieces of cloth, and to
remove the cause of his complaint. (1682, November
30th).[1]"

As was to be expected the council and the magistrates
persist in their refusal to receive young Krehl on the
roll of burgesses. "We will not admit boys instead of
men" they say. "When Your Grace recommends some
one as a new member to the nobility, either his or his
ancestors' merits are considered, but we can find nothing
in Krehl; he being still so young that he can neither
carry on an ordinary conversation nor do useful services ;
and as to the old one he is so obstinate and importunate
that he not only ruins the guilds, but also disgraces
the magistrates by his slanderous counter-statements and
reports. The money he has accumulated in Prussia has
made him insolent. Let him pay a fine of 1000 gulden."[2]
This was in February 1683. In September of the same
year Krehl's goods are at last restored after a severe letter
of the Duke threatening to mulct the magistrates of 2000
thaler. A good many more letters were required before
the matter was finally settled by the Duke in a written
order to the Königsberg authorities to admit young
Krehl without fail and delay, in default whereof the
threatened fine would certainly be exacted.[3]

Sometimes the Scottish applicants for the honour of
citizenship, when they did not rely on the intercession of
royalty, preferred curious claims in their favour.

Hans Abernethy from Aberdeen, for instance, states on
a similar occasion that he had married the daughter of

[1] *Kgl. St. Archiv*, Königsberg.
[2] *Kgl. St. Archiv*, Königsberg (Kaufmännisches Archiv).
[3] Letters dated 17th of January 1684, 7th of February and 7th of
April 1684.

the bailie's man,[1] and that he had provided the town of Danzig with butter for the last ten years. Jacob Hill and W. Tamson also married daughters of citizens, and have carried produce into the city. Alexander Demster (end of the XVIth Century) married the daughter of the clerk at the Corn Exchange,[2] "by whom he got nothing." He had also for charity's sake taken his two sisters-in-law into his house after their father's death, "one of them almost deaf."

No less remarkable were the conditions attached by the authorities to the enrolment of new burgesses. In Christburg, one Donalson has in a case like this to promise only to marry a German girl on pain of losing his privileges (1640).[3] In the town of Posen not only had the candidates to present the town on their admission as citizens with "leather buckets" or a musket ("sclopetum"), but they had also to conform to religious tests. In the year 1667 three other Scotsmen — Jacobus Joachimus Watson, George Edislay from Newbattle, and Wilhelmus Aberkrami (Abercrombie) from Aberdeen, are with others enrolled as burgesses after having produced their birth briefs. But this condition is added, that they should on Sundays and festival days go and hear the sermon at the Parish Church of S. Mary Magdalene and embrace the Roman Catholic faith within a year. In 1630 three Scotsmen—Erasmus Lilitson (?) from Aberdeen, and Gilbert Blenshel (?) and Georgius Gibson from Culross, produce letters from the King of Poland and are admitted as citizens on the pledge of Jacobus Braun, a

[1] "Schulzendiener." There was a lower grade of citizenship at Danzig and a higher one. A higher fee was charged for obtaining the latter, which comprised the merchants, and, in general, the better class people of the community.

[2] "Haberschreiber," Clerk of the Oats.

[3] Schmidt, *Geschichte des Stuhmer Kreises,* Thorn, 1868, p. 132 f.

merchant at Posen. They promise to be present at all
the Catholic services on festivals, and pay the large sum
of 900 florins "as wages for the poor workmen."

It is only just, however, to add that these are the only
two instances found out of a large number of Scottish
names in the Civil Registers of Posen where a similar
interference with the religious belief of the candidate occurs. In two other cases the applicants are
called "Calvini," but no condition like the above is
added.[1]

In Königsberg David Grant is one of the few Scots
who had gained the heart of the magistrates. Considering that he had lived quietly and retired for thirty years
in the town, and that neither his neighbours on account
of his domestic life, nor the guilds of citizens on account
of injury done to their trade ever complained of him;
considering also that he, after the death of his first wife,
married the daughter of a German citizen, whereby he
became related to and befriended with good and well-to-
do people, and that the ministers of the Church give him
an excellent character for piety; considering lastly that
the guild of merchants intercedes for him, the magistrates grant him permission to acquire his own house and
to keep it, without, however, establishing a precedent
(Sept. 5, 1622).[2]

Significant is the addition made when Thomas Smart
from Dundee was admitted into the ranks of Danzig
citizens; it runs: "but he is to refrain from buying up
noblemen's estates" (1639).[3] Read together with the

[1] See the list of Scottish citizens at Posen, a most suggestive and
interesting document, in Part III.

[2] *Stadt Archiv*, Könisgberg. This is the only example of the magistrates looking favourably upon the civil claims of the Scots. But what
an imposing catalogue of virtues was demanded in exchange!

[3] *Kgl. St. Archiv*, Danzig, xxiii. D. 28.

notice to be found in a document in which John and Andrew Tamson complain "of having lent more than two tuns of gold to noblemen of the Polish kingdom on the security of their estates, of which large sum nothing could be recovered in consequence of the Cossack warriors" (1653), this speculation in landed estates does not seem to have been a very profitable one.

Curious to say that in very many cases the young Scottish burgess who had encountered such great difficulties in gaining admission, now rapidly rose in the public estimation of his fellow-citizens. We find him in positions of trust as mayor, councillor, elder or president of the guilds. For the latter also had been obliged to open their gates most reluctantly at first, more willingly after the second generation of the Scot, retaining its Scottish name but born in the country "of right, free German kind," as the old documents call it, had grown up within the walls of a German city. In Königsberg, where popular prejudice and hatred of the stranger made itself much more noisily heard than at Danzig, there appear as members of the guild of merchants in the year 1690— Charles Ramsay, son of Gilbert, another Charles Ramsay, Jacob Kuick, Jacob Hervie, John Brooke, Adam Fullert and William Ritch. In the same year Thomas Hervie, a young merchant, applies for admission, stating that he was already a burgess, had been duly sworn in and was quite ready to submit to the laws of the guild. The elders thereupon declare their willingness to admit him as a guild brother on this condition that if he did not marry within a year's time, he should lose his civil rights as well as his guild privileges. And since the reception of one unmarried was uncommon, not only were the laws read out to him, but he was also given to understand that he would do well to consent to an extra fee for admission to the guild. This admonition proved so effective that he subscribed ninety gulden, adding voluntarily another ten gulden for the treasury; setting, as the document quaintly adds, "a glorious example to his successors; and many were the wishes for his prosperity and happiness. May God keep him strong and in good health, so that he may work with much profit and acceptance in this honourable guild!"[1]

The elders or presidents of the guild had each year on the accession to their office to deliver a long speech, which was duly reported in the minute-books. Now this must have been a hard task for some of the Scottish members. It explains, perhaps, why a good many bought themselves out, among them the above named William Ritch. In a marginal note of the minute-book of the guild we find this addition (1690): "the money has not been paid yet, Ritch having gone to the wars in England."[1]

But not only in the guilds, in Church and State matters also the Scots after they had settled in the towns, took an active part. They contributed liberally to all public undertakings and to all charitable institutions, especially the hospitals; they were among the most active of the great German patriots who helped to shake off the yoke of a foreign tyrant.[2] But their own Scottish community or "nation," as it was then called, always remained nearest to their hearts. Their care for their own poor had almost become proverbial. There is not an important event in their families which did not find an expression in a donation to "our dear poor." In the dusty—very dusty—records of the Church of SS. Peter and Paul and

[1] *Willkürbuch der Kneiphofischen Kaufmannszunft* (Roll of the Merchants' Guild at Königsberg). For complete list of Scottish members from 1602-1750 see Part III.

[2] Compare *Scots in Germany*, pp. 272 ff. and elsewhere.

St Elizabeth, the two Presbyterian places of worship at Danzig, the congregations of which were largely joined by Scotch and Dutch,[1] we find numerous and touching instances of this. Gourlay in 1682 gives two hundred gulden to the poor-box in memory of his son killed at Blois in France; T. Carmichael contributes twelve gulden after the death of his "Söhnlein" Jacob; Col. Patterson gives six gulden on the occasion of the baptism of his son, whilst Chapman (1619), Lumsdel, Ramsay (1672), Thomas Leslie, Robert Tevendale and D. Davidson[2] on a like occasion contributed ten gulden each. Now as some of the Scottish families boasted of many children, the poor must have fared rather well. We are glad to read that the same Carmichael was comforted for the loss of his " Söhnlein " by the birth of another son in 1691 and of another in the following year: the Scottish poor profiting each time twenty - four gulden. The Turner brothers, Andrew and William, also show the same liberal spirit, and so does Alexander Ross who at one time sends his contribution accompanied by the words: " A debt of

[1] The Dutch had their own "Church Books" written in Dutch, but of Scottish records written in English no trace could be discovered.

[2] Davidson wrote a sketch of his own life. The manuscript is in the Town Library of Danzig. He was born at Zamosc in Poland in 1647. His father, born 1591 at Edinburgh, came to Poland in 1606, served six years as a boy and three years as journeyman, after which he commenced his own business. Later he came to Danzig where he "by the advice of his friend Robert Tevendail," married a daughter of Al. Aidie, the scholar. In 1682 he was enrolled as citizen and became President of the Board of the Smallpox Hospital, then a most important institution and one much favoured by the Scots in their last wills. He was also an elder at St Peter's Church. His daughter married one John Clerk in 1699 and received as dowry the large sum of 25,000 gulden. In his will he left large bequests to the poor, exhibitions for Polish students of the Calvinistic faith and legacies to the widows and orphans of Danzig. His name is also written Davisson.

due gratitude to the Great God for the safe delivery of his beloved wife " (1702).[1]

The same national spirit prevailed among the Scottish nation of Königsberg. Unfortunately we have hardly any Church Records there, beyond what was told in our third chapter of "The Scots in Germany "; but the following document, dated May 27, 1636 [2] will go far to prove it. It is signed by the Burggraf, *i.e.* the representative of the Sovereign who was at the same time the President of the Board of the Great Hospital in Löbenicht, and runs :

" This day there appeared before us the representatives of the whole Scottish nation dwelling in this city and made known to us how they were unanimously of the opinion that it would be necessary and proper to have their own room or lodgment in the hospital, in which not only their servants but also their countrymen could find a refuge, comfort and assistance when they came here by land or by water and were according to God's will taken ill or fell into poverty. Now since they know of no other place so well provided for and fitted up as the large hospital of Löbenicht, where in such cases of necessity the sick would best be cared for, they therefore applied to us and urgently requested us to let them have a room and a small room for the sum of 1500 mark and an annual perpetual rent due at Easter 1637 of twenty mark. In answer to this request we, the masters of the hospital, have promised the above representatives of the Scottish nation to build them a room thirty-six feet long and broad, also another small apartment of about eight feet width but of the same length as the large room ; in

---

[1] Much prettier in German : " Aus schuldiger Dankbarkeit dem grossen Gott vor (sic) glückliche Entbindung seiner Eheliebsten."

[2] *Kgl. St. Archiv*, Königsberg, Schieblade xxxii. 33.

the meantime we have assigned to them for their use a vacant room situated near the gate, which they will have to give up as soon as the new rooms have been built. These new rooms they will have to keep in repair for all time and to furnish with beds, bed-clothes, tables, seats, wardrobes and other furniture, and they will have a right to make use of the rooms as their own property for their children, servants and countrymen, should illness or poverty overtake them (which God prevent). But they ought to apply in such cases to the master and bring a letter from one of their elders to prevent imposition. The sick shall then be taken in willingly and shall be furnished with the needful food and drink, wood for heating purposes, light and other necessaries as far as the means of the hospital allow; and in order that there be no want of good and faithful nursing, a man and a woman, whom the Scots may select and submit to the approval of the hospital governors, shall be appointed for these rooms. In the case of death all moneys owned or acquired during the illness, all goods and clothes shall become the property of the hospital. The same rule applies to those afflicted with *morbo Gallico*, who shall have been brought into these or other rooms at the request of the elders for their recovery; only that in such case the person afflicted with this abomination of the French shall be holden to pay his medical fee to the barber. Signed with my own hand,

THE OBERST BURGGRAF."

In their marriages also a strong national tendency shows itself. It is true, in a great many cases the daughters of German citizens were chosen, especially in the second generation, and very often, it is to be feared, for the purpose of getting on socially as well as politically. But

E

wherever there were no such reasons, as a rule, the Scots-man preferred his own blood. Unfortunately, shall we say, the choice among Scotch girls was not a large one; but then there were the widows. The widow of a Scots-man in Germany never had to wait very long before she was led to the altar again by one of her own nation. Numerous entries in the marriage register of the Presby-terian Churches of Danzig prove this. The very first name we meet is that of James Burges, who in 1573 marries the widow of Simon Lang. In 1647, Alex. Nairn, a Scotch lieutenant, marries John Irvin's widow; H. Saunders leads Davidson's widow to the altar in 1651. Other entries are: Hans Morton marries Mary Robertson; Jacob Meldrum, Christina Balfour in 1629; William Balfour marries Anna Pilgram in 1631;[1] Jacob Littlejohn, Barbara Edwards (1634); George Dempster marries Elizabeth Steven; and Thomas Philip, the daughter of Hans Kant (1635); Elizabeth Muttray (Aberdeen) is chosen by Albert Bartelt (?), a Scotch glover; John Wood marries Maria Robertson (1654); and Francis Gordon, the Consular Agent of Britain in 1655, Margaret, the daughter of James Porteous, a late minister in Scotland.

At the christenings, too, godfathers and godmothers were mostly chosen from amongst their own people. Hans Tam-son has a "Söhnlein" baptised in 1631, godfather and godmother are Williamson and Anne Pilgram. For David Biel's son Nathaniel Andrew Thin, "noch ein Schottsmann," and James Smith's wife perform the duty (1632); whilst William Balfour is godfather to David Moritz's (Morriss) son Henry, and again to Arnt Pilgram's son Jacob, together with Jacob Meldrum's wife and the German Sühnefelt.[2]

---

[1] William Balfour married a second time in 1636. His wife was Maria von Hoffen.

[2] See the Records of the Churches of SS. Peter and Paul and of St

If Scottish children or widows required guardians, or a Scottish plaintiff or testator, witnesses: again we invariably come across Scottish names. All business transactions that had to be carried on by commissioners or delegates lay in the hands of Scotsmen. Thus David Nisbet gives Jacob Rhodo (?) at Danzig, power to call in certain moneys owed by A. Guthrie (1619); or David Maxwell as the assignee of the brothers George and Alexander Bruce "de Carnok," gives a receipt to J. Rowan at Danzig for a certain sum of money, whereby two contracts entered into at Culross and Edinburgh become void (1627). Thus Patrick and Thomas Aitkenhead depute R. Tevendale and D. Davidson concerning the property left by David Aitkenhead (1689).[1] Or Anna Moir at Danzig appoints George Falconer to receive a legacy left to her children from the hands of Dr William Skene, the Rector of the High School at Edinburgh. Or the City of Aberdeen writes to one Chapman in Danzig to act as trustee for Mrs Janet Cruikshank, who is to receive three-fourths of the residue from George Cruikshanks' widow (1672).

A very common event was the solemn declaration of the coming-of-age of a young Scot. For this purpose one or two of his friends accompanied him before the magistrates, pronounced his apprenticeship finished, and gave him a verbal testimonial of good character. Hundreds of those cases are recorded. We shall only mention a few at random. Hans Morton at Danzig receives a certificate of good conduct from his brother-in-law Orem, and from Andrew Bell, and is declared of age "as a braidmaker."[2]

Elizabeth at Danzig. The latter church was sold in consequence of the terrible distress after the French occupation, there is now only one Presbyterian Church there, that of St Peter, a very old, fine building.

[1] Edinburgh, Nov. 16th. *Kgl. St. Archiv,* Danzig.

[2] Feb. 10th, 1660.

Jacob Grieff receives the certificate from his two guardians and is declared of age (1619). Frequently this was accompanied by a short speech of the young Scot, in which he declared his gratitude to the guardians and absolved them from all further responsibility.

In clannishness like this the Scot must have found a source of happiness; for though now settled in a town, the hostilities of the trade and the ill-favour of the magistrates, consequent upon it, were by no means diminishing. Twice in Königsberg did they reach quite an acute point; in 1612 and again in 1683. The orders to banish the Scots from the town had been given, and but for the energy and the wisdom of the Duke would ruthlessly have been executed. The Duke again was influenced by the British ambassador Georgius Brussius,[1] who had been sent for the very purpose of. assisting and protecting the Scottish subjects of His Majesty the King of Great Britain.

Protesting against the narrow-minded policy of his capital, the Duke writes on the 3rd of February, 1613: "That according to the laws of your town you refuse civil rights to the Dutch and the Scots may pass. But I do not find in your laws, or anywhere else, the least cause why those foreign nations should not be suffered in this country, nor why they should not have their own houses. On the contrary, this town of Königsberg derives great advantages and profit from the commerce and trade of these nations. Moreover, it might prove a dangerous thing to proceed to extreme measures and give

---

[1] He was sent in 1604 by James VI., and was a native of Caithness. His birth brief issued by the Comes de Caithness (1591) is still preserved at Danzig, as well as his University Certificate, dated Würzburg, 1594, (*Kgl. St. Archiv*, Danzig, Handschr. I. B. C. 32). He had studied law at Würzburg for four years.

cause to pay us back with the like coin; the commerce of our towns might easily be injured thereby. For these and other important reasons it is our will that the foreign tradesman as hitherto, so in the future, shall not be prevented from acquiring house-property, it being not only inhuman and against good manners to deny any Christian nation, that lives with us without giving any offence, the *jus hospitii*, but also *per indirectum* deducible from your conduct, that you, by such heavy taxes and unbearable innovations, wish to drive the Dutch and the others out of this town of Königsberg altogether. This would be a thing which we, for many and grave reasons, could not approve of and much less permit.

HANS SIGISMUND."

How there could be any doubt as to the Duke's way of thinking after an energetic letter like the above is beyond comprehension. Yet the struggle went on to the end of the century — the justly - aggrieved Scots against dense magistrates and jealous trades; again the narrow-minded policy of the magistrates against the fairness of the sovereign. Obstinacy on both sides. In 1617 the Scots and the Dutch complain that they could only bury their dead at a much higher fee than that exacted from the citizens of Königsberg, and that in some cases burial was refused to those who had not received the Lord's supper from the hands of a priest on their death-bed; and from a petition to the Churfürst of the year 1622 it appears that the Scots had been threatened with expulsion. They write very indignantly as follows: "It could easily be proved from the annals of Prussian history that of the Scottish nation in this duchy, not only in the time of the Teutonic Order, but also since Prussia became a duchy, honest and upright merchants have been suffered by the three towns of Königsberg.

These merchants have always shown themselves duly submissive to their rulers and the city authorities, so that no great insubordination or unpleasantness occurred. But now they have not only refused us habitation, but given us to understand by public notice that we must leave this town at Michaelmas, and with our households betake ourselves elsewhere. This decree appears to us all the more grievous as our nation has been *in possessione ultra centenaria*, a possession which it has never given up, so that the rule applies *uti possidetis ita possideatis*. But may God prevent that our nation should rely upon the rigour of the law; it has always preferred the way of supplication and humble petition. Moreover, our intention has always been, and is still, to risk our very lives [1] for the Crown of Poland and the Duchy of Prussia. We can prove by many examples how in war the Scots performed many glorious deeds. Therefore we do not expect that Your Highness will, as long as we live peacefully and like our neighbours, showing due reverence for Burgomaster and Council, consent to the steps taken by the three towns of Königsberg, whereby we would be cast off as 'vile members.'[2] Such a step would be a disgrace in the eyes of the whole world, which the Scottish nation could never extinguish. Moreover, those of us who perhaps did not obey the law at times have always been duly punished. We have hoped that the decision of this matter would have been deferred until Your Highness's home-coming. We would then not have doubted that a way would have been found to satisfy the magistrates. But since this was not done, we now humbly pray Your Highness to postpone the decision, or to remit the quarrel to Your Ducal Court

---

[1] "Leib und Leben, Gut und Blut aufsetzen."
[2] "Stünckende Glieder."

of Justice. We can then show that we are *in naturali et civili possessione*, and that we cannot be expelled out of it by the three towns."

The Churfürst, in reply, sends a very angry letter to the magistrates, expressing his astonishment that they dared to assume an authority which did not belong to them. He commands them to postpone the matter until his return. We read no more of an expulsion, but the magistrates bewail the fact that their office was slighted much more by the present than by the former rulers, their decrees continually blamed and set aside, and that everything was either comprised under the title of regal rights or esteemed a lesion of royal prerogatives.[1]

Matters reached another climax in the years 1680-1690. It appears that in that time new taxes had been laid upon the Scots, whose unpopularity had increased with their increased success in business.[2] Moreover, as this was the time of religious controversy within the walls of the Protestant Church, the *odium religionis* had made itself felt in spite of the most urgent protests on the part of the sovereign of the country. Already in 1680 the Churfürst Frederick William had written to Königsberg requesting the authorities not to oppress

[1] *Stadt Archiv*, Königsberg.

[2] One more letter of complaint to the Duke from the merchants of Königsberg may here be introduced, because it proves to what extremes, both in statements and expression, trade jealousy had by that time driven the writers. They say in article 5, "because it is plain that strangers and those unfit to acquire civil rights, especially the Scots, have usurped most of our trade . . . it is all the more a matter of complaint that this is not done secretly, but under the plea of just privileges. These people have, like a cancerous ulcer, grown and festered; they cling to each other, keep boarders, hire large houses, nay, sometimes oust honest citizens by offering a higher rent, furnish several stores, and this not because of their large capital—most of them are only commission-merchants—but because four or five of them collude, so that if we were

the Scotch and English. In the following year the latter again bitterly complain against the severity of the magistrates, and ask for the liberty of acquiring civil rights, and of buying and hiring houses. The English Ambassador also at the Court of Prussia, Robert Southwell, interceded for his countrymen in a French letter, in which he says:

"Trois années passées pour l'interest particulier des magistrats de la ville ils ont été traités comme s'ils s'en étaiant rendus indignes quoy-qu'ils n'ont jamais en le malheur de le faire. On impose sur eux des impositions personelles comme le tribut par teste, ce qu'on ne pratique ailleurs contre les étrangers, on les taxe comme s'ils possedoient des fonds de terre, sans leur permettre de s'approprier aucun fonds, ni même d'acheter les maisons où ils habitent ni un lieu pour s'ensevelir,[1] on leur demande un tribut de chaque cheminée[2] . . . on se sert de toutes extremités pour lever ces deniers, jusqu'à mettre en prison ceux qui ne s'y conforment."[3]

The opinion of the Churfürst was not long withheld. In 1681, on the 28th of March, the sovereign writes

---

to admit one as a burgess publicly we should secretly create half-a-dozen of them, who would prowl about the country towns from east to west, and finally leave by the gate with a patched knapsack, not, however, without leaving in their place at home a couple of green boys, who would afterwards carry on no better. . . . The great damage the Scot Jackson in the Crooked Lane is doing to our trade in spices under the cover of old Schönfeld is as plain as the light of day. In his and in Wobster's open shop not natives, but two or three Scottish boys are trained the whole year round to our ruin. We therefore pray you," etc., etc. Then follow the usual proposals for inhibiting the trade of the Scots, banishing them out of the town during winter, and so on.

[1] This charge is denied by the magistrates, who say that the Presbyterian burying-place was on the Neue Sorge (now Königstrasse).

[2] No, the magistrates say; not for each chimney, but a smoke-tax.

[3] Names, names! from the magisterial benches. *Stadt A.* Königsberg.

from Potsdam: "We can not allow that the strangers, especially the Scotch and the English, be thus oppressed or expelled, but it is our will that every kindness should be shown them. You will have to take care, therefore, not to oppress them unfairly."

And again, on the 20th December 1681 : "We command you to remove all those new taxes which in fairness cannot be claimed from them, to show them good-will, and not to hinder them from hiring or living in decent houses."

Similar letters were sent in 1682, in January and April. "We again command you, with all our authority, to look to it lest the Scots be oppressed unfairly. This we do in the interest of your own city."

In spite of all this, the matter dragged on till the year 1693, when it needed another strong letter from the Churfürst to make the magistrates desist from an expulsion of the Scots.

This humane spirit of the rulers showed itself everywhere. Letters of protection are issued to Andreas Porter and Hans Adie in 1590 at Königsberg, and concessions are given to sell on the public fair to Jacob From and Andrew Wright (1620); also to the brothers Lawson to visit the fairs in the districts of Welau, Memel and Tilsit (1698). The widow of a drowned Scottish soldier, Charles Ray, obtains permission to carry on her small trade (1697). Or, take the case of Mary Anderson, who had taken refuge in Königsberg after the destruction of Wilda, a village in Posen, by the Russians. She had been driven, for the want of other means, to gain a living by making caps and bonnets, but was greatly annoyed by the guild of furriers, who took the finished goods from her by force. A letter of protection is issued to her in 1668.[1]

[1] *Kgl. St. Archiv*, Königsberg.

About the same time, one George Hotcheson appeals to the Duke and claims exemption from having soldiers quartered in the little house he built for himself at Tragheim, one of the suburbs of Königsberg. The reply states that if the house was not built as a permanent residence, or for the purpose of letting it, but only as a summer-house to be used in the time of the plague, no soldiers should be billeted in it (1663 and 1667).

Gradually only, very gradually, and not till the eighteenth century had well commenced, did the Scots in Prussia enjoy civil rights and privileges.

But even the enrolled Scottish citizen had often to suffer from the ill-will of the German fellow-citizen. A very curious and instructive case of this sort is recorded from Neidenburg. In this small town, to the south of Königsberg, a Scot, with the name of Duncan, had settled, and for more than twenty years attended to his business. In 1603, he had a quarrel with the magistrates on account of a house which he had bought and of his having added cloth to his stock-in-trade. So far, this was only the common form of trade jealousy. But the matter went much further. Let us listen to poor Duncan's story in his own words. "Some people in Neidenburg," he writes, "not only prevent me from brewing my beer, but also try to hinder me from erecting on my own ground, bought by me twenty years ago, instead of the old coach-house another building to contain an upper room and a closet. In consequence of this, when the old building had already been taken down and the new foundation laid with all the wood-work ready, they send Wolf Geschell and Dominick Uttman to me on holy Easter eve to let me know that I was not to proceed with the building or else they would pull it down again. Whereupon on Easter Monday I complained to the governor, and asked for protection;

which he promised, bidding me at the same time go on
with my building; he would order the aforesaid two men
in virtue of his office to leave me in peace.   But when I
was away at Thorn on Tuesday, and my carpenters had
completed their work, Dominick Uttman, being then vice-
consul, in the absence of the burgomaster sent from
house to house, ordering every one under penalty of three
marks to be present at nine of the clock on the following
morning at the town-hall, with their axes and spears for
to tear down my new building.   At the appointed hour
on Friday, the alarm-bell is rung to call the inhabitants
together.   But because many did not approve of proceed-
ings so violent, and consequently stayed away, he again
commands them under penalty of ten marks and imprisonment in the tower to come forward, and when the bell
had tolled twice at one o'clock, he, Dominick Uttman, as
the author of this tumult, marches off with those who had
gathered together; although many others, and especially
the judge, whom my poor terrified wife had implored for
protection, tried to dissuade him, representing to him that
the governor and burgomaster as well as myself were from
home; yet he, having some of the town council with him
who were, together with himself, urging the armed rabble
on, caused ladders to be raised against the house, and
mounting to the top they strike, cut, break and throw
down at their pleasure, until the whole upper story is
demolished.   Even strangers that passed, crowded together, especially some of the Polish nobility who, viewing
the turnout, deplore the great destruction, and express
their detestation of the crime in words like these: 'In
other places people are enjoined to erect pretty buildings,
in Prussia they are forced to pull them down.'   Some of
the rioters, stung by this remark, were drawing back,
when Dominick ordered the beadle to use his whip, as if

they were a herd of cattle; and the town carpenter, who did not want to participate in these acts of violence, and had said to him he would rather sit in the dungeon for some weeks than assist in these unlawful doings, he had cast into prison after the rioting was over. He also caused my servant girl, who had jokingly asked one of the rioters to come in and have something to eat after a hard day's work, to be suddenly taken up in the lane unawares and to be put in prison for some days, so that I, poor man, can find neither justice nor protection in Neidenburg."

Duncan, who, as will be noticed, did not want an eye for the picturesque, afterwards obtained permission to go on with the building.[1] He was to pay to the magistrates the sum of twenty gulden as ground rent and one mark annually, but he was not allowed to light a fire in his house. As to his dealing in cloth, he was not allowed to sell common cloths outside the public fairs. Fine cloths, however, at one and more gulden a yard, he was at liberty to sell and to cut. To this decision was added the note: " Let him behave reverentially and be obedient to the magistrates, and do not let the latter be too hasty." The permission given to sell cloth at all was, however, very distasteful to the guild of cloth merchants. They complain again and again against Duncan and his son-in-law as the " blood-suckers " of the country.

It was pitiful, indeed, that to a life already so full of trouble from within, new trouble should be added, arising in their own home. We have already mentioned the various begging missions of King Charles II. and the names of those who, according to an extraordinary knack of this monarch always to appoint the worst persons to the worst place, were put in charge of them.[2] We are enabled now

---

[1] Brussius (Bruce) also interceded for him as a 'mercator honestus' (1606).   [2] See *Scots in Germany*, p. 202 ff.

to give additional details which will show the different attitudes of the King of Poland and the Kurfürst of Brandenburg towards the scheme of extracting money from Scotsmen now living within these territories.

The first information we get of this plan is contained in a letter of Frederick William to the members of his council in the Duchy of Prussia, dated 1651, 20th of January. In it he simply declares that a *subsidium charitativum*, as he calls it, be collected from the English and Scots living in his domains. Two months later, on March 30th, after due consideration he says, in a circular letter to all his Magistrates and Councils: "We have decreed that for the distressed Royalty [1] of Great Britain, ten per cent. should be collected from the Scots and English within our territories. But after those Scots and English who have settled in our towns at this time and have borne all civil burdens and contributions *have humbly besought us not to impose this extraordinary tax upon them*, it is not our intention to grieve our subjects and citizens with a double and heavy tax, but we shall be satisfied, if only those Scots who are not domiciliated are applied to, but the others who have obtained civil rights and are settled in our towns passed by in the meantime."

Scarcely had this letter been dispatched when on the following day a new letter was sent after it. Apparently the Churfürst was in great difficulties; on the one side his sense of fairness, on the other hand his distressed royal brother and the strong appeals of the hot-headed King of Poland. He now writes: "We do not see that anything worth speaking of could be collected from the vagabonds and pedlars alone, for there are not very many of them who would be able to contribute anything at all. It would be very disreputable if we were to send such a

[1] " Die bedrängte Königliche Würde."

trifling sum as a contribution. We consider it necessary, therefore, and wish to impress it upon you, and request you to send for all the inhabitants of the Scottish or English nation in our Duchy of Prussia and to represent to them in *the most moving terms* how they for the love of their country and respect for their King should not refuse to pay this subsidy willingly ; with this additional assurance that no precedent should be established thereby."

The temper of the Scottish and English residents in Prussia with regard to this matter is very well expressed in the memorial which the latter presented to the magistrates of Königsberg on the third day of October 1651.

" We have communicated with our countrymen, the English settlers in this town, of whom there are only four, respecting the contribution of a subsidy to His Majesty in Scotland. Now we would like very much indeed that we were in such a position as to be able to appease the restlessness and the disturbed state of our native country by it and to remedy all misfortune. But such is the condition of our dear fatherland that if we were to obey this request at once, and the people there came to know of it, not only our property but our lives and those of our own families would be forfeited after those that would assist the King having been declared traitors by Parliament. What have we done, that by a contribution like this, our total ruin should be wrought ? We who are only guests here and have never mixed ourselves up with the quarrel between King and Parliament, but have simply attended to our business and as factors to the orders of our principals ? In so doing we have contributed large sums to the treasury not only but also enriched the community of this town. We can prove from our books that the duty paid by us amounted annually to 30,000 gulden. All this would cease if we and our principals and the whole English and Scottish trade were to be driven out from here. And how could it be otherwise since all the more important ports are in the hands of the Parliament? The only way to save our lives and our property and that of our friends in England would be to emigrate to other places such as Danzig, Elbing, etc., where this request has not only been rejected but the person and the property of the English been taken under the protection of the authorities, whilst their trade was declared free and all magistrates enjoined to petition His Majesty the King on their behalf."[1] This document was signed by John Cottam, Thomas Taylor, Joseph Wynde, and John Burges.

In the meantime Croffts, one of Charles' messengers, had not been idle. He was very anxious to know the result of his appeal. We find him writing from Thorn to the magistrates of Königsberg, requesting them to send the details of the collection (June 14th, 1651); and again seven weeks later from Danzig to the Council Boards of Prussia. He had commissioned Colonel Seton to go to Königsberg and confer with the magistrates there. He concludes by saying: "The matter suffers *no* delay since the King presses me for a detailed account which I cannot give without having received a definite answer from you."[2]

It seems almost incredible that this could have been said and done in the face of Charles' letter, in which he disavows Croffts, and which was dated Dec. 9th, 1650. One is almost tempted to believe in a forgery, as was actually done by Johannes Casimirus, the King of Poland, who, in an angry letter of Sept. 1651, threatens the Scots in his kingdom with expulsion because they made

[1] *Stadt Archiv*, Königsberg.
[2] See Part III.

"certain forged letters the pretext of not paying the contribution."[1]

But the royal missive was no forgery, as we know from a letter issued by the magistrates of Danzig to the Scots who had asked for a Latin translation of it. It officially sets forth its genuineness. The signature had, by comparison with other letters of the same writer, been found genuine, the seal intact, and the whole document free from any suspicious feature.[2]

The half-heartedness of Frederick William, the Churfürst, also appears, from a letter of protection issued on the first of June 1651 to the following six Scotsmen:—Hans Dinings (Dennis?), Hans Simson, Gilbert Ramsay, Andrew Ritchie, Hans Brown and Hans Emslie, in which it is expressly stated that the bearers as inhabitants and citizens of Königsberg paying taxes to the Prince, were in nowise obliged to give the tenth part of their possessions to His Royal "Dignity" in Great Britain, as the other Scots in Poland. The letter granted them safe-conduct for themselves and their goods, especially in their journeys to and from the fairs of Elbing and Danzig, where otherwise their property might have been confiscated at the instigation of the British Orator, because of their non-payment of the subsidy. At the same time, it certified that they were settled in Königsberg and not at Danzig; therefore not under the jurisdiction of Poland.

Little remains to be told of this sad tale of double-dealing. The *subsidium charitativum* proved no success. All Croffts got amounted to about £10,000, as we have seen, and how little of this sum ever reached the King will perhaps never be fully known.[3]

---

[1] "Sufforeta veritate . . literas quarum praetextu ab hac contributione immunes esse volunt."

[2] See Part III. [3] See *Scots in Germany*, p. 48.

The reader of these old records concerning the Scots in Germany cannot fail to be greatly impressed by these facts : the comparatively inoffensive lives these colonists led, their unbroken energy and the quick way they ascended in the second or third generation to positions of trust and eminence.

Barring that large and undesirable element that swept across the Northern States of Germany during the great flood of Scottish emigration—an element the greatest crimes of which seem to have been its youth and poverty —we seldom find the Scot implicated in criminal cases. We say "seldom," of course, in consideration of the long centuries of their settlement and their vast numbers, which at one time must have exceeded by far the thirty thousand mentioned by Lithgow. Neither was the moral atmosphere of Germany in the XVIIth Century particularly fit to inspire and invigorate any man's character. Requesting the reader to keep both these points in view we shall now give a few examples of the Scot as he appeared before the German Courts.

In the minute books of the Courts at Bromberg we are told of Jacobus Herin (Heron), Scotus, who is accused of having sent his *famulus* David Heron to attack a Scotch tailor, with the name of Alexander, whom he wounded (1598). Heron replies that David was *nobilis et sui juris*, of noble birth and of age, and not his *famulus*. He himself knew nothing of the crime, having on the day of its committal been absent in Thorn on business (*mercatum*). The same books relate how a Scot with the name of Wolson (Wilson), who had been president of the court of bailies in the absence of the Starost, was called before the council of the town, and accused of having suppressed certain important documents to the detriment of the place (1671). He, however, appeared only to deny the competency of the court, and " went away." [1]

In Stuhm, in the year 1594, a virago strangles her husband, David Trumb (?), a Scot, by means of his own suspenders, and throws his body out on the field of one Junker Brandis.[2] The small town of Hohenstein reports that two and a half years ago a quarrel and fight took place between some Scots and some peasants (1604).[3] On Dec. 10th, 1555, Alex. Paton, David Alston and George Fleck appear before the court at Neuenburg. During a quarrel, George Fleck had wounded Alexander in the left hand, and he had to get it dressed in the town. The parties settle the matter amicably for the sake of good friendship, on condition that Alexander pay the barber. Jacob Forbes, in a case of manslaughter, is indignant at the Governor of Rastenburg for distraining a sum of money whilst he was quite willing to come to terms peaceably with the family of the deceased, whom he had killed by accident only and not by malice (1569).

To a similar charge, one Albrecht Braun has to answer, but it is not quite clear in his case whether he was a Scot or not (1586).

Hans Wilandt, a Scot, in the town of Konitz, must retract his insults and swear not to offend Andrew Bernt, a jeweller, again (1587); whilst some years later, on the 13th of April, 1598, Alexander Nisbett has to vouch for the honesty of a certain purchase of corn. In Tilsit, John Irving and his workman Anderson are taken before the bench on account of desecrating the solemn day of

---

[1] Schöffenbuch, B. 1, fol. 74c, and Acta consularia, B. 9, fol. 356.

[2] Geschichte des Stuhmer Kreises v. Dr Schmidt, Thorn, 1868, p. 132 f. (*History of the District of Stuhm*).

[3] This notice is interesting also from a linguistic point of view, the word for quarrel or fight being " parlament."

repentance by selling some goods to a Pole. He is admonished and fined in one thaler (1684). In the same town, Jacob Murray is brought up to pay his rent after having been called on forty times. He pleads great poverty, and promises to pay within a week (1687).[1]

Very curious is the case of Hamilton, or Hammelton as the German records spell his name. He was a citizen of Tilsit, a cooper by trade, poor, "so that he seldom kept strange servants, but managed to get along with the help of his two grown-up sons, leading a respectable life," as a certificate says, which the town, at his request, issued in 1687.

Now the peace of mind of father Hamilton is greatly disturbed by the slanderous behaviour of three or four other coopers, Germans, who in a letter had accused his son Christoph of having fraternised with the son of the executioner at Königsberg. Nothing could be more disreputable, more hurtful to the moral feelings of those days, than to have any intercourse with those social outcasts, "unehrliche Leute," as they were called in German, of whom the executioner was the foremost and the most formidable. Accordingly, Hamilton appeals to the law, and the following judgment is given on the 15th of March 1688:

"Whereas Master Andr. Lorentz, Master Abraham Kraus, as well as David Kraus and Johann Lorentz, coopers by trade, defendants, have written to the cooper-guild at Königsberg accusing Christopher Hamilton, the plaintiff, of having in a public beerhouse fraternised with the executioner's son, which, though denied by them, has been sworn to by two witnesses, and whereas they have refused to arrange matters amicably, the Court of Bailies decide that the defendants go to prison for a

[1] *Kgl. St. Archiv*, Königsberg.

night and a day, binding them over to hold the peace. Thereupon they were at once marched off to the cells." [1]

Hot temper seems to have been the origin of many of the reported crimes. Already in 1517 a case of that kind is reported of a Scot from Dumblane, Henry Gorm, aggravated by an attempt of robbery. It was, however, privately settled by the Danzig magistrates.[2] In Schöneck, a Scot is imprisoned on suspicion of having killed a man, but he is released on the testimony of Captain Sutherland, who testifies on his oath that the deceased was accidentally drowned (1599).

In Jastrow, Hans Forbes, father of the Burgomaster, Balthasar Forbes, was placed in the dock on the charge of having shot a man. Having sworn that it had not been done maliciously, he is fined in 150 gulden (1607).[3] Very tragic is the story of Barry, another Scot of the same town, who quarrelled with his wife because she at one time had left him, accusing him of criminal relations with his step-children. Barry himself then brought the matter before the court and had her sentenced to death. It was only through the intercession of the Starost, the president of the court, that the stubborn man was brought to a more conciliatory frame of mind, resulting in an amicable adjustment, "because she had done it in great rashness."

Rather frequent were the contraventions of the many

---

[1] *Kgl. St. Archiv*, Königsberg, E. P. Fol.

[2] *Kgl. St. Archiv*, Danzig, D. xvii.

[3] Cp. Fr. Schulz, *Chronik der Stadt Jastrow*, 1896, pp. 55-57. Since 1602 there were eleven Scotch families in Jastrow: Andr. Barry, Andr. Swan, Hans Forbes, Andr. Sym, Jurge, " a Schott," Thos. Hilliday, Elias Dennis, Jacob Krudde (?), Adam Darby, John Duncan, Hans and George Smedt (Smith). In the year 1647 there were only two left who could be called of Scottish nationality.

trade prohibitions. In this respect, as we have said, the Scottish moral code was lax. We do not wonder, therefore, at William Hutney, John Ray and William Turry having been called before the authorities to show reason why they had unlawfully imported into the kingdom and sold English cloths, which did not bear the mark of the city of Danzig[1] (1630); or at one Mallisson from Elbing, who is caught fishing sturgeon in forbidden waters (1661). An offence sure to excite the reader's pity is that of Andrew Law, who is unable to live at peace with his mother-in-law, the widow of Andrew Morrisson, and is on that account brought before the magistrates of Neuenburg in 1643.[2]

The worst cases seem to have taken place in a small town of Western Prussia, called Deutsch Krone. Here, at the beginning of the seventeenth century, two or three rich Scottish merchants ruled, and ruled with a high hand. They were the Wolsons, the Lawsons and the Malsons. The mischief commenced with John Malson in 1609 killing a man who had been a furrier by trade. Two of his countrymen become surety for him; but in the following year he is himself attacked and killed by two noblemen with the name of Jurno. John Lawson, who had taken upon himself to pay the alimentation money to the children of the slain furrier, and who seems to have shared the violent temper of his friend, killed a Jew a few years later, a crime for which he was promptly called to account by the Woywod, governor, of Posen, the officially appointed protector

[1] "Quod pannos Anglicanos contra constitutionem nullis signis Civitatis Gedanensis notatos in regnum invexissent et venales exposuerunt." *Kgl. St. Archiv*, Danzig.
[2] *Kgl. St. Archiv*, Königsberg, W. Pr. Fol.

of the Jews. But his extradition is refused by the Mayor of Krone, who maintains that he alone represented the proper authority (1615). Of Walson and his money-lending we have already spoken in another place; how he was accused of wearing the apparel of the rich and how tight a grip he had on the needy Polish nobility. Later in life he turned Roman Catholic, and wrote a last will and testament in favour of the Jesuits, which was, however, contested by the magistrates of the town (1642).[1]

There are, of course, a number of other smaller civil cases of debt, pilfering and so on, but on the whole, here again we have an example of a people's moral worth being in the inverse ratio of the full enjoyment of its liberties. Not much energy is called forth by basking in the sun; it is in fighting that hearts of oak are made. Any other nation but a sturdy one, physically and mentally, would have succumbed to a life so full of privations. But the Scot was reared in hardship and poverty and on plain food; his saving disposition made him gather property under the most adverse circumstances; his fidelity to his superiors was beyond suspicion, and having once obtained by his wealth or the favour of the great a position of influence, his shrewdness and his clannishness made him use it to the most far-reaching advantage. In the face of never ending hostilities this was necessary.

Even at the approach of death the Scots dared not lay their weapons down. They had to contend against two curious laws: the *jus caducum* and the *quarta detractus*, as they were respectively called. By the former the property of a man dying childless, or of a

---

[1] Cp. *Scots in Germany*, p. 55, and *Geschichte von Deutsch Krone*, by Fr. Schulz, 1902, p. 50.

stranger dying in the land, if not claimed within a certain time reverted to the Crown ; the latter gave the Crown the right to retain one-fourth of 'the property of the deceased stranger, provided that the other three-fourths went out of the country.   The official who looked after the interest of the State was called the Fiscal.   It is only natural that these laws proved a very fruitful source of dispute between Scotland and Germany. It was customary, therefore, in olden times for the Scottish claimant to provide himself with letters of introduction and recommendation from King or Queen before he started on his voyage to the Baltic ports, in order to prove his rights to the property of a deceased relative.

Thus both Queen Mary and Henry Darnley supply David Melville with letters of recommendation, who went to Danzig in order to claim the inheritance of his brother James, after the latter's death from the plague two years previously (1566).[1] James VI. recommends Captain Arnot, who goes to Germany claiming an inheritance of his wife, the daughter of William Forbes, a citizen of Danzig (1581, July 11th) ;[2] and in 1594, Joannes Strang, of Balcalzye, who is about to start to the same city, on a similar errand.   Or the magistrates of Perth certify that Jacobus Stobie has been empowered to regulate certain matters of inheritance at Danzig by the parties concerned (1589).

Richard Bailly presents a letter from the magistrates of Edinburgh with respect to the inheritance of the late Robert Baillie of Danzig, from which it appeared that the rightful heirs of Robert, who had died childless, were Maria, Jeanet and Margaret, daughters by a second marriage of Jacob Baillie, late minister of Lamington, in the county of Lanark, the father of Robert.   These three daughters

[1] *Kgl. St. Archiv*, Danzig. XCIX. A.

transfer their rights to Richard Baillie, the bearer (1665).[1]
Thomas and Patrick Aikenhead appoint Robert Tevendail,
or Tevendale, and Daniel Davidson, citizens of Danzig,
trustees for the assets of David Aikenhead, a Polish merchant.[2]

We also find the town of Dumfries on a similar occasion
issuing a letter to a certain Greer or Grier, who went to
Danzig to claim the inheritance of his brother (June 20th,
1594).[3]

On the other hand, the magistrates of Königsberg
inform those of Glasgow that they desire to intercede for
one Hannibal Spang, son of Colonel Andrew Spang,
who claims an inheritance amounting to one thousand
"Imperiales" (1661).

But all these recommendations from high and official
personages could not prevent frequent friction between the
Fiscal and the Scotch heirs. Sometimes, and for certain
periods and districts only the Kings would transfer their
claims to the inheritance of a stranger to certain persons of
merit as a favour; as when the King of Poland granted the
estate of John Tullidaff, who died at Neumark in 1618,
and whose property reverted to the Crown to Robert
Cunningham, "nobilis de Bernys *aulico nostro*" in grateful recognition of his faithful services, or when the same
King Sigismund presents Colonel Learmonth[4] with the
inheritance of a certain Fritz in 1619.

A very interesting case, illustrating this law of reversion,
happened in Bromberg in 1625. A Scot, with the curious
name of Michael Nosek,[5] had just died there and the

---

[1] See Part III.   [2] Edinburgh, Nov. 16, 1689.

[3] The witnesses to the letter are Robert Cunningham, Andrew
Cunningham and "Albertus Cunningham, notarius publicus et scriba."
Kgl. St. Archiv, Danzig.

[4] See Part II.   [5] The name is evidently Polonised.

"royal notary," Nicholas Gurski, a nobleman, demands the inheritance as a donation of the king. The bailies are about to hand over the property of the deceased when John Varuga and John Brommer, a medical practitioner, lodge a protest. Finally, the decision of the court is as follows: Considering

1. That the deceased Nosek had deposited an authenticated and unobjectionable birth-brief;

2. That he had done military service under King Stephen in Livonia;

3. That he had made Bromberg his domicile, acquiring real estate there;

4. That he had sworn the oath of fealty to the magistrates;

5. That he had married according to the rites of the Roman Catholic Church, and had begotten children;

6. That he had earned his living in an unobjectionable way; and

7. That he has paid taxes, and had borne other civic burdens : *he has acquired the rights of a native. The "jus caducum," therefore, can not be applied to his case, although his wife and his children had died before him, and his property was left to relations of his wife and to charitable institutions.*[1]

The so-called *quarta deductus*, or the right to deduct one-fourth of the inheritance for the Crown was applicable to Scottish *citizens* also. The Fiscal's duty was to have an inventory made of the deceased Scotsman's property. For instance, in 1590, a Scot dies at Johannesburg. Three of his countrymen—Andrew Robertson, Daniel Nicholl and Alb. Meldrum—undertake the work of appraising in the presence of the clerk. The goods, in

[1] Bromberg, Städt. Gerichtsbücher (Court minutes) : B 3, fol. 251b. and 354b.

this case mostly pieces of cloth, are taken to the Castle and there re-valued. Whatever was retained for the necessary use of the house must be brought to account and finally the quarter fixed, after the deduction of the debts due. If the property was small, the rulers of the country often refused to claim it. Thus, George Frederick, Markgraf of Brandenburg, writes from Königsberg in 1601 to his magistrates in the country: "Whereas, two years ago, two Scotsmen named Jacob Chalmer and Richard Watson, travelled together to Livland, and quarrelled on the road till they came to blows, and Watson was slain by the other; whereas, also, the culprit fled, and the property of the killed man fell to the Crown; but whereas, thirdly, the fugitive has not only come to terms with the deceased's friends in Scotland, but His Majesty of Scotland has also written requesting us to give up whatever may be left of the dead man's goods in our Duchy to the bearer Alexander Crichton, who has arranged with the representative of our treasury concerning the "fourth;" we command all our governors and magistrates to deliver the said inheritance to him without fail, and to assist him against Hillebrant Watson, who has already seized upon a great part of the property."[1]

In 1633, there dies at or near Memel a Scot with the name of Butchart, leaving "much cattle, money and outstanding bonds." A good deal of his money was invested in Königsberg and Tilsit, and Paul Greiff, the Elector's receiver, was not slow to prosecute his inquiries. "In this way he discovered at the house of a Scot, called Jacob Guthrie, the sum of two thousand gulden, which he at once distrained until the deceased's brother should arrive from Scotland. Now, as the fourth of the 30,000 gulden left by Butchart were claimed by the Elector, though

[1] *Kgl. St. Archiv*, Danzig.

Memel was at that time in the hands of the Swedes, he wrote a letter to that town maintaining the assets to have been accumulated within his own territories, and asking for a new inventory.[1]

A long exchange of letters between the Churfürst and his councillors took place with respect to this same law at the death of a Captain Trotter in 1653. Forty-three years later, Frederick III. of Prussia decided that according to the treaties concluded with England in 1660, and again in 1690, the quarter could not be claimed of the inheritance of Thomas Scoles, a native of Hull, who had died at Königsberg in 1697 or 1698.[2] As to Scotland, the treaties seem to have been forgotten until the year 1725, when Allan, a Scotch merchant in Königsberg, died, leaving a pretty considerable fortune. The magistrates inquired of the Churfürst concerning the "quarter," and were told to write to England in order to ascertain whether or not a duty was levied there on property left to Prussian subjects in Prussia. In his answer, the Fiscal at Königsberg pointed out that in a convention between the Dutch and the English, it had been agreed that the subjects of neither country should come under the *jus detractus* ; [3] and that afterwards in 1661 an agreement with England was arrived at, according to which *subditi suæ Majestatis Brittannicæ*, *i.e.* comprising the Scots, should enjoy the same privileges as the Dutch. The Churfürst is not quite satisfied in his own mind by this reply. Scotland is not England, he writes back, and a different custom may obtain there. Therefore an assurance ought to be de-

---

[1] *Kgl. St. Archiv*, Königsberg.

[2] In 1692, when Thos. Taylor died at Kneiphof, the fourth was claimed but not insisted upon if William Garforth, the heir, would remain in the country. *Kgl. St. Archiv*, Königsberg.

[3] "Quod utriusque subditi a jure detractus eximant."

manded from Scotland that in a similar case no quarter would be levied in that country either (May 1st, 1725). Thus the matter drags on till 1727. A certificate issued from London is not considered sufficient. The sister of the deceased, after having sent various petitions, at last appoints a delegate or trustee, who succeeds in procuring the necessary documents from Dundee and Aberdeen. The former city says : " To all and everybody reading this letter, we Bessy Allan, the widow of the late John Leitch, baker in Aberdeen, but now the wife of Alexander Reid, inhabitant of Old Aberdeen, with the consent of said Alexander Reid for his portion, and Agnes Leitch, eldest daughter of the said John Leitch, now the wife of Alexander Webster, shipbuilder in the port of Dundee, send our greeting. Since the late George Allan, merchant and dyer at Königsberg, left certain moneys to the above-named Bessy Allan, his sister, and to Agnes Leitch, his niece, we appoint Christoph Heidenreich our attorney. Signed by W. Cruikshank, W. Chalmers, and others."

From Aberdeen, the following document was sent in 1729 : " As His Majesty the King of Prussia consented to hand over a certain legacy to our citizens, Bessy Allan and Agnes Leitch, without deducting the regal fourth part or any other part, on that condition that we should bind ourselves to forward any sums of money left in succession to Prussian citizens likewise free of duty, if such case should arise, we testify that not only has hitherto nothing been detracted but we also promise faithfully on the part of this town not to do so in future." [1]

Examples of this kind could easily be multiplied. In 1737, for instance, Alexander Fairweather, a native of Montrose, died at Goldap, a small town in Western

---

[1] The original is written in Latin. *St. Archiv*, Königsberg.

Prussia. He left to each of his sisters, Catherine Fair-weather, the wife of James Smith, at Irvine in Ayr, and to Marjory Fairweather in Montrose, the sum of three hundred gulden. This legacy the magistrates of Goldap had in the meantime put on interest, and they now claimed the fourth part of it. David Barclay, a merchant in Königsberg, who had been appointed trustee, appeals to the King; but only in 1740 the legacy is given free, reference being made to the treaties mentioned above. About twenty years later, Alexander Moir died at Königsberg, leaving the large fortune of 38,000 gulden, of which the greater part went to three brothers and sisters at Danzig. About five thousand gulden were left to his nephew, Samuel Cutler in London. Here, also, the question of the fourth part arose.

Sometimes it happened that Scotsmen or Scotswomen, settled in Germany, acquired property in Scotland by the death of a relative; as when the magistrates of Dirschau write to the town council of Aberdeen stating that Jacob Koliszon (Collisson) had sold his portion of the inheritance of his father Duncan in Aberdeen to one Andrew Walker, (May 2nd, 1542), to whom he remitted at the same time the money due for teaching him the weaving trade. Likewise, Hans Anderson and Albr. Kuk struck a bargain with reference to a house in Aberdeen in-herited by the former (1567).[1] Some years later the sisters Elizabeth and Isabella Murray, the latter being the widow of the late John Dale, a Scot in Danzig, appear before the magistrates of this city. They had inherited some houses in Aberdeen from their grand-father John and their father Andrew Murray, and appoint Robert Munro their trustee. The situation of the houses

---

[1] Altstädtisches Schöppenbuch—"Bailie's Minute Book of the Alt-stadt," Königsberg.

is accurately described.[1]   In 1597, Alexander Morell (or Norell) at Danzig, son of the late James Morell, sells his father's house in Edinburgh, situated on the west of the Erleus Street (?), for 1500 gulden.   A case somewhat similar occurs in the year 1632, when George Forbes, only son of the late Andrew Forbes, declares before the court that he gives his movable and immovable goods, moneys and so forth, especially a house in Aberdeen, "situated near the lower Kirkgate, between the houses of Samuel Mason and Robert Patterson," to Marian Moor for her use during her lifetime; after her death to Peter Moor and his heirs "as a reward for the many benefits received from his hands" (Aug. 18th).

Again, in many instances an arrangement was made by the Scottish heirs, by which property left to them in foreign countries was sold to third parties, as when in 1589 James Wright appears before the court at Linlithgow, certifying that he had transferred his part of the inheritance of his late brother, who died at Johannisburg in Prussia, to George Nicholl from Edinburgh, by whom he had been fully compensated;[2] or, in 1619, when William Allanson from Glasgow, died at Belgard in Pomerania, and his inheritance was sold to one William Kammer (Chambers), at Colberg.   In this case, however, a birth-brief and two letters of surrender from the brother and sister of the deceased were required, and even then the magistrates were not satisfied.   Only after a letter of King James himself in favour of Chambers,

---

[1] *Kgl. St. Archiv.*, Danzig, xxxiii., D 14, 20a.   "In platea inferiori ecclesiæ inter ædes seu domum Capellariæ S. Stephani ex australi parte inter ædes Thomæ Philipson ex Boreali parte inter ædes seu domum quondam Andreæ Dortie orientem versus et inter viam regium occidentem versus sitas."

[2] *Kgl. St. Archiv*, Königsberg.

dated Greenwich, June 12, 1621, in which it was stated that "Camerarius" had acted quite properly, the property was released.[1] Or, when in 1628, Thomas Melville, a citizen of Aberdeen, "who cannot talk German very well," declares at Tilsit that he had sold the shop left to him by the late Hans Philipp in that town, to Thomas Hay, also of Tilsit, for the sum of 300 gulden.[2]

But, apart from the legal aspect, the wills and bequests of the Scots dying in Prussia and Poland are very often highly interesting on account of the insight they afford into the domestic life of those days and into the character of the deceased.

Very frequently the assets left were exceedingly small, hardly worth enumeration in a special inventory. Yet, however small, a charitable bequest, either to the Scottish poor-box or to one of the Danzig or Königsberg hospitals or otherwise, is always there. Take the case of Alex. Wright mentioned above. The whole of the money left amounted to nine thalers and eighteen groschen, of which sum one thaler and fifteen groschen was to be handed to the schoolmaster. Besides this, there were found sixteen pieces of coarse linen; two and a "half parcels of red trousers;" one parcel of veils; two pieces of ticking; fifteen of linen; one piece of green cloth for aprons; one half stone of cummin, and one fourth of pepper.[3] There were also a horse and a cart, but they were claimed by the

[1] *Kgl. St. Archiv*, Danzig.

[2] *Kgl. St. Archiv*, Königsberg. The Scottish heirs in this case had much trouble given them by the young clerk of the deceased, John Laurie, whom they suspected of having kept back certain goods.

[3] In an edict against the Scots they are called "apothecarii," not exactly druggists but dealers in drugs. Spices formed a valuable item of their stock-in-trade. Itinerant drug vendors were also known in Scotland in the Middle Ages.

Duke and valued at ten gulden. With very many of the Scottish small merchants something like this must have been their stock-in-trade.

Equally modest were the assets of Hans Patrzin (Patterson) from Aberdeen, who died at Konitz in 1574. An inventory of his property was made on "Thursday before Holy Easter," as the old records tell us, "by Alex. Symson, a burgess of Tuchel, and another Scot . . . and there were found twelve gulden of outstanding debts and goods valued at sixteen gulden which Symson was told to convert into cash and to hand over to the relations of the deceased, in case the inheritance should be claimed within a year and a day. If not, he is to deposit the money with the magistrates."

By the side of this, for the sake of contrast, we shall now put the last will of William Robertson, who died at Danzig in 1670. It was translated from the "Scottish into the German language" by one Robert Mello, a broker and an interpreter ; but this was done with a total disregard of grammar and idiom, making it difficult at times to arrive at the proper meaning of the document :

"I, William Robertson," it runs, " of legitimate birth, am the son of Thomas Robertson, citizen and merchant of Ross, in the Kingdom of Scotland, and of his wife, Christina Lefries, and I was born after they had lived together in matrimony for some years. I, William Robertson, do write this my last will and testament ,being in sound health, God be praised. I ordain that my body shall be buried in St Peter's Church. To the clergyman preaching the funeral sermon I leave eight thaler, to the Smallpox Hospital 300 gulden, to the Scottish Poor Fund 300 gulden. To William Robertson, my brother's eldest son, my god-son, the money owed to me by Archibald

Campbell on the lands of Hillpont (or Killpont?) in Lothian, Scotland, namely, 20,000 mark Scottish; moreover, I bequeath to him the money I sent to Scotland in 1665 with George Skene, *i.e.* 2438 thaler in specie. . . . I give and bequeath to this my godson, after my death, everything that is in my room at Danzig; my large cashbox and all in it, my small chest of drawers with all my linen . . . my upright bed, including bedding, my coverlet, my two pillows, my sheets and mattresses . . . my wardrobe with all its contents, my big basket (?) and my small basket, my four chairs, my bottle-stand, my large wardrobe with my cloak and coat in it, my hand-tub, my tankard with the lid of English tin, my close-stool lined with tin . . . three doublets of satin and three caps of sable and other two of marten; two coats lined with sable and marten; a small silver bowl, another silver bowl gilt, a small clock and other things; my silver tankard, three brass candlesticks, and a coat lined with fox. All these articles I give to my godson William; and more, as soon as my debt has been collected from Patrick Simson, which, at eight per cent. interest, will amount to more than 8000 thaler in specie; and from Alexander Kemp 12,000 mark Scottish. To my friend and relative, James Abercrombie, I leave 2000 mark, besides what he received from me long ago. The rest of my debts when called in I leave to Jacob and Johann, the two brothers of my godson. My mirror and my carriage I give to William Robertson, my godson. As executors I appoint James Campbell, Writer to the Signet, my friend Jacob Abercrombie, my brother's son William, and my friend W. Anderson. When this money has been received, let it be invested in landed estate in Lothian and not lent on written security. Ye know, dear friends, that God gave me the opportunity in His grace to be helpful to my friends; therefore I pray you to take a special care of this my last will and testament, as you must give an account on the last day to the Judge of all things."[1]

Another large fortune was left by Jacob Balfuhr who died childless in 1622. His wife received 14,000 gulden; Andreas, his brother, about 7000. Legacies were given to Margaret Balfuhr, daughter of the late Duncan Balfuhr; to William Balfuhr, son of the same; to Christina Balfuhr, daughter of the late William Balfuhr. Moreover, to David Balfuhr's stepson 500 gulden, the interest of it to go to the mother Isabella till her death. To each of the two children of his late brother Duncan at St Andrews 500 gulden; to William, his brother Duncan's son, who is now in the service of the testator, 400 thaler; to Stephen Balfuhr, who is now serving his time abroad, 500 gulden; and to Christina Balfuhr, in Danzig, at her marriage, 1000 gulden. To the son of his late brother William in St Andrews 500 gulden. Likewise to each clergyman of his own persuasion at Danzig 50 gulden; to the Hospital of St Elizabeth 100 gulden; to the Scottish Poor-box 100 gulden, besides another hundred gulden to be distributed among the poor after his decease. Lastly, his servant, Daniel Robertson, on account of his faithful services, shall have as much added to his due wages as to amount to 400 thaler, and his servant girl, Elsie, shall have 50 gulden.[2]

George Kilfauns in 1657 leaves three fourths of his fortune to Christina Hebron (Hepburn). As legacies he gives to each of the four Presbyterian clergymen ten ducats, five ducats for his funeral sermon, ten ducats to the poor; twenty for the poor of the Scottish congregation. His brother Hans is to receive the remaining fourth.

[1] Danzig, Jan. 4, 1670.
[2] *Kgl. St. Archiv*, Danzig. See also *Löschin, Beiträge*, ii. 69.

Mrs Smith, née Leitch, leaves "half a house" in the Heilige Geist Gasse at Danzig, together with the sum of 1000 gulden, to the daughter of Catherine Lermonth. She also bequeaths 700 gulden to the Scottish Poor-box (1660).

W. Garioch leaves a certain sum to the Scottish community, and to the Small-pox Hospital at Danzig. He left only distant relations in Scotland "with whom he had not corresponded for the last thirty-two years" (1669).

The will of John Turner, written in English, was deposited in Aberdeen with a George Skene; but it appears that he left another will at Danzig with reference to the property not disposed of in the Scottish document. As the testator had died childless, his cousins William and Andreas, merchants in Poland, are declared heirs. The following legacies are bequeathed: To John Turner in Poland, 6000 gulden; to William Lumsdel, 1500; to Peter Dunbar's and Thos. Smart's widow, 100 gulden each; to the Scottish Poor-box, 300; the Elizabeth Hospital, 200; the Small-pox Hospital also 200 gulden (1688).[1]

A very wealthy man Jacob Carmichael must have been, who died at Krakau in 1696. His brother Robert succeeds him. A taste for art jewellery seems to have distinguished him, for he left, besides many silver and gilt articles, one diamond ornament, one ruby necklace and pendants, six diamond rings, one signet ring set with diamonds, one ring set with emeralds, two bracelets and three strings of pearls.

At Danzig again, one Robert Gellentin bequeaths to the Scottish Poor 300 gulden, to the Smallpox Hospital 300, and to the preacher of his funeral sermon '*pro labore*' the goodly sum of 200 gulden.

---

[1] Cp. *Scots in Germany*, p. 60.

Of Daniel Davidson's charitable bequests we have already spoken.

Good common sense is shown in the will of Robert Chapman, who died in 1675. He makes his sister's son, William Tampson, his heir. "Taking into consideration," he says, "that he has a good heart, and is a youth of good promise, and that my mother"—she had married a second time—"has plenty of means as it is, and has been richly blessed by God."[1] He then gives various legacies to the Small-pox Hospital and other hospitals of the city, leaves to the poor of the Scottish congregation 300 gulden, and to Alb. Duggel (Dugald), "a poor Scotsman," thirty gulden.

Now and then these last testaments give rise to legal wrangling and quarrels among the heirs and creditors themselves. One of these last, named Laurence Gream (Graham), after the death of George Hutcheson, opposes James Masterton from Edinburgh, "who wants to make himself paid first" (1649). A similar case occurred somewhat earlier, in 1642, after the death of Laurence Orr in Insterburg, when the son of Regina Oliphant, living in Scotland, thus writes to the Elector of Brandenburg: "I cannot help complaining that William Oliffant cunningly tries not only to deprive your Electoral Highness of the quarter but also his brothers and sisters and their children of the inheritance left by his late brother Conrad Oliffant, late inhabitant of your Highness's town of Insterburg. Under the pretence of being a burgess, he demands possession of the goods; but as there are four other heirs his portion can only be one-fifth."[2]

---

[1] Again the archaic flavour of the German is totally destroyed by the translation. The sentence reads: "Da sie aber ohne das in guten mitteln sitzet, und von dem lieben Gott reichlich gesegnet, in ansehung er gutes Gemüthes und ein Jüngling von guter Hoffnung ist." *Kgl. St. Archiv*, Danzig. [2] *Kgl. St. Archiv*, Königsberg.

Very remarkable is the last will of Robert Porteous or
Porcyus, as his name is written in Polish documents
We have in our former volume[1] been able to give a very
few details only of this successful Scot. Further researches
have brought to light other circumstances of his life,
enabling us to complete the portrait.[2]

When still a young man, Porteous emigrated to Krosno
in Poland previous to the year 1623, when his name occurs
in a business transaction. Where his Scottish home was
is not very certain. His being called "de Lanxeth"[3] on
a painting in the Church of St Peter and Paul at Krosno
may probably point to a place "Langside," which again
would refer us to Dalkeith and neighbourhood. A certain
violent rashness of his character early manifested itself.
When serving his time with a certain Johann Laurenstein
he caused his master the loss of 50 florins, and a short
time later he is mulcted in the same sum for wounding a
man in a quarrel. The records in the Episcopal Archives
before the year 1627 call him a "heathen," that is a
follower of Calvin or Luther. In that year he embraced
the Roman Catholic Religion of which he remained
a most devoted member to the date of his death. He
also married in 1627, then twenty-six years old, the
widow of one Bartholomew Mamrowitz, whose maiden
name was Anne Hesner. She was his senior by eleven
years, and had a son Paul, who is frequently mentioned
as a Doctor of Medicine in the testament of Porteous.

[1] *Scots in Germany*, p. 60.
[2] Rev. Ladislas Sarna, *Opis powiatu Krosnienskiego*, Przemysl,
1898. *Cf.* pp. 266-68, 277, 283 f, 290, 318, 335-338, 495-505.
[3] The additional "h" lengthens the preceding "e," and makes the
syllable sound like "aid."

Three of his own children, two daughters and a son, died.

The commercial enterprise of Porteous soon extended over Lithuania, the whole of the Austrian empire, Prussia, Silesia and Scotland, and was encouraged by several privileges granted to him by successive kings: Sigismund III. in 1632, Ladislaus IV. in 1633, and John Casimir in 1649.[1] They also permitted him freely to dispose of his property. The chief trade of Porteous consisted in Hungarian wines, of which he practically held the monopoly. This gave cause to the citizens of Krosno to complain of his high handed manner of doing business: buying wine at 50 florins and selling it to the town at 200. Moreover, the town was compelled to borrow money from him, the only very rich man in Krosno, and this also he used for his own advantage.

Nobody, however, could deny that Porteous, if inclined to carry out his own will in a manner rather imperious, was a man of strict honesty. A story is told of him confirming this. Once there arrived for him a cargo of wine from Hungary. When they were lowering down the casks into his cellars, it was thought that one of them was unusually heavy. On being opened how great was Porteous' surprise when he found it to be filled with ducats instead of wine. He informed the owner in Hungary immediately, but received for an answer: that what was once sold was sold for ever. Not satisfied with this Porteous brought the matter before the courts of justice, and the money which was owned by nobody was finally devoted to pious purposes. To this honesty he joined a most generous public spirit, not only for the

---

[1] The exact dates are: 20th April, 11th of February, and 8th of February.

benefit of churches and hospitals, but also of town improvements.

Porteous died in 1661.[1] His brother Andrew survived him, but seems to have left Krosno. Another brother Thomas is strangely enough not mentioned in his will. Other relations of his were John Dawson (Dasson), a nephew, and Francis Gordon (Gordanowitz), who had married a cousin of his.[2]

The Parish Church of Krosno looked upon Porteous as its " secundus fundator." He restored the nave and the vaults which had been destroyed in a previous conflagration ; he covered the roof with copper ; he presented to it new bells, a baptismal font, many precious vestments and paintings, and a set of bells.[3] His own burying vault is below the Chapel of St Peter and St Paul. It has remained undisturbed, though other graves had long since to give way to new sanitary improvements of the town. His funeral was attended by over a hundred members of the Catholic clergy, who at the request of the Bishop of Przemysl thus honoured their benefactor. It almost seems a pity that, according to a chronicler of the time, each of them was given 3 "imperiales" for his trouble.

Porteous' last will in its chief enactments reads as follows : "As it is the duty of everyone, especially of a Christian, to redeem his soul, bought by the most precious blood of the Son of God, I, Adalbert[4] Porcius, citizen of the Royal town of Krosno and a merchant, being of sound

[1] Not in 1651 as erroneously stated on his portrait in the Chapel of St Peter and Paul.

[2] The name of Porteous continued in Krosno up to the 18th century.

[3] The biggest of these weighs 50 cwt., has a circumference of about 14 feet, and a height of about 4 feet and 6 inches. The circumscription contains, besides the names of the makers, that of the donor, Porteous and his coat of arms : three stars, a book, and a sword. The date is 1639.

[4] Porteous so called himself after his Patron Saint.

body and mind, and not knowing when my last hour shall strike, make the following declarations in writing : As I, by the grace of God, commenced my life in the Christian Roman Catholic Religion, I shall also end it according to its teaching. I therefore commend my soul into the hands of our God and Creator; but since it was joined to a sinful body and could not therefore be without sin and offences in God's eyes, I wish that it should for its eternal redemption have an advocate here below, for which purpose I set aside certain portions of my property. My body being made of earth, may again return to earth, and be buried in the Parish Church of Krosno in the vault of the Chapel of the Holy Apostles Peter and Paul which I have founded. As to my moveable and immoveable property, I shall, according to the privileges granted me by three successive Kings of Poland, and in order to avoid quarrels amongst my relations, make the following dispositions which I beg my executors to obey in all points for the salvation of their souls :

" For the renovation of the belfry of the Parish Church, the covering of its roof with sheet-copper, and the making of iron shutters, also for the raising of the steeple by ten yards in order to hang the bells, I bequeathe 6000 florins to be paid by my executors.

" The lustre made of brass and stag's horn, which is now in my large room, I also bequeathe to this Chnrch, and request that the same may be hung up above the magistrates' and judges' pew in the centre. For wine and wax for the two chapels of Peter and Paul, and of Adalbert, my Patron Saint, I leave the sum of 200 fl. Moreover I assign to these two chapels my farm [1] . . . and that field which is situated . . . for the renovation

---

[1] Here follows the exact situation.

of several church vessels or for other repairs. If necessary
the wine and the candles for the two brass candlesticks and
the gilt wooden one are also to be paid out of these farm
rents. Whatever remains of the rent is to be put aside
in a separate box, and to be placed in the treasury well
locked, the key of it to be kept by the priest. All sacred
utensils, cups, vestments and sacred silver vessels which I
bought for these chapels are to be used in them only, and
not in other churches. Should one of my relations wish
to buy the said farm and field, he may do so on condition
of his investing 1000 florins in safe and unencumbered
property for the purpose of redemption. . . . No pay-
ments of the priest out of these funds must be made
without the consent of the clergymen of Krosno. But if
the farm be sold to strangers, let it be done to the best
advantage of the chapels, so that new sacred vessels may
be bought, and all repairs duly carried out.

"As the clergyman of the Church at Krosno is but
poorly paid, I bequeathe the sum of 1200 florins to be
invested in good security, the interest of which will go
to him. For this he will say two masses for the repose
of my soul in the Chapel of St Adalbert, one for my
wife and one for my relations, on Mondays and on
Thursdays. . . . Myself as well as my wife, now resting
in God, having been members of the Confraternity,
called St Anne, it is my wish that our souls should be
remembered at Mass, and I assign to the Priest of the
said Confraternity the sum of 300 florins; but as the
Confraternity of St Anne already owes me 160 florins,
only 140 florins shall be paid to it out of my property,
the interest to be used only.

"To the Organist I leave 600 florins on condition of
his taking his degree at the Academy of Krakau, and I

G

impose upon him the duty of singing the Litany Omnium Sanctorum with his school-children after Vespers on Wednesdays in the Chapel of St Peter and Paul, and on Fridays in the Chapel of St Adalbert the Litany of the Sacred Heart. He has also to insist that his scholars obey the call of the Church Bells on Saturdays and on the days preceding each Holy Day, when they will dust the pews. To the Bellringer I leave 200 florins, the interest of which he is to receive; he shall be obliged, however, to summon those of the Church Beggars who are strong enough, to assist him in cleaning the sacred paintings, and he is to ring the Angelus on the big Bell every mid-day about 12 o'clock. To the bellows' blower I give and bequeathe in consideration of his small salary, 100 florins. For the beggars in the porch of the Church I bequeathe 200 florins, of which legacy they will receive the interest monthly from the hands of the clergymen on condition that they clean the font every month and the two brass candlesticks as often as it appears necessary. . . . The house which my step-son Paul Mamrowitz bought of me I leave to my brother Andrew and to the said Mamrowitz, Doctor of Medicin. They will also have to share in equal parts my clothes, tin-vessels, guns, horses, grain, flour, pictures and other things. My farm Suchodol. . . . I likewise leave to my brother Andrew and Paul Mamrowitz. One of them may live on the farm, as I have done, and pay half of its proceeds to the other, or they may live there alternately as they may think desirable. . . .

"Having enjoyed the trade monopoly in Krosno I leave to the said town for the repair of the town-walls and the bridge behind the Krakau Gate, which has been allowed to fall into decay, as well as for the improvement of the pavement, the sum of 2000 florins. It is my wish that this should be done as soon as possible, as it will not be difficult for the town to provide carts. Let my servants get their due wages and a decent sum of acquittance besides, and let them pray for my soul to God.

"To George Hay I leave 1500 florins in the hope that he will remember my kindness, and conscientiously hand over everything to my executors so as to avoid the judgement of God. . . . To my steward I give 50 florins, to my head coachman 100 florins, to my head cook Elizabeth 40; to the younger cook 15 florins besides their due wages, so that they may buy suitable mourning. . . ."

After enumerating certain other legacies left to the Brotherhood of St Anne, of which, as we have seen, both the testator and his wife had been members, Porteous continues :—

"Having acknowledged all through life His Majesty John Casimir as my gracious King and Protector, I wish to give him a further proof of my loyalty by leaving to him the sum of 10,000 florins. I also present to him an altar made of pure gold. My relations Francis Gordon and John Dasson (Dawson) will attend to this my request. . . . To the Revd. priest Prazimorski I leave 2000 florins and 3 casks of wine; to the Bishop of Przemysl, my benefactor, likewise 2000 florins and 3 casks of wine, with the humble prayer that they would accept these gifts and assist in the carrying out of my last will. My brother Andrew and Dr. Paul Mamrowicz will see that all my creditors who can duly prove their claims be satisfied.

"As to my funeral, I cannot say of course what the expense will be, but I request my executors to invite the clergy of all the neighbourhood, to receive them hospitably, and to give each of them one thaler. Before the funeral let all poor beggars be treated to a dinner. I leave besides 50 pieces of linen at 6 gulden each, 50 pieces of Krosno Cloth at 16 or 18 florins, for distribution among the poor. Should there be found ready made linen and common cloth in my house, only so much must be bought as will complete the number of pieces."

Porteous requests the treasury of the Government to assist in calling in his outstanding debts, of which one part is to be employed for the payment of the soldiery. Debts under 100 gulden are to be entirely remitted; all other debtors are allowed 10 per cent. in their favour and in no case is there any great rigour to be employed.

"All my moveable and immoveable possessions in the Crownland of Hungary, as well as my claims against Hungarian noblemen, merchants and citizens, I leave to my sister's son, Johann Dasson, and to Francis Gordon and his wife, with the strict injunction to be guided entirely by my information written in the Scottish language and signed by two witnesses.

"In Danzig also I have some outstanding money with Thomas Gielent for potash bought from me. All this I leave to John Dasson, according to the wishes expressed in my Scottish codicil.

"As additional 'Protectors' of my last will I name 1, His Majesty our most gracious King; 2d " . . . Here the Testament of R. Porteous suddenly comes to a close, the last page being torn off.

No wonder that his memory is still honoured in Krosno. A portrait of himself, his wife and his brother, probably the work of later years, is still to be seen in the Church of St Peter and Paul. Very different from the wills of most of the Scots Porteous left nothing of his vast wealth to his countrymen as such or to the Scottish "Nation."

How important a part was played by this Scottish "Nation," and how in every place where there was a large number of Scots such directing body was established and demanded implicit obedience, we have frequently had occasion to remark. It is seen also in a succession case of Jacob Kyth (Keith) in the year 1637.

It appears that the late Jacob Hill owed the late William Kyth, a brother of the above, who died in 1636 on his journey to Jaroslaw, a sum amounting to between five and six thousand gulden, but the Scottish 'Nation' at that town thought it right, for reasons not stated, to reduce the sum to two thousand seven hundred gulden. Jacob Kyth agreed, and gives the children of Hill a receipt for that sum.

Looking over these last wills and testaments, which only represent a small portion, we arrive at the natural conclusion that the most influential Scotsmen settled in Germany were merchants. They possessed houses in good localities,[1] they traded oversea and overland, their services were much sought after by kings and nobles. Their natural propensities and their characteristic mental features made necessarily for success in this branch of human industry.

Whilst in France we hear of nothing but of the heroisms

[1] Alex. Anderson buys a house in Neuenburg in 1590. "Honestus Kilianus Makkien Scotus civis Bidgostiensis" (Bromberg) sells his garden and shed behind the hospital of St Stanislaus to Michael Normanth (Anglicus or Scotus) for 50 gulden (1615) ; Hans Wricht in Memel is in possession of 2 hides of land and 21 "morgen" (1650) ; Gilbert Baillie in Königsberg obtains permission to sell 2 hides of his lands in 1665 ; the Irwings in Memel also owned considerable property (1740); the family of Davisson were in possession of the Schönfeld estate near Danzig, not to speak of the great number of those that acquired house property in the large towns, especially at Danzig and Könisberg—a fact brought to our knowledge in many a trade complaint.

of Scottish warriors; it was the Scottish trader in Germany who chiefly left his imprints upon the country of his adoption, ready when the times demanded it to show a heroism quite as great as that of his more celebrated and more loudly acclaimed countryman-in-arms.

But there were a good many handicraftsmen among the Scottish emigrants also, Scottish linen-weavers being among the very earliest settlers of Danzig.[1] Numerous were those that had to do with wool and cloth, as weavers, dyers, tailors, braidmakers and clothiers. Another large class represented the leather trade, such as shoemakers, belt and harnessmakers, and tanners; a few of them were brewers and distillers, notably the Barclays in Rostock[2] and James Littko (Lithgow) of Danzig. We have only come across one butcher, one pastry-cook, a few coppersmiths,[3] one or two coopers, one or two jewellers, one letter-painter, but no joiner, carpenter, or mason. Very soon, as we have seen, we find the Scot occupying positions of trust, as councillors of state, governors, magistrates, bailies, presidents of guilds in Poland, as well as in Prussia, Pomerania, and Mecklenburg. Their foreign extraction and language did

[1] Cp. p. 53 in *Scots in Germany*. It is curious to notice how long these Scottish weavers remained in their old settlement of Alt Schottland, south of Danzig proper. There exists an agreement of the year 1517 (June 8th) between the guild of linen weavers in Danzig and the Scottish masters of the trade on the Rivers Radaune, and, as we have seen, on the Bishop of Leslau's territory, concerning trade difficulties and the obligations of the Scots towards the maintenance of the Chapel of St Thomas (*Kgl. St. Archiv*, Danzig).

[2] There was a Paul Barclay, brewer, in 1592; Henry Barclay enrolled as a citizen in 1659 and Ludwig in 1685, all of them "Groszbrauer" = brewers on a large scale.

[3] Handicraftsmen were preferred in bestowing civil rights on the Scots. Hans Witte, a coppersmith from Cupar, obtains citizenship at Danzig in 1575, because his craft gave him the preference. He had to promise, however, not to carry on any trade, and not to keep any lodgers, but strictly to attend to his handicraft (Bürgerbuch, *Kgl. St. Archiv*, Danzig).

not even prevent them from serving the state in the capacity of post-office clerks and postmasters. In the annual account book of Marienwerder (1607-8) we find that a Scotsman attends for two weeks to the letters at the magistrates' office for the fee of three marks, by the command of the elector; and at the end of that century one Low was postmaster at Danzig. Princes liked to have Scotsmen for their trusty waiting-men, as well as for their body-guard. Thus the Duke of Mecklenburg, Frederick William, in 1697 kept two Scotsmen as running footmen, John Macnab and John Macullen; and among the citizens of Cassel in 1618 occurs the name of Alexander Arbotnit (Arbuthnot), a footman or "lackai."[1]

Of the eminent position many Scotsmen in Germany took in the world of letters and science we have spoken at length elsewhere.[2] A special mention deserves Gilbert Wachius (Waugh), prorector of the school of St Peter and Paul at Danzig;[3] and the Latin poet, Andreas Aidie, whose son Alexander occurs as one of the contributors to the Marshal College Fund. He was headmaster of the High School at Danzig from 1609 to 1613, and his appointment so pleased King James that in 1611 he wrote a special letter of thanks to the Magistrates.[4]

The next generation of Scotsmen in Germany had, of course, a much easier life to lead than their fathers. Being

[1] *Casseler Bürgerbuch*, edited by F. Gundlach, 1895.

[2] *Scots in Germany*, Part IV.

[3] He left 50 gulden to the Scottish poor at Königsberg in 1692.

[4] "Quod pro aliis Andream Aidium gymnasio vestro praefecistis . . . nobis gratum est, favoreque vestro haud indignum 'futurum plurimum speramus." *Kgl. St. Archiv*, Danzig. Aidie wrote several philosophical works—*e.g.*, "De subjecto et accidente," "De Fossilium et Metallorum natura; "De somnüs." He is also said to have written a commentary to the Nicomachean "Ethics of Aristotle" (Cp. *Athenæ Gedanenses*, Lips. 1713).

born in the country of "rechter, freier, deutscher Art," as the German phrasing then was, all the former disabilities disappeared. They were now no longer classed with the Jew, especially as the type of the vagrant Scot gradually became extinct,[1] and was supplanted by the type of the plodding, well-to-do citizen. Marrying into rich and influential German families, they rose in favour and social distinction in the same measure as they lost much of their nationality. Let us adduce a few examples of this.

Alexander Niesebet (Nisbet) from Edinburgh appears as a citizen of Elbing towards the close of the sixteenth century. He built the two houses in the Schmiedegasse next to the Schmiedethor in the corner. He married first the daughter of a town councillor, and when she died, in 1614, another councillor's daughter. His own child Catherine became the wife of Johann Jungschulz, Mayor of Elbing, and died one year after her father in 1618.[2]

William Patterson, a colonel, married a daughter of Adrian van der Linde, an old Patrician family of Danzig (1664).[3]

Thomas Gellatlay from Dundee, born 1590, emigrated to Danzig, where he changed his name into Gellentin. He was of good family, and connected with the Wedderburnes of Dundee. In 1623 he married Christine Czierenberg, daughter of the town councillor Daniel Czierenberg of Danzig. A daughter of his second marriage became the wife of Reinhold Bauer (1657),

---

[1] That the Scots themselves were smarting under this common classification appears from a short but valuable note which says: "Dietrich Lobstan, 'the Scot at Wehlau,' as he is called, craves permission for carrying his goods about the country unrestrainedly, so that he might get out of the great distress, misery and wretchedness into which the Jews had brought him (1570), *Kgl. St. Archiv*, Königsberg.

[2] *Elbing, Stadt Bibliothek*, MS. F 48.

[3] *Danziger Stadt Bibliothek*, MS. xv. f. 467.

and the mother of C. Ernst Bauer, burgomaster of Danzig.[1]

Charlotte Constance Beata Davisson, a daughter of Daniel Davisson and a great granddaughter of Daniel Davisson, who came as a struggling Scottish merchant to Poland, married in 1783 Carl Friedrich von Gralath, twice burgomaster of Danzig and the historian of his native town; whilst her aunt—*i.e.* her father's sister—became the wife of a town councillor Broen.[2]

The process of Germanising was a rapid one. It first showed itself in the names which were adapted to the German pronunciation: Wallace becoming Wallis, Cochrane Cockeren, Mackenzie Mekkentsien, Taylor Teler, Wood Wud, Allardyce Ardus, Crawford Craffert, Moir Muhr, Murray Morre or Morra, Morris Moritz, Rutherford Riderfarth, Bruce Bruss. Sometimes the meaning of the name was rendered by a German equivalent. Thus Miller was changed into Möller, Smith into Schmidt, Gardiner into Gertner, Cook into Koch; or Polish endings were added to the name such as Ross = Rossek or Rosek, Cochranek, Tailarowitz, and so forth.

The Christian names also underwent a metamorphosis. Where the original immigrants only changed their James into Jacob, John into Hans, Andrew into Andreas, we now meet such names as Dietrich, Gottlieb, Ulrich, Albrecht, Otto, and so forth. Wherever these names occur we have a sure sign of the bearer belonging to the second generation, which not unfrequently affords us a welcome clue to an approximate date.

[1] *Danziger Stadt Bibliothek*, MS. xv. f. 440 f. Carl Ernst Bauer married a daughter of Jacob Wright and Anne Horn. Thomas Gellatlay's great grandfather was one Walter Gellatlay of Templehall and Borrohall, who had married Isabella Wedderburne, John Wedderburne's daughter, of Dundee.

[2] *Kgl. St. Archiv*, Danzig, MS. Bb. 31.

It is in this and the later generations of Scotsmen generally that we find, too, a much greater number of literary men among the Scottish settlers. Their educational passion had not deserted them. Especially large is the number of Scottish names among the clergymen of the new Presbyterian Churches.

But with all this process of Germanising going on till hardly the name remained to testify to an extraction foreign to the fatherland, still even to this day one finds and gladly notices among the descendants of the Scottish settlers the old origin remembered and cherished, like the far off echo of an old tune or the dim halo around a sacred head. Sometimes it takes the form of certain pronounced mental or moral qualities, sometimes that of a predilection for the English tongue, or of a longing for the country where their cradle stood, most frequently that eminently characteristic one of long pedigrees, intricate, and hard to unravel.

The heart-throb is still there; but now it is the heart-throb without the pain of separation.

It now remains to cast a glance at the foreign relations between Scotland and those parts of Germany we are concerned with during the sixteenth century and later. We have already mentioned the various plenipotentiaries and factors sent by Scotland to protect the interests of the Scot abroad. The Scottish kings never lost an opportunity of interceding for their subjects, and the German Powers were eager to rely on the support of Scotland. One of the acts of the last Hochmeister of the Teutonic Order of Knights, Albrecht, better known as the first Duke of Prussia, was the mission of Dietrich von Schönborn to England and Scotland, professedly to ask for help in military expeditions against Poland, secretly, if secondarily, to devise a common plan for checking the growth of Protestantism. He went in the year 1522, and so well pleased was Albrecht with his reception at the Court of King James, that he sent this sovereign a valuable cuirass as a present in 1523. In return James in 1522 issues a proclamation emphasising his friendly feelings towards the Order, and enjoining his subjects to grant and afford the skippers and merchants, subjects of Albrecht, every possible safety and liberty of trading in all his lands, *cum omnibus mercenariis et rebus quibuscunque*, with all their goods of whatever description, *in terra vel marique*, both on land and sea.[1]

Many letters were again exchanged on the subject of piracy, in 1535 and notably so in 1592 and in 1593, with regard to the " Grite Jonas " and "Noah's Ark," [2] and in 1597 when a ship had been plundered at Burntisland.

In 1508 the King of Scotland desires Danzig to promote in every way the exportation of ships' masts,[3] whilst twenty years later Edinburgh writes a letter to the magistrates of the same city apologising that no compensation had as yet been given for goods which had been unlawfully taken from the Danzigers in the harbour of Leith. But the commission appointed had not been able to arrive at a decision on account of the rising that had taken place in other parts of the country.

Other diplomatic exchange of letters takes place between the two countries in cases of succession; they have been dealt with in another place.

Very curious is a more recent attempt to establish a Scottish colony on a small scale in Prussia, and it also led to a good deal of official correspondence. In the year 1823 the Hon. David Erskine wrote as follows to Privy Councillor Kelch at Königsberg from Dryburgh Abbey :—

---

[1] Dated Edinburgh, Nov. 3, 1522. *Kgl. St. Archiv*, Körrigsberg.

[2] *Kgl. St. Archiv*, Danzig. See also *Scots in Germany*, p. 19, 27.

[3] Cp. *Scots in Germany*, p. 22.

" Sir,—Having been requested by Mr Thomas Kyle, late of Fenns, in this part of the country, to inform you that he is known to be a first-rate agriculturist and gentleman farmer, and that few indeed understand husbandry in all its branches better than he does, he is very anxious that you would inform His Majesty of Prussia of the grant of 2000 morgens of land awarded to him by His Highness, Prince Hardenberg. Should this be confirmed to him, I know several young gentlemen of good families and connections who wish to turn their mind and time to agriculture in Prussia, among the number my present wife's brother, who is an officer in His British Majesty's service, and another officer also who is connected to me by marriage, with several others; as they are aware of the superior abilities of Mr Kyle in that department his establishment is of the first moment to them, and they only wait to learn from him of his being fixed in Prussia to follow him immediately; and as the year is advancing they are anxious not to lose time in commencing ' opporations ' (sic).

" You, sir, may wish to know who it is that is addressing you; exclusive of my near relationship to the Earl of Buchan, with whom I now always reside from his Lordship's advanced age (82), I was married to his brother's daughter (Lord Erskine, late High Chancellor of England). I am an officer in His Royal Highness the Duke of York's Rangers (Yagars).[1] I also belong to the Household of His Royal Highness the Duke of Clarence. I past three of my early years in Deutchland (sic), in Lauenburgh and Hamburgh, but having been thirty years out of Germany I have very much forgotten the language, and dare not venture to write it to a native. My heart still warms to Germany where I was most kindly treated, and I shall

[1] The writer means "Jäger" = chasseurs.

ever remember it with gratitude.—I have the honour to remain, etc.,   DAVID ERSKINE."

Kelch then asked Kyle at Königsberg to come and see him, when he was told that the latter had resolved to settle on a Prussian domain of about 2000 morgen, if the conditions were favourable, and to farm it according to the Scottish methods of cultivation.   "I told him," Kelch writes to the Government, " that first of all ready means were required, and that there would be plenty of opportunities of buying estates advantageously at the present juncture.   I also drew his attention to the farm of Kobbelbude,[1] which was shortly to be sold by auction. He is going to realise a capital of about eighteen hundred pounds, but he has not given me any vouchers for it. This Thomas Kyle is the same with whom I negotiated last year by order of the Government with regard to the acquisition of another estate, when the affair was broken off."

Finally, Kyle received the following official reply: "The farm of Kobbelbude is already disposed of.   We beg to draw your attention to the fact that your knowledge as an experienced agriculturist has been testified to sufficiently in the private letter of Mr Erskine and other private persons, but that this is not sufficient for the County Council in whose hands the administration of the province is put, and which can only be persuaded to favour the settlement of foreign agriculturists by an improvement held out to inland farming.   Neither have you given us sufficient proof of funds large enough for the acquirement and management of such an estate.   As long as you cannot lay before us certificates of your knowledge in practical husbandry from qualified and official bodies in your own

---

[1] Close to Königsberg.

home, we are afraid that we cannot hold out to you any hopes of realising your plans of settlement in Prussia.[1] "

Thus somewhat ignominiously did this rash plan of improving the Prussian methods of agriculture end.

In conclusion we wish to warn against an erroneous impression which the foregoing sketch of the Scottish settler's life in Eastern and Western Prussia might not unnaturally produce upon the minds of our readers.

Looking at the thousand and one obstacles put in the way of the stranger Scot, looking at the almost cruel mockery which forbade the '*umbfarende*' pedlar to traverse the country and earn his bread by the toilsome sale of his pack on the one hand, and then closed the gates of the towns against him, when he wanted to exchange the vagabondage, for which he was reproved, for a settled life to which he had been invited; one feels at first sight inclined to assume some particularly aggravated feeling against the Scot on the part of the Germans; some specially prepared hatred and malevolence to be used with or without discretion at certain frequent intervals against him.

But this assumption would be wrong. The Scot was not the only recipient of these strange gifts of hospitality. He shared them with the Jew, the Spaniard, and above all with the Dutch, who vied with the Scot in their enterprise and the number of their settlements[2] throughout the north-east of Germany. He would have shared them with an angel from heaven if such a one could have been induced to live in Prussia. The gifts were doled out

[1] *Kgl. St. Archiv*, Königsberg.

[2] A very interesting pamphlet on these Dutch settlements has just been published by B. Schumacher under the title : *Niederländische Ansiedlungen im Herzogthum Preussen zur Zeit Herzog Albrechts*, Königsberg, i. P. 1902.

quite irrespective of the person, they were the outcome of a principle under which all Europe, as under a barometrical minimum, then suffered.

There is not the slightest doubt that a German or any numbers of them, that had landed in those days on the coast of England or emigrated to Scotland trying to pursue their trade to better advantage, would have been treated in the same fashion. They could not have been treated otherwise, except by a few enlightened minds born before their time.

This, if it does lessen the severity of our judgment on the Germans of those days, does not lessen the pity and the sympathy felt for the persecuted.

Many of them have succumbed " uncoffined and un-knelled"; of others we are told on many a stately stone and in the turgid eloquence of many an epitaph ; many again have survived and bear witness in their names of the old flood of Scottish emigration. All have left, very literally and very legibly, their footprints in the sands of time.

It is with the memory of those among them that have neither obtained fame nor wealth that we were specially concerned here, and to them we would fain have erected a humble cairn in the long row of sand-swept Scottish graves on the shores of the Baltic.

PART II.

MILITARY, ECCLESIASTICAL AND OTHER MATTERS.

No:3.

GEORGE KEITH
Last Earl Marischal

ARMY—CHURCH—AND OTHER MATTERS.

ONE of the earliest, if not the earliest record of Scottish military assistance being given to the Powers of the Baltic, is to be found during the Crusades of the Teutonic Order against their neighbours, the Lithuanian heathens, or Letten as they are called, in the last decade of the fourteenth century. Then Scottish knights among the knights of all Europe flocked thither to offer their swords in the cause and the propagation of Christianity.

The death of Lord William Douglas of Nithisdale in 1390 or 1391 is related to us by various Scottish, English, French and German sources, all of which have been enumerated in our previous volume.[1] To these may now be added the oldest Hochmeister Chronik dated about the beginning of the fifteenth century.[2] It mentions Lord Douglas in these words: "Do erslugen die Engelischen gar eynen erbarn graffen awsz Schotten do grosse leide umb was undir aller herrschafft, wen her was gar eyn truwer man leibes guttes und ere"; *i.e.* "There the English slew a very honourable earl out of Scotland on whose account there was great grief amongst all the Lords, for he was a very staunch fellow in body, possessions and honour."[3]

Simon Grunau also, a Dominican monk, who wrote

---

[1] See *Scots in Germany*, pp. 274-278. The newest Douglas Book by Sir H. Maxwell refers very briefly to the murder of Lord William. Of course it did not occur in a war against the Turks as stated there. The Turks at that time were very far off indeed.

[2] Dr Hirsch, *Scriptores Rerum Prussicarum*, iii. 620.

[3] The writer of the Chronicle seems to refer to Königsberg.

a Prussian Chronicle about the year 1526 makes mention of Douglas, adding the words: "It was he whose father allowed himself to be killed in order that his master the King might live."[1]

Of the various embellishments of this story we have also spoken previously. Curious it is that the fact of a gate at Danzig, the Hohe Thor, having once been called the Douglas Gate, and of its having been adorned with the Coat of Arms of this nobleman, should occur in the following three Scottish writers: the author of the *Atlas Geographus*, Hume of Godscroft, in his Douglas book, and John Scot in his *Metrical History of the War in Flanders*. The last of these has the lines:—

> "And at Danskin even in our own time
> There was a gate called Douglas Port
> Now re-edified again and called Hochindore.[2]

To these must be added the testimony of an English merchant, who in his description of the city of Danzig writes: "Upon account of a signal service which one of the Douglas family did to this city in relieving it in its utmost extremities against the Poles, the Scotch were allowed to be free burghers of the town, and had several other immunities granted them above other foreigners, but now excepting the successors of those who were so incorporated they have no distinction or privileges, but indeed *a better half of the families are of Scotch extraction*." He then mentions the Hohe Thor being called Douglas Gate even in his time (1734).[3]

---

[1] The Chronicle has been published by Perlbach, i. 676 and 679.

[2] *Metrical Hist. of the War in Flanders*, 1701-1712, by John Scot. a soldier. Published in the *Scottish Brigade in Holland*, iii. 522 (*Scott. Hist. Soc. Publications*).

[3] A Particular Description of Danzig by an English Merchant, lately resident there. London, 1734.

In Danzig, where the beautiful Hohe Thor still stands, restored and freed from its former encumbrances, nothing is known of this story. But then Danzig is rather badly off for a good history, and at some future time a verification may be found of what, till now, must be considered tradition only.

Skipping over a period of nearly two centuries we arrive at a period where Danzig was sorely pressed by the enemy.

In 1575 a scion of the royal family of Bátori had been called to the throne of Poland as Stephen IV. Danzig, though nominally belonging to Poland, refused to acknowledge him and declared for the German Emperor, Maximilian II., who promised the town important trading privileges. Even after the death of Maximilian in 1576, its opposition did not cease. Stephan, therefore, laid siege to it, but its defence was so obstinate and so skilful that he had to withdraw very soon, express his regret, and pay 200,000 gulden as an indemnity.

For this war Scotland, the great recruiting depôt of Europe, furnished a force of six or seven hundred men. They were drawn not, however, from Scotland itself, but from the Scottish forces in Holland. The first indication of it we find in the Calendar of State Papers when (August 3, 1577) Walsingham writes to the Regent : "It may please you, therefore, to stay such of that (the Scottish) nation as lately served in Holland, who, as I am informed, are otherwise minded to repair to the service of the town of Danske, for unless the matter be speedily compounded their cause requires speedy relief."[1] To Danzig they went, anyhow, and, as it appears, by sea.[2] They were commanded by Colonel William Stuart and the Captains

---

[1] *Kgl. St. Archiv*, Danzig. Militaria.

[2] Some of them under Gourlay, Trotter and Tomson, arrived at Danzig in the middle of June 1577 ; others on the 20th of August.

Gourlay, W. Moncrieff, John Crawford, John Tomson, John Dollachy (?), Alex. Morra and Will. Rentoun. Their engagement was to last till May 1578; good pay and plenty of ammunition and provision was promised. We also hear that their sergeant-major was called Ambsteroder (Anstruther), their surgeon (Feldscheer), John Orley, their Provost, Robert Schwall, and their preacher (Predikant), Patrick Griech (Greig), the latter drawing two hundred gulden as his pay.

Now powder and shot seems to have been forthcoming in abundant quantities—we are told in the treasury-accounts of Danzig that at one time fifty-four schock (*i.e.* three score) of slow-matches at an expense of eighty-one gulden were handed out to the forces—but it was somewhat different with the officers' pay, and some little pressure was required on the part of the claimants. Captain Murray addresses the Magistrates on this matter, and scornfully states that he has wasted a whole week and got nothing, and William Moncrieff writes a long letter with respect to the same business.

" Gestrenge, edle, ehrveste, erbare, nahmhaffte, grossgünstige Herren ! " he begins with that waste of adjectives which delighted the soul of the German official at that time. " After offering you my very willing and humble services, I beg to draw your attention to the fact that I have, a few weeks ago, brought all the men under my standard from the Netherlands at my own expense to this good town to serve against her enemies. I have thus laid out in food, conveyance and other expenses more than six hundred thaler, by which I was compelled to pawn my best clothes at Holschenore[1] in Denmark. Though I did formerly apply to you for a reimbursement, I received only the

[1] He means Elsinore. Cp. *Kgl. St. Archiv*, Danzig. Militaria. See Part III.

answer that I must put down all my expenses with regard
to the soldiers serving under me, carefully in writing, and
send it to the magistrates, when I should duly receive
what was right. Now to put down every item in connection with my said expenses clearly and distinctly, is
quite impossible, for I have kept no account-books. I
therefore leave it to you and to your decision, and trust
that I shall receive what is due to me, with which I shall
be well content. Hoping to receive a favourable reply,
your humble servant,

"WILHELM MONKRIEFF, Captain."

Matters, however, seem to have been settled amicably,
for we soon read of the valiant deeds of the little Scotch
garrison. They were the chief stay of Danzig in all her
troubles, say the State Papers, "They have done so
much noble service that they have got great fame for
their country in these parts." [1]

Poor Gourlay had to pay with his life. An old
chronicler of Danzig tells us that he, being wounded
under the arm, wanted to jump into a boat, but he jumped
short, and in his heavy armour he was drowned. [2] His
funeral was a very solemn affair. "All the Scots, with
their muskets under their arms, went first with their
colours, and drums beating. After the coffin came the
magistrates, the bailies and the burgesses."

Colonel Stuart himself had a narrow escape. "On this
Saturday, December 7th, 1577," writes an old chronicler,
"the Scottish colonel, a handsome and imposing warrior

[1] See Löschin, *Geschichte Danzigs*, i. 235. Cal. of State Papers
(Foreign) 1577-78, p. 460.

[2] See Curicke, *Der Stadt Danzig historische Beschreibung*, 1657.
"Gourlay welcher mit schwerer Rüstung in ein boht springen wollen
aber weil er zu kurz gesprungen und über das unter dem Arm wundge-
schossen war, ist er ersoffen."

of royal blood, went for a ride with the horses he had lately bought, outside the town, and exercised them opposite the hills near the shooting range of the citizens. But when the enemy noticed this, he rushed out of his cover, wanting to attack him. He, however, with his men, quickly galloped towards the Heilige Leichnams Thor, where he was under the cover of the guns, and the enemy dared not follow him.[1]

After the siege had been raised the services of Colonel Stuart were asked for by the Danish King, but Danzig would not let him go before all the Scots had been paid off for "fear of a rising"[2] (1578). As to the "Predikant" or military chaplain, as we would now say, he held services after the manner of the Presbyterians, in the Church of St Nicholas, also called the Church of the Black Friars, whilst the Pastor of St Elisabeth also celebrated the Holy Communion in the same way for the benefit of the levied Dutch and Scottish troops.[3]

Danzig seems to have retained some at any rate of the Scottish soldiers in her pay. We read now and then of

[1] "An diesem Sonnabend ist auch der Schotten Oberster, ein feiner und stattlicher Kriegsmann von königlichem Geschlechte mit seinen Pferden die er gekauft hatte vor die Stadt spazieren geritten und tummelte sich bei dem gebürge an der Bürgerschieszstange. . . . Wie aber der Feind solches merkte, stürzte er aus dem Gebürge heraus und wollte ihn berennen. Er rannte aber flugs mit seinem Volk nach dem Heil. Leichnams Thor. Do durften sie nicht unter das Geschütz ebenteuern und zogen sich zurück." *Kgl. St. Archiv*, Danzig. Handschr. Ll. 92.

[2] *Kgl. St. Archiv*, Danzig. Missivbücher. Letter to the King of Denmark, dated February 21, 1578. Colonel Stuart is in Edinburgh in 1590 writing to the Danzig Magistrates on behalf of the Danish Councillor Ramel, who had lent King Sigismund money to redeem the Crown Jewels which the latter had pawned.

[3] Duisburg, Versuch einer topographisch historischen Beschreiburg, Danzigs i. 163, 170 f.

Scottish names, the bearers of which "now served in this town's soldatesca."

Hans Krafort, for instance, and Oliver Ketscher, both soldiers, testify before the Magistrates of the town that the late Hans Rehe (Ray), born in the Kingdom of Scotland, did serve as a sergeant under Colonel Fuchs in the Russian War, that he was killed during the siege of Smolensk, and buried with all martial honours (1634). Or when Major-General Gaudi explains that Jacob Black, born at Danzig, who had served in his company as a dragoon, had died on the march behind Casimirs four years ago (1662). Very numerous, of course, were the Scottish officers in the service of the King of Poland. To the names already mentioned we may here add those of Captain James Murray, who in 1627 commissions Jacob Rowan at Danzig to collect his pension;[1] Captain Reay who figures in a rather curious case of wrongful imprisonment; and Major-General Count von Johnston, who was also Colonel of a Regiment of Cuirassiers.[2]

In 1624 King Vladislaus IV. grants to the Scot, Thomas Fergusson—'_egregius_'—who had served under Jacob Wilson and Captain Kirkpatrick as a sergeant against the Russians, permission to return to his own country, characterising his conduct during the campaign as brave and honourable (1624).

Very sad was the case of Alexander Ruthven, who lost his life in the service of Poland. It is on account of his widow that Edinburgh addresses the following letter to the Magistrates of Danzig in the year 1605: "We make it known to you that to-day appeared before us the noble Margaret Munro, the widow of the late Colonel Alexander

---

[1] _Kgl. St. Archiv_, Danzig, Schöppenb.
[2] See _Geschichte der Familie von Johnston_, by M. von Johnston-Rathen; printed privately, 1891, p. 42.

Ruthven, and explained to us how her late husband had
spent and lost all his property in various wars in Poland
and Sweden, so that after he had sacrificed his life in the
service of the King of Poland she had hardly enough to
live with her orphan children.   Her only hope was placed,
next to God, in the liberality of His Majesty, King Sigismund III., whose Chancellor and Field-marshal, Johannes
Zamoscius, had promised him, when he was about to meet
his death at the siege of Volmer, to see that the King
would provide for his wife and children liberally ; and
as she herself for the want of means and otherwise is
prevented from accomplishing such a long journey to call
upon His Majesty and General Zamosc, she by the terms
of this letter solemnly appoints George Bruce to approach
the said persons in her name, and to remind them of their
promise, and to act in all matters relating to her deceased
husband as her representative, with this only limitation,
that he shall have no power to arrange about money
matters and pensions unless George Smyth, a goldsmith,
and George Hepburn, a merchant, both citizens of Danzig,
consent and approve.   She makes these two her trustees,
and empowers them together with her representative,
George Bruce, to administer all matters relating to the
late Alexander Ruthven, to pay his debts, or to call in
debts just as if she had been present herself; and she
will consider everything that has legally been done by
these her representatives as binding, pledging at the same
time all movable and immovable possessions she owns at
present or may own in the future.   In testimony whereof
we have ordered our first secretary, Alexander Guthrie,
to append the seal of our city to this document.   Given
at Edinburgh, on the sixth of April, one thousand six
hundred and five." [1]

[1] *Kgl. St. Archiv*, Danzig.

Another well deserving officer in the Polish Army was Peter Leermonth, whose name occurs in the Minute Books of Marienburg in 1619. He is called "nobilis," and the King, in granting him the property of a late stranger, which according to the *jus caducum* fell to the Crown,[1] says of him: "He showed himself a brave and active soldier, not only against the Duke of Sudermannia, but also during the whole of the Russian War when we were besieging Smolensk . . . and again in the reign of our son, Wladislaus Sigismund, he fought very bravely, and was an example to others (*et aliis dux et auctor existens ad pugnam*)." It is well known that the Russian Poet Lermontoff's Scottish ancestor Learmonth came to Russia about this time. The poet's father's name was Petrowitsch, showing that Peter was a family name.

It would fill another volume to write exhaustively on the Scottish officers in the service of Poland. Their numbers were, as we have stated, very large, their services much appreciated. It is owing, no doubt, in great part to these services that so many Scottish families were ennobled and enrolled among the Polish nobility in the sixteenth, seventeenth and eighteenth centuries. We find the following names who were granted titles of nobility by the Polish Crown: Bonar, Chambers (1673), Mackay, Macferlant, Ogilvie, Murison, Miller, Guthrie (1673), Forseit (Forsyth), Patterson, with the surname of Hayna, Gordons, Fraser, Halyburton, with the surname Stodart, Watson, and Karkettle, the last two at the end of the eighteenth century.[2]

Prominent among the Scottish officers of Gustavus

---

[1] See above.

[2] Cp. Emilian v. Zernicki—Szelika, *Der Polnische Adel*, Hamburg 1900. Pp. 57, 91, 254, 324 and elsewhere.

Adolphus, King of Sweden, was William Lewis,[1] who emigrated to Sweden at the beginning of the seventeenth century. His ancestral home was Castle Manor in Peebleshire. He also saw a good deal of service in Germany. In the camp of Altbrandenburg he was made colonel on the 17th of August 1631. In 1640 he was garrisoned with his regiment in Stralsund, Pomerania. His grateful King acknowledged his faithful services by bestowing upon him the estates of Panton and Nurmis in Livonia. Colonel Lewis died in 1675.

A descendant of his was Lieutenant-General Friedrich von Löwis of Menar, who, in 1813, for several months commanded the Russian army during the siege of Danzig, Danzig then an important fortress. His portrait and a memorial tablet is to be seen in the Waisenhaus Kirche (Chapel of the Orphanage) at the last named place.

How this portrait got into the Orphanage is told in the records of the institution. According to them a letter of recommendation to the heads of all the villages in the territory of Danzig had been granted by the magistrates to the Master of the Orphanage, who intended to set out on an expedition with some of his pupils in order to collect contributions in money and in kind for the institution, and to relieve the great want and distress occasioned by the protracted siege of the town. It must be remembered that Danzig at that time was held by the French, and that it was besieged by Russians and Germans, under the chief command of Alexander, Duke of Würtemberg, to whom General Frederick von Löwis of Menar acted as second in command. "On the 24th of August," our records continue, "at half-past nine in the morning, one

[1] To this day there are "Löwis of Menar" in Livonia. Baron K. von Löwis of Menar at Riga had the kindness of furnishing me with the above data.

hundred and thirty-four orphans, accompanied by their teacher, sergeant and some nurses, left the orphanage and moved in procession, and singing the old hymn, 'When we are in the depth of woe,' to the Church of St Mary's in the town, where the senior clergyman and chaplain of the institution delivered an address and pronounced the benediction. Then the children went to the melody of the hymn, 'Now God be merciful,' to the Langemarkt, the chief square of Danzig. Here one of them spoke a few touching words of farewell. Everybody crowded around them, and even the poorest showed their sympathy by some little gift. It is told that an old apple-woman divided her whole barrel of fruit and vegetable amongst them, a present not to be undervalued in those days of famine and distress. With their master Gehrt at the head, the procession then moved out of the High Gate, past the little village of Ohra. But here their difficulties commenced. Scarcely had they passed the French outposts, when to their dismay they beheld at no great distance the Russian outposts, who had advanced as far as the "Three Boars Heads." Now, as neither the French would allow them to return to the city nor the Russians to proceed on their errand of mercy, they had to encamp where they were under the sky, starvation staring them in the face.

"At last, General Frederick von Löwis, moved by compassion and himself deeply afflicted by the recent loss of a young and promising boy, succeeded in effecting their release. The Duke of Würtemberg having written to him on the occasion of his sad loss, he replied that his grief would be greatly assuaged if the poor orphans of Danzig received a free pass. Upon this the Duke allowed them to proceed.

"They were first placed in the monastery of St Albrecht, where Löwis had his quarters, later they found an asylum in the little village of Ottomin, where they were well fed and clothed by good Samaritans, until, in January 1814, Danzig was restored to Germany, and they were allowed to return to their old home.

"In memory of this act of kindness on the part of the Russian General, the following tablet was placed in the Orphanage chapel: 'During the siege of Danzig under Alexander, Duke of Würtemberg, Friedrich von Löwis, Imperial Russian General and Knight, our deliverer in the fatal days between the outposts at Niederfelde, from the 24th of August to the 8th of September 1813.'"[1]

An additional glimpse of Scottish officers in Germany is afforded to us in the history of the City of Thorn,[2] which was occupied by Sweden from the year 1655 until 1658, when it was retaken by Polish and Austrian forces. The garrison at that time consisted of two thousand five hundred men, amongst them the Scottish Body Guard numbering five hundred, whilst some of the other regiments were also commanded by Scottish officers such as Colonel Cranston, Hatton and Douglas.

The following officers were serving in the Guard :—

        Colonel Hamilton.

        Majors Mercer and Wilson.

        Captain Eske (Erskine).

            ,,   Ramsay.

            ,,   Orcheson (?).

            ,,   Lawson.

            ,,   Robertson.

[1] Kindly communicated by the Directors of the Orphanage at Danzig. Frederick von Löwis was the son of Major-General Fred von Löwis and Eliz. Clapier of Cologne. He was born 16th Sept. 1767, at Hopsal in Esthonia, and died as Livonian Marshal after a brilliant military career against the Swedes, the Poles and the French in 1824 on the 16th of April.

[2] E. Kestner, *Beiträge zur Geschichte der Stadt Thorn*, 1883, p. 203 f.

Lieutenant Fraser.

,, Jamieson.

,, Stirling.

,, Montgomery.

,, Kurning.

,, Macdougall.

,, Lenegis (?).

,, Karr.

In the chronicles of the time the excellent discipline of these troops is praised.

Once again, at the beginning of the eighteenth century, the city of Danzig entrusted the post of commander of its forces to a Scotsman. This was Major Sinclair, who was called out of Holland in 1698. He was an energetic, able man, and took an interest in the improvements of the city. In 1704 he was made Colonel, and he died as Major-General in 1731, when he was buried with great pomp in the Frauen or Marien Kirche, where there is still to be seen a monument erected in his memory.[1]

In the armies of Brandenburg and Hanover also Scottish officers were found in great numbers during the seventeenth and eighteenth centuries. In the Brandenburg Prussian service such names occur as Captain Trotter (†1653), Captain Hamilton (1669), Lieut.-Colonel Black (1665), and Colonel Spang. Very likely the following letter of introduction also refers to an officer. It was written by one Robert Stewart from Danzig in 1611, and addressed to the Elector of Brandenburg, Johann Sigismund. The writer recommends " Joannem Drummond," his countryman, who is honest and of good birth, and

---

[1] Köhler, *Geschichte der Festungen Danzig und Weichselmünde* (1893). Pawlowski, *Populäre Geschichte*, Danzig, p. 142. There is a long Latin inscription on the tomb, but no biographical details. His coat-of-arms that used to hang up above the monument has disappeared.

possesses famous friends. "The very great friendliness and condescension with which Your Highness received me may excuse the boldness of interceding for another friend. I most urgently commend him to your favour and kindness."[1] In more recent times we find no less than four Hamiltons mentioned in Königsberg: General Hamilton (1810), Colonel Hamilton (1819), and two other Hamiltons, non-commissioned officers (1832). A Colonel Leslie also occurs in the town of Preussisch Holland (†1821).[2] In the Hanoverian army the most eminent Scottish names in the seventeenth century are: Graham, Crichton, Gordon, Ramsay and Stuart; in the eighteenth: Henderson, Macphail and Robertson, and in the nineteenth: Mackenzie, Murray, and General Sir H. Halkett. Of these the Robertsons or "von" Robertsons, as they are now called, are distinguished by a long and honourable service. The first of them, belonging to the Strowan branch of the family, came to Germany about the middle of the seventeenth century, and entered the army of the Prince of Celle as a Major. He returned to Scotland in 1687 and died on his estate of "Clerkensheede," a name which has not yet been identified. Another Robertson was Governor of Nienburg in Hanover; a third, Captain in the Hanoverian Guards; a fourth, Knight of the Bath and the Order of Guelph, fought at Waterloo, where he was dangerously wounded. He died in 1849. Grandsons of his are still living in the North of Germany.

[1] ". . . Joannem Drummond conterraneum quem constat bene oriundum, amicos enim claros habere, et ipsum ni fallor satis probum; Serenitatis Vestrae humanitas et incredibilis clementia qua me ipsum excepistis eo me audaciae protraxerunt ut pro alio etiam Serenitatem Vestram interpellari audeam, quo-circa eundem solitae Vestrae benignitati et clementiae iterum atque iterum commendo." *Kgl. St. Archiv*, Königsberg. *Hzgl. Brief Archiv.*

[2] *Kgl. St. Archiv*, Königsberg. *Testaments Akten.*

A great many of the second generation of Scotsmen followed the calling of the Church. Among the preachers of the Presbyterian Church of St Peter and Paul at Danzig we find Sam. W. Thomson towards the end of the eighteenth century and his successor, Peter J. Buchan. Thomas Burnet was the first preacher of the Scottish congregation there about the year 1692, when Scotch services took place in his private dwelling in the Frauengasse. From the great number of entries in the Church books of St Peter and Paul and of St Elizabeth, however, we conclude that from an early date the bulk of the Scots attended divine worship in these German Presbyterian Churches; though they may have formed and did form an ecclesiola in ecclesia, having their own poorfunds and so forth. They also had their own "Umbitter," a sexton or low church official, who was sent round to the members of the congregation announcing deaths, and funerals and marriages. His name is given as David Grim (Graham), and he died in the hospital of St Elizabeth in 1667, at the age of seventy-eight. Not only did the Scots of Danzig attend the services of St Peter and Paul, but they had clergymen of their own nation or extraction at that church as well, though of course the sermons were delivered in the German language. Two Buchans, Jacob and Peter, and probably father and son, were preachers there from 1749-1776, and from 1804-1814 respectively. Besides these the name of S. W. Turner occurs in the list of clergymen (1781-1806).

Among the Lutheran clergy of Danzig, as far back as 1624, a Scot, Magister Adrian Stoddart, deserves mention. He was born in 1598, and filled other responsible positions in the government of the town besides being Dean of the Parish Church of St Mary's. His portrait is still to be seen in the vestry. The most valuable Chronicle of Curicke is dedicated to him.

In the remaining Province of Western Prussia we find no less than five Lutheran clergymen of the name of Achinwall, the same family that has already furnished us with the name of the famous Professor of Jurisprudence and Political Economy at Göttingen. The eldest of these was Thomas Achenwall, born 1695, at Elbing. He afterwards became clergyman of the Heilige Drei Königskirche in his native town, and died in 1755. The next is another Thomas, a cousin, born at Elbing in 1702. He became preacher at St Mary's Church there and died in 1764. The third is his son Gottlieb Thomas Achenwall, born in 1731. After having taught at Elbing for some years, he was called to the village of Fürstenan as clergyman in 1759. His son Daniel Thomas Gottlieb, born in 1766, came as minister to Lenzen (1804) and died there in 1807. The last of the Achinwall theologians was Thomas Christlieb, born at Elbing in 1751; ordained in 1778, he officiated in various churches, latterly in St Mary's. He died in 1810.[1]

Another Scottish clergyman at Elbing was W. Rupsohn (Robinson) who was born in 1664. Having

---

[1] The following is a table of descent of this remarkable family :

THOMAS ACHINWALL (Auchinvale) 1615-1674.

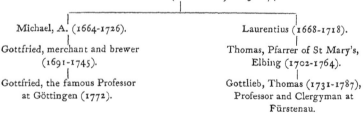

Michael, A. (1664-1726).	Laurentius (1668-1718).
Gottfried, merchant and brewer (1691-1745).	Thomas, Pfarrer of St Mary's, Elbing (1702-1764).
Gottfried, the famous Professor at Göttingen (1772).	Gottlieb, Thomas (1731-1787), Professor and Clergyman at Fürstenau.
	Daniel Thomas Gottlieb at Lenzen.

studied at the University of Rostock, he spent some time in travelling through Germany, Belgium and France, not so much for the sake of scenery, but in order to enjoy the intercourse with famous men.[1] After his return in 1689, he was chosen clergyman at the Heilige Leichnam Kirche[2] in Elbing, an office which he held until 1718, the year of his death.

In Nassenhuben, a village not far from Danzig, and where there was a Presbyterian Church, no less than four clergymen of Scottish descent officiated. Gilbert Wachius was the first. He came there from Königsberg in 1694, and was called to Bremen five years later, where he died in 1720. Alexander Davidson from Danzig succeeded him in the ministry. He died in 1725. Of John R. Forster we shall have to speak later. Finally we have in this same village the name of S. W. Turner, whom we have just mentioned as having been called to St Peter's at Danzig in 1781.

In other places of Western Prussia such as Thorn,[3] Thiensdorf,[4] Graudenz,[5] Rosenberg[6] and Preussisch Mark,[7] we find clergymen of Scottish extraction filling the ministry.

Turning to Eastern Prussia the names of four Andersons occur since 1775. We have two W. Crichtons, Chaplains and Doctors of Divinity at Königsberg; the elder of these came from Insterburg, became preacher in the Royal

[1] This was the main object of travelling in those days. To travel for the sake of natural scenery is altogether of modern growth.

[2] Corpus Christi Church. See Stadt Bibliothek, Elbing, MS. F. 48.

[3] Th. Albert Young (1719-1745) and Ernest Wauch (1789-1791).   [4] G. Kraffert (Crawfurd), (1721-1737).

[5] Dan. Lamb (1703-1708).

[6] Michael Scotus, 1738. He was first in Neidenburg.

[7] Th. Marschall from Elbing (1708-1710). See Rhesa, *Presbyteriologie von Ost und West Preussen.*

Orphanage (1715-1718), and, since 1730, Court Preacher and Consistorialrath in Königsberg. He died sixty-six years old in 1749. His son William, born 1732, at Königsberg, was for a time Professor of Theology at Frankfurt. In 1772 he succeeded his father.

Another Court Preacher, there used to be three, was J. Thomson, born at Warsaw in 1675. After having occupied the post of headmaster of the reformed School at Königsberg he entered upon the chaplaincy in 1707.[1]

In the Polish Presbyterian Church at Königsberg, mention is made of a clergyman named Chr. Henry Karkettle, who died in 1751.

In Rastenburg, Ernest Fr. Hammilton officiated;[2] in Pillau, David Hervie, a native of Königsberg, but of Scottish descent,[3] whilst in 1665 Jacob Glen was a minister at Stallupöhnen.

In Tilsit we find besides A. Dennis, who died in 1699, a clergyman named von Irwing, a native of the place, where the Scottish Irvings were widespread. Another Wach, born at Goldap, occurs as clergyman in the village of Tollmingkehmen.

With regard to Jacob Brown who was appointed to Königsberg in 1685,[4] there exists a remarkable letter addressed to Hofprediger Schlemüller, on the 3rd of April 1668, by the Churfürst, showing and completing our evidence of the desire of the numerous Scots to enjoy the worship of God in their own tongue many years before.

"Your Reverence will remember," it runs, "how about two or three years ago, some of the Scottish Nation here held private meetings in their houses and had sermons,

---

[1] He died in 1732.   [2] 1755-1783.   [3] 1707-1775.
[4] *Scots in Germany*, p. 190 f.

about which people in the town spoke very harshly, under the name of false and forbidden doctrine, asking our government very earnestly and humbly to stop such suspicious conventicles. Now when we caused an enquiry to be made into the matter of these secret gatherings and found that a Scottish exile of pure doctrine and good morals and an adherent of the Reformed (*i.e.* Presbyterian) Form of Religion had come hither to visit his good friends, but was not able now to return to his native country on account of the naval war lately broken out between Holland and England, and further that he, not wishing to eat his bread in idleness, desired to preach the Word of God to his countrymen in their own tongue ; we have in order to remove all grounds of suspicions and complaints and to assist them in this praiseworthy undertaking, graciously been pleased to allow them to continue their religious exercise publicly after the close of the service of the Reformed Church on Sundays, in the Hall at the Castle.

"But as we have now been informed, shortly before our departure, and not without very great surprise on our part, that the said Scots against our prohibition continue their private meetings, that there were some points in their doctrine not altogether sound and that all this would be brought forward as a great ' gravamen ' at our next diet, we desire your Reverence (it being very necessary to prevent this) to let these people know in our name, that, because the diet is approaching now and we are in nowise anxious to see a matter allowed by us disallowed by them,[1] they should discontinue both the public as well as the private exercise of religion in their own tongue. But if afterwards they desire to have their own preacher besides our two Court-Preachers,

---

[1] The meaning of this sentence is not quite clear.

they may duly petition for it, when, we have no doubt, His Electoral Highness will graciously consider such a request."[1]

It is curious to observe not only the liberal and humane views of the Prince, but also his dread—so often the dread of a military hero who knows of no fear in battle—of having his previously and magnanimously given privilege denounced, torn to shreds by discussion, and perhaps cancelled by the diet. The Scottish predilection for private religious meetings as well as the extreme importance attached to points of doctrine and their "soundness" is again highly characteristic.

We know the further development: how Brown was found wanting in some minor doctrinal matters, how the Elector interceded for him, and how he, after having promised to teach or do nothing against the mode of worship in Königsberg, was finally appointed preacher to the Scottish congregation.[2]

Going across the strict boundaries of the two Prussian Provinces we may add to this already long list of Scottish Presbyterian Clergymen the name of C. Musonius (1545-1612), son of the Scot, Jacob Musonius, at Lobsens, in the Province of Posen, and that of his brother Simon who died in 1592. Some of their descendants were likewise ministers. We even hear of Scotsmen preaching to Polish congregations, for instance Andrew Malcolm, who was Presbyterian clergyman at Züllichau in Silesia, his congregation consisting of a colony of Polish immigrants.

In Pomerania about the year 1650 one Hamilton occurs as the clergyman of Wachholzhausen, not far from Treptow, whilst in Mecklenburg Ludovicus Barclay, Archdeacon at Rostock, took a prominent position among

---

[1] *Kgl. St. Archiv*, Königsberg. See the original in Part III.
[2] See *Scots in Germany*, p. 190 f.

the learned theologians and writers of sermons of the day.

The interest taken by the General Assembly of the Church of Scotland in the religious well-being of their countrymen abroad has been illustrated in our previous volume. Once again in 1722 the Assembly took occasion to write to those far-off parts of Europe. The Protestant Church of Lithuania was in a pitiable condition at the time, chiefly for the want of funds and for their inability to give their young candidates for the ministry a suitable training. On the seventh of May in the year given, the National Synod assembled in Edinburgh takes this sad condition of the sister Church into consideration, and deliberates on the "friendly request" to train at its own expense two Lithuanian Students at the University of Edinburgh. Finally they resolve to spend the four distinct collections from Lothian and Tweeddale, which were formerly devoted to the bringing up of other students, for the said purpose of educating two Lithuanian youths at the University, beginning at Martinmas 1723. They commission Jacob Young of Killicantie to gather in these tithes, and send copies of their resolution to the Prussian ambassador at London, Baron von Wallenrode, as well as to the Rev. Boguslaus Kopyewitz at Vilna.[1] The letter written to the Reformed Synod of Lithuania in connection with this matter is dated May 17th, 1722[2] and runs :—

"DEAR AND HONOURED BRETHREN,—The Reverend Boguslaus Kopyewitz, minister of God's Word at Vilna, when he was here in 1718 as a delegate of the Reformed Church of the Grand Duchy of Lithuania, witnessed with his own eyes, with what great pity for his brethren who profess a purer faith among your

[1] In Livonia, Russia.   [2] *Kgl. St. Archiv*, Königsberg.

people, the story of your afflictions, as read by him in your letters, had filled the Scottish Church then holding her National Synod, and how heartily she advocated a collection of funds on your behalf. The event has sufficiently taught us that our lay-brethren have been animated by the same feelings towards you as we ourselves. We have handed over to you all the money except nine pounds and two shillings of British money, which small sum not being considered large enough for the purpose, was given to Samuel Chien, a student of Divinity, and a Pole, as a donation. As a further proof that the kind feeling of our Scottish Synod towards you has remained unaltered, and that our mind is most ready to spread the Kingdom of our Saviour and most willing to assist our brethren tied to us by the same Reformed faith, the members of the Synod commissioned me to let you know in their name, that they have, in consequence of your letter, by their resolution, a copy of which is enclosed, provided for the board and the education at the University of Edinburgh, of two students, who will have to be recommended by your certificates. We hope that this proposal of our Synod will be agreeable to you, and a fresh token not only of its interest in your own Synod but of its sincere love towards those among your nation who are united to us by the true teaching of Christ. It remains for me to add with how great a pleasure I received the commission of communicating this to you by my letter, having thus an occasion of assuring you of my own sincerest wishes, with which I beg to sign, Reverend and dear Brethren, in brotherly love, your humble servant,

GULIELMUS MITCHELL,

May 17, 1722. *Moderator.*

Verum Exemplar Epist. ab Ecclesia Scoticana ad Synod. Reform. Lithuaniensem.[1]

How zealously the Scots attended the German Presbyterian Churches of St Peter and Paul and of St Elizabeth at Danzig, and how eagerly they availed themselves of their ordinances is shown in the Church registers and books which have been kept and preserved uninterruptedly since the year 1573, that is to say only about fifty years after the introduction of the doctrines of the Reformation.[2] In the marriage registers we find between the years 1573 and 1699 over one hundred Scottish names, from Jacob Burges who marries Anne, Simon Lang's widow (1573) to D. Nichols, who marries Anne Merivale a hundred years later. In the lists of baptisms from 1590 to 1632, about seventy Scottish names occur, amongst them Mackomtosh, Cochran, Skoda, Hewell and Grieve, names that we do not find elsewhere.

In the fifty years dating from 1631 to 1681, finally close on sixty Scotsmen and Scotswomen were buried in St Elizabeth's alone, a great many also in the Church of St Peter and Paul, two or three in the Church of St Mary (Frauenkirche) and three in St Johann's. Of one Daniel Beer, it says, "a Scot of ninety-five buried in the Churchyard of St Barbara," another whose name from Fergus became "Vergiss" seventy-two years old, was buried in the Churchyard of Corpus Christi. The notes, short as they are, very often are extremely interesting. Of Edward Kincaid we read that he was a late "Feldprediger" (Army

---

[1] *Kgl. St. Archiv*, Königsberg. See also Part III. The name Chien occurs amongst the Scots in Poland, so that the above named student would have been a "Scoto-Polonus."

[2] According to Simon Grunau it was the son of a Scot from Nürnberg, with the name of Matz Köningk, a councillor and very eloquent, that first brought the message of Luther and his books into the town of Dantzke. Grunau, III., 115. But Grunau is not an authority of the first order.

Chaplain) in the army of the Swedish General Baner (1641); another, Jacobus Ross, is described as a late lieutenant and an innkeeper; the name of Johann Cant is accompanied by the following note: "a Scottish lieutenant who died on his way through Danzig fifty-six years old" (1652).[1] Gertrud Uphagen is described as Lieutenant Jacob Stuart's "housewife" (1658), Catherine Watson, seventy-seven years old, as the "Scotch" Catherine (1639), and of Alexander Watson we are told that he was "a Scottish youth of twenty-four who was wounded on the walls of Schöneck."[2]

Besides these entries we have the more enduring records of numerous tombstones and mural tablets, many of them adorned with their proud Scottish coats-of-arms, in the two Churches of St Peter, St Elizabeth and St Mary at Danzig.

Danzig, always ready to receive the sea-tossed Scots in the shelter of her harbour, has now granted them a last safe anchorage.

The Scottish traveller, who gets into ecstasies of delight at the sight of the foreign Campo Santos under the brighter sky of Italy, would do well to remember that here also far in the "rude North," forgotten and lonely, is a Campo Santo intimately connected with the life-history of his own people: the true Campo Santo of the Scot abroad.

On those Scots in Germany eminent in the walks of life we have now to make a few remarks. To the notices given concerning Alexander Alesius, the celebrated Scottish Reformer, we may add that when he threw up his pro-

[1] "Ein schottischer Lieutenant, so auf der Durchreise gestorben." Another Cant or Kant, Andreas, was a tanner and dwelt in Petershagen, a part of Danzig. In 1661 he is described as a "musketeer under Sergeant Major Goltz in the army of the Elector of Brandenburg."

[2] "Ein schottischer Gesell so einen Schuss ufm Thurm zu Schöneck empfangen." For a complete list see Part III.

fessorship at Frankfurt on the Oder, so poor seem to have been his circumstances that Johann Friedrich, the Duke of Saxony, had to provide forty ducats as travelling money for him;[1] that his name occurs written on the fly leaf of a Latin Bible (1549) belonging to the German reformer Scribonius and that his chief work was his Lectures on St Paul's epistles to the Romans.[2]

There is another Scottish professor at Frankfurt mentioned with the name of *Johann Walter Leslie*, who died in 1679. He wrote various theological works;[3] whilst on the Roman Catholic side mention must be made of *William Johnston*, who was a Jesuit and taught Philosophy and Theology at Grätz in Austria. He died in 1609.[4]

Other descendants of the Scots took to the Law. To complete our list given elsewhere we may mention the names of Christof Pathon or Patton who was a lawyer at Elbing in 1648,[5] and of John Immanuel Hamilton, the son of the above named clergyman, who became an advocate and professor of Philosophy at Halle University and died as a judge at Stargard in Pomerania in the year 1728. Another Pomeranian solicitor, John Mitzel (Mitchel) was born in 1642, at Stralsund, and went as a lawyer to Rostock after having finished his University course at Helmstädt. In 1670 he became Professor of Jurisprudence at Königsberg, where he died in 1677.[6]

To the famous Scottish doctors of medicine must be added the name of John Patterson, who was Imperial

---

[1] *Corpus Reform.*, II., 885.

[2] *Omnes disputationes D. Alex. Alesii de tota Epistola ad Romanos*, 1553.

[3] Wrote: *De Animo, De regimine Ecclesiastico*, etc.

[4] He wrote among other works an *Epitome Historiae Sleidani* and a *Commentary on Isaiah.*

[5] *Stadt Bibliothek*, Elbing, M.S., Q. 117.

[6] He wrote among other works: *Oeconomia juris provincialis Ducatus Borussiae ; De Tutelis ; De Principiis juris ; De Testimoniis foeminarum*, etc.

Physician, and lived in the small town of Eperies in
Hungaria, in the latter half of the XVIth. Century.

In the walks of Science and Natural History the Forsters,
father and son, were eminent. Their ancestor, George
Forster, emigrated, together with the swarm of his countrymen, about the year 1642, when he settled at Neuenburg,
in Eastern Prussia, as a merchant. His son Adam removed
to Dirschau not far from Danzig, where he also obtained
citizenship. A grandson of his, George Reinhold, became
famous as the companion of Cook, with whom he sailed
round the world from 1772 to 1775. He was a man of
a very unsettled disposition, and quite incapable of adapt-
ing himself to the exigencies of life. After having been
a clergyman at Nassenhuben, a village with a Presbyterian
Church near Danzig, he turned to the study of Natural
History and made a scientific journey, by order of the
Empress Katherine, through the Colonies of the Government of Saratow (1765). A year later we find him in
England supporting himself as a teacher of German and
Natural History at Warrington. After his voyage with
Cook, he ruined his chances with the English Government
by allowing his son, who had accompanied him, to publish
a diary of his travels, in contravention of the Government
order forbidding any printed publication except its own
official report. The D.L. of Oxford was the only reward
he reaped for his scientific researches during his voyage.
It was only by the generous act of Frederick the Second
of Prussia that he escaped imprisonment for debt. In
1780 he was appointed Professor of Natural History at
Halle, where he died in 1798. He understood seventeen
languages and stood in the first rank of the Zoological
and Botanical scholars of the day.[1]

[1] Johann Reinhold Forster wrote an *Introduction to Mineralogy*; a
Geschichte der Entdeckungen und Schiffahrten im Norden, Frankfurt on the

His son, Johann George Adam, accompanied his father as a botanist, though he was then only seventeen years old. He then studied at Paris and in Holland. Being of the same roaming disposition as his father, he was for a short time Professor at Kassel, but changed this pleasant place for Vilna in Russia. A Russian voyage of discovery to the Northern Regions of the Pacific Ocean was abandoned on account of a war with the Turks (1787). In his disappointment Forster accepted the offer of a librarianship at Mayence. Here in very rigid Roman Catholic surroundings his cosmopolitan views as a Republican were strengthened. He joined a Republican Club, of the town, then in the hands of the French, was sent to France in 1793 to advocate the French occupation of the left border of the Rhine and spoke and wrote much in favour of his political ideals. But, having seen Paris, his was a rude awakening. Moreover, the German army retook Mayence in 1793 and Forster was thus rendered homeless. His plan of visiting India was cut short by his death in 1794. He belongs to the classics of German style and is a model of clear and spirited diction, whilst he was among the first to rouse the feeling for the beauties of outward nature, a merit which has been warmly acknowledged by Humboldt.[1]

Other Scottish families still existing in Germany are the Barclays. We have seen that a great number of them settled in Rostock in the XVIth. Century. They

---

Oder, 1784; *Beiträge zur Länder- und Völkerkunde*, 1781-1783. He also issued a Magazine of recent Travel, Cp. *Deutsche Allgemeine Biographie*.

[1] One of the younger Forster's chief books was his *Naturgeschichte und Philosophie des Lebens* (*Natural History and Philosophy of Life*), 1789, in six volumes. He was also the first to introduce *Kalidasa's Sakuntala* to German Readers.

all descended from one *Peter Barclay*[1] who immigrated from Scotland and became a burgess in 1657, as a silk merchant. His eldest son called himself Joannes Barclay "de Tolli."[2] Peter's other son Ludwig was the clergyman. Descendants of his on the female side are still alive.

Of the *Spaldings* in Mecklenburg who have now spread over the whole of Northern Germany and of the services they rendered to their adopted country in the calling of arms and in the learned professions, we have already spoken. The third Scottish family that settled in Mecklenburg were the *Gertners* (Gardiner). *John Gardiner* from Brechin in Scotland was made a burgess of Schwerin on the 19th of July 1623. His son was enrolled in 1647 and afterwards rose to the dignity of "Rathsherr" (councillor).

The *Muttrays* at Memel, of which family descendants are still living at Danzig and elsewhere, trace their origin to Thomas Muttray who is said to have accompanied James II. to France in the year 1688. He afterwards came to Memel when the King of France did not prove the liberal supporter of the adherents of the fugitive British prince, he was expected to be.

The *Simpsons*, another Scottish family in Memel, which spread from there all over Prussia, came originally from Cupar Angus in Forfar. An old birth brief, dated 1680, is issued there. It seems that they first settled at a small place about twenty miles north of Memel called Heiligen Aa,[3] from a river Aa which emptying itself into the Baltic at the same time formed the boundary between Kurland and Szamaiten. Besides the Simpsons, tradition

[1] He is called "ex perantiqua et illustri baronum de Barclay familia.'

[2] The Russian General of the same name, who became Field-marshal and Prince (1761-1818), is said to belong to the same stock.

[3] "Aa" means water. "Heilig" is "sacred."

ALEXANDER GIBSONE
British Consul at Danzig

mentions the names of Muttray, Douglas and Melville as settlers. They traded with the produce of Szamaiten, corn and flax, which they chiefly sold to Danzig. The inhabitants of Memel, feeling themselves aggrieved at this proceeding, lodged a complaint with the Crown of Poland, at that time exercising supremacy over the Duchy of Prussia; and effected an interdict of King Vladislaus, dated February 6th, 1639, by which all trading across the Heilige Aa was strictly prohibited. His captains received orders to burn the place. To this day, there is a fishing village called Heiligenaa on the borders of Curland, but the harbour has long ago been choked with sand. Simpson and the other Scots fled to Memel, where they soon held positions of influence and trust. The Simpsons trace their descent from one Andrew Simpson, whose son, Jacob, was married to Barbara Young, a descendant of Magister Will. Young of the Ruthven family and of Catharine Bruce (Robert Bruce). They are related by intermarriage to the Macleans, Muttrays and Stoddarts.

The *Macleans* also are numerous in Prussia; some of them call themselves " of Coll " from the island of that name in the Hebrides group; others hail from Banff; on a tombstone in the churchyard of St Salvator at Danzig, the home of Maria MacLean, who died seventy years old in 1806, is given as Duart in Scotland, which is on the island of Mull. This is all the more interesting as among the many thousands of Scotsmen emigrating to Prussia and Poland in the centuries spoken of, very few from the far West and of Celtic blood are to be found.[1]

As to Baron *Gibsone*, the proprietor of the large Neustadt estates which he left to the husbands of his

---

[1] The Scots were known in Prussia for their fair hair; a dark Scot is immediately called " de swarte Schotte."

nieces, the Counts Keyserling,[1] he caused his nephews John and Alexander Gibsone to come over from Scotland to Danzig in order to take up his business, as we have seen. Of these the second, Alexander, did a large export trade of grain under the style of "Gibsone and Co." He took for partners other two young Scotsmen, Marshall and Stoddart, of whom the latter, after Gibsone's death, carried on the business, leaving it to his son Francis Blair Stoddart,[2] who is the present owner of this well-known house. Alexander died unmarried. His elder brother John, generally called Baron Gibsone, who was at the same time the elder brother of Sir James Gibsone Craig of Riccarton, lived at Potsdam, was a member of the Prussian Court, and as such accompanied King Frederick William III. on his flight to Königsberg in 1807. He instructed the Crown Prince, later on King Frederick William IV., in the English language. Like his brother Alexander, he was an active member of the "Tugendbund," a secret association for the rousing of the nation against Napoleon. Later in life he resided some time at Rome, and to judge by his correspondence with Wilhelm von Humboldt, then Prussian ambassador at Naples, appears to have been something of a political agent for Prussia. He died only fifty-three years old and is buried in the old churchyard of Potsdam, along with his daughter,

---

[1] See *Scots in Germany*, 270 f.

[2] There were Stoddarts or Stodderts in Danzig in the sixteenth and seventeenth centuries, but a connection between these and the present bearer of the name cannot be established. The father of the Stoddart who came to Danzig in 1832, served in the English Navy against Napoleon and died as Vice-Admiral. Originally, the family hailed from Peeblesshire, and Selkirkshire, where they owned the property of Williamhope on the Tweed and Hartwoodburn. Many members of this old family are buried in St Mary's aisle by the shores of "lone St Mary's silent lake," or in the venerable graveyard by the manse of Yarrow.

JACOB KABRUN OF DANZIG

Cecilia, who outlived him more than sixty years, and was a friend of Alexander von Humboldt and the famous Mendelssohn family in Berlin. Of his sons, the eldest, William, and the youngest Gustavus Adolph died unmarried. William went back to Great Britain, established a mercantile house at Liverpool, and was appointed German Consul there. After having given up business, he travelled a good deal and died very aged at Scone, in Perthshire. His younger brother, Gustavus Adolph, was an officer in the British navy, was sent home an invalid from India and died on the Hamburg roadstead, where his father had gone to meet him.

John's second son, Alexander, remained at Danzig and took to ship owning under the firm of Alex. Gibsone & Co. about the year 1820. He was greatly esteemed by his fellow-citizens, who conferred on him their highest honours appointing him president of the Chamber of Commerce and of the Town Council.

Of his three sons, the eldest, Alexander, was a student who finally settled at Nuremberg where he worked for many years voluntarily at the great Museum Germanicum ; the third son, Thomas, an officer in the East Indian navy, died in India, twenty-three years old at the time of the mutiny. The second son, John, who alone of the brothers is alive, inherited his father's business in 1853, and enlarged it considerably, so that he was known as one of the largest shipowners in the Baltic. Being also entrusted with a good many honorary offices by his fellow-citizens, he now chiefly devotes his time to the building of labourers' cottages, being honorary secretary of the so-called " Abegg Stiftung," a legacy left for this purpose in 1870.

As neither Mr Gibsone nor Mr Stoddart has any direct heirs bred to the business, the mercantile firm of

Gibsone, so well-known in Danzig for several hundred years, is doomed with their demise to disappear.

Casting back a look over the vast numbers of Scotsmen in Prussia in the seventeenth century, far exceeding the thirty thousand mentioned by Lithgow,[1] and noting their gradual assimilation and absorption, we do not wonder at the statement of the anonymous English Merchant, and Resident in Danzig, of the eighteenth century, that one third of that city was of Scottish blood, nor at the other statement of the German scholar of the nineteenth, who attributes the stubbornness and the shrewdness of the Eastern Prussian to the influx of the Scots.

Let us rather hope that some of the higher qualities of the Scots also: their tenacity of purpose, their sense of duty, their great charitableness, their saving disposition and their general trustworthiness contributed something towards shaping the character of the inhabitants of these remote German Provinces; provinces, that may no longer now be looked upon with that stolid indifference or cheerful ignorance which is generally vouchsafed abroad to German geography and ethnology, but must be considered as the Canada and the Australia of the seventeenth century, into which much of the best strength and blood of Scotland has been poured, if to less glorious advantage, still not all in vain and always to the incentive interest and delight—let us hope—of the student of this phase of exterior Scottish history.

[1] "Scots in Germany," p. 32.

PART III.

DOCUMENTS.

BENEDICTUS ARBUTHNOT

Last Lord Abbot of Ratisbon

DOCUMENTS.

I.

Edict of 1556.

SIGISMUNDUS Augustus D. G. rex Poloniæ gratiam nostram Regiam. Intelleximus complures ex vagabunda gente Scotorum cum rebus mercibus—que suis per regnum et dominia nostra passim discurrere eoque fieri ut non modo hominibus nostris honestæ victus comparandi rationes maxime præcludantur, sed multæ etiam fraudes imposturaeque in mercandis vendendisque rebus impune fiant. Quia vero non dubium est quin ex hac jam usitata licentia discurrendi eorum praesertim hominum qui lucri gratia nihil non audent, maximum ad homines nostros, nisi consilio tempestive occurretur, sit perventurum incommodum, cupientes ejusmodi licentiam autoritate nostra tandem cohiberi, mandamus sinceritati ac fidelitati vestrae omnino habere volentes, ut pro ratione officii sue hoc genus hominum vagum nullis certis legibus et jurisdictioni subjacens emptione venditioneque rerum ac discursu per regnum et dominia nostra prohibeant arceantque neque permittant commoda hominibus nostris quoquo modo praecludi et impediri non obstante literis si quae posthac in contrarium ex cancellaria nostra prodierint: quas nullius roboris esse volumus ac jubemus pro gratia nostra non aliter facturi. Datum Varsoviae, *Dec.* 18*th*, 1556.

II.

Edict against the Scots issued by Sigismund III.

SIGISMUNDUS Tertius Dei gratia Rex Poloniae. . . . Significamus praesentibus literis nostris quorun interest, universis et singulis cum post felicem nostrum e patrio regno in has alterius regni nostri partes reditum in oppidum nostrum Kcyna divertissemus, supplicesque nobis ejusdem oppidi incolae inscripto certa gravamina, quibus a Judaeis, Scotis et aliis ceteris vagis hominibus premuntur, obtulissent, pro eisque nonnulli consiliarii nostri intercessissent ut eorundem oppidanorum, qui et nostra et reipublicae onera ferre consueverunt, potiorem quam Judaeorum vagorumque hominum rationem habere dignaremur, Nos cum plurima nostra reipublicae interesse videamus, ut civitates et oppida quae in pace regnis ornamento in bellis autem praesidio tempore felicis regiminis nostri ad meliorem deveniant condicionem, in diesque locupletentur pro regali nostra munificentia et favore, quos subditos nostros prosequimur, faciendum esse nobis duximus ut praerogativas et libertates infra scriptas in vim privilegii aeternis temporibus duraturi, ipsis dare et concedere dignaremur, damus et concedimus praesentibus hisce literis nostris primum quidem quoniam, ut intelleximus, in praedicto oppido numerus Judaeorum augetur ne ob eam causam invictus quaerendi ratione cives ab eis in posterum magis impediantur statuimus. . . . . Deinde cum Scoti apotecarii et alii externi vagi homines jus civitatis non habentes non solum nostrorum hominum victus, rationem sua negotiatione praeripiant, sed et alia regno nostro detrimenta adferant, volumus et ordinamus, ne tales ullam postea mercaturae exercendae potestatem in foris septimanalibus praedicti oppidi habeant. Postremo cum nobis relatum est hocce oppidum non modo a Judaeis et Scotis sed etiam a revenditoribus frumentorum gravari . . . volumus et statuimus ne revenditores . . . in foro publico . . . ante meridiem frumenta coemant. . . .[1] (*Sept.* 12, 1594).

III.

Letter of Duke Albrecht the Elder of Prussia to Kaspar Nostiz.

Es ist allhier bei Uns gegenwärtiger Zeiger Wilhelmus Scotus erschienen und hat vermeldet, wie ehr aus Schotland umb des Evangelii willen vertrieben, unns auch umb eine gnedige Steuer zu seiner unterhaltung gebeten, als haben wir aus gnaden ein Chleydlin desgleichen 4 Gulden zur Zehrung geben zugesagt. Ist demnach unser Bevhell du wollest Ihme ein Chleydlin daneben die 4 Gulden aus der Kammer geben lassen. (*Sept. 9th,* 1549).[2]

IV.

The eighty Articles drawn up by Patrick Gordon for the Scots in Prussia (1616).[3]

Titulus Primus.

1. *Institutio fraternitatum et seniorum Electio.*—Societas ista Scoticae gentis in tres fraternitates distincta erit quarum prima erit Samlanden secunda Notlangen, tertia in ea ducatus parte quae superioris terrae nomines censetur.

2. Hae fraternitates iisdem legibus et conditionibus

---

[1] Posen, *Kgl. St. Archiv,* Dp. Exin, N. 1.

[2] *Kgl. St. Archiv,* Königsberg.

[3] *Kgl. St. Archiv,* Königsberg, Etats Minist. 20 A.

erunt astrictae, mutuamque operam et opem in omnis fraterni amoris et officii vinculo, ad omnes honestas actiones asserendas et propugnandas et contrarias puniendas profligandasque ex privilegii praescripto invicem praestabunt.

3. Quotquot in singulis supra dictis locis mercaturam exercent, tempore publicarum nundinarum loco opportuno quotannis semel convenient et communi aut saltem majoris partis consensu quatuor suae gentis homines pietate prudentia et experientia praestantes sensores eligent, qui ceteris juxta privilegii tenorem praesint.

4. Quicunque ad hanc electionem citatus non comparuerit mulctabitur 2 fl.

5. Si quis vero communi consensu aut plurimorum suffragiis electus officio fungi detrectaverit, praeterquam quod e fraternitate excludetur, mulctam solvet 5 fl.

6. Seniores hi ipsa electionis hora publice coram fraternitatis sociis solenne juramentum praestabunt se sincere nullo habito amoris, aut odii, divitiarum aut paupertatis, beneficii aut incommodi aut ullius denique personae respectu officio functuros.

7. Similiter singuli singularum fraternitatum socii praesentes et futuri, pari solemni juramento ad debitam obedientiam senioribus jus secundum Privilegium dicentibus praestandum tenebuntur ; aut ab omni popularium suorum conversatione extrusis, omni mercaturae genere contumacibus interdicetur.

8. Nemo Seniorum in officio ultra unius anni spatium permanebit nisi denuo ad id legitime electus fuerit.

9. Singuli seniores anno elapso rationem officii sui fraternitatis sociis una congregatis aut ad id deputatis reddent sub pœna 10 fl.

10. Si quem Seniorum in officio existentium negotia sua aut in patriam revocaverint aut alio migrare coegerint

uniusque mensis ante discessum spatio fratres praemonebit et officii rationem reddet sub pœna 10 fl.

11. Quotiescunque generale per universum ducatum subsidium colligetur (quo tempore solum a fraternitatibus nostris ad Reipubl. usus contribuendum est) seniores in singulis fraternitatibus Collectorem idoneum constituent qui pecuniam collectam in aerarium deferet et quietationem recipiet.

12. Ad generale autem subsidium solvendum singuli pro modo census obligabuntur nisi forte nonnulli civitate donati cum concivibus solvere teneantur.

13. Seniores convenienti loco et tempore (non inter convivandum aut confabulandum, aut alias ubi et quando non decet) jus dicent; ne privilegii auctoritas aut officii ipsorum respectus vilescat.

14. Ut senioribus modeste se gerentibus reverentia merito debetur; ita eosdem fratribus suis arroganter insultare non convenit.

15. Si quis seniores praesertim vero officio fungentes irriserit aut ulla injuria affecerit, totius fraternitatis arbitrio in eum animadvertetur.

16. Quicunque vero propter sententiam adversus se latam minaciter murmurans non impetrata venia se subduxerit mulctam luet 2 fl.

17. Legitime citatus non comparens persolvet 2 fl.

18. Arrestationum literae seniorum Chyrographo signentur alioque nullius erunt efficatia.

19. Violator arresti praeterquam quod causa cadit persolvito 1 fl.

20. Et quo convenientius negotia quaecunque expediantur, Seniore scribae fidelis opera utentur qui omnia scripta comprehendat ad perpet. rei memoriam.

21. Si qui fraternitatis socii ullum hominem ullo modo offenderint, seniores pro eorundem delictis aut debitis satisfacere non erunt obligati.

22. Neque quisquam in fraternitatum Catalogum conscribet a praesenti die et anno nisi qui septem fl. intra biennium sit numeraturus.

Titulus Secundus.

De Divino Cultu.

23. Quia timor dei initium est omnis Sapientiae sine quo omnia humana consilia successu carent: Unus quisque commoda utens valetudine singulis diebus Sabbathi publicae concioni in ecclesia, ut verbum Dei attente et reverenter audiat, tempestive aderit sub p. —2 fl nisi necessitas legitimi negotii aut longinqui itineris impediverit.

24. Similiter omnes et singuli semel ad minimum quotannis ad Communionum Coenae Deae in timore et dilectione accedent, digne ad tam sacrum opus praeparati sub p. 10 fl.

25. Absentiae autem causam praetexentes, seniores serio admonebunt: quorum salutare consilium si aspernati fuerint hi eosdem Ecclesiae deferent: quam si non audiverint a fraternitatis consortio secludentur, donec vera poenitentia ducti. Deo et proximis reconcilientur.

26. Nemo tabernae mercatoriae foris aut fenestras tempore Concionis ad merces divendendas aperiet s. p. 2fl.

27. Ne quisquam inutiles de Religione quaestiones, disputationes aut controversias proponere, aut ad propositas respondere praesumet, quia ut captum indoctorum superant, ita nil nisi malitiosas et noxias plaerumque rixas et contentiones gignunt s. p. 1 fl.

Titulus Tertius.

De heris et servis.

28. Quia praecipuum fraternitatum nostratum robur hic

consistit necessarium est ut utrorunque munus diligenter expendatur Proinde nemo servum sufficienti vitae antea honeste actae testimonio carentem conducet, alioqui si quod damnum servus is commiserit, herus illius pro illo non modo respondebit et satisfaciet sed etiam mulctam representabit, 5 fl.

29. Quicunque vero testimonium vitae et morum non habuerit persolvet 2 fl.

30. Et quicunque conscius erit aliquem ejusmodi testimonio carere nec senioribus significaverit, is itidem persolvito 1 fl.

31. Nemo servum novitium linguae Germanicae aut negotiandi prorsus imperitum assumet nisi integrum quadriennium ad serviendum se obligaverit, sub p. 10 fl.

32. Neque etiam servitio et mercaturae autea assuetum conducet nisi ad biennium adstrictus fuerit sub p. 2 fl. nisi forte fraternitatis ejusdem socius sit.

33. Si quis servus antea exactum servitii terminum herum secum derelinquerit, nemo eundem conducet aut assumet donec seniores causam et occasionem exploraverint, s. p. 10 fl.

34. Et quicunque sive herus sive servus deliquisse aut offendisse deprehendetur, arbitrio seniorum pro modo delicti punietur.

35. Si quis herus aut servus aliquam bonorum sibi concreditorum partem deglutiverit, decoxerit et luxuriose comsumpserit et fuga supplicium evitare voluerit singulis fraternitatis sociis integrum erit eundem sub arresto detinere ubicunque deprehensus . . fuerit: ut bona quae adhuc supersunt, recuperentur et culpae reus seu arbitrio severe castigetur. Sumptus vero legitime in hoc negotio facti ex bonis recuperatis persolventur.

36. Servus pervicax hero irreverenter obganniens persolvet 15 gr.

37. Servus vero herum ad monomachiam provocans aut in herum manus injiciens violentes, solario amisso, fraternitatis beneficio privabitur atque si in malitia perseveraverit justo supplicio afficietur.

38. Sin herus servum verberibus durioribus aut damno insigniori absque justa causa affecerit, seniorum censurae se submittet ut servo afflicto satisfaciat et injuria damnosa reparetur.

39. Nullus cum servo alieno privatim inibit conditionem ante exactum debitum servitii prioris terminum, s. p. 5 fl.

40. Si quis quovis modo ad aliam fraternitatem transfugerit, seniores ibidem requisiti eundem eo unde venerat remittere teneantur.

Titulus Quartus.

De Circumforaneis, aleatoribus, ebriosis et id genus aliis turpiter vitam transigentibus.

41. Quoniam multi nimia licentia et otio luxurianter divitiarum tamen et judicii expertes, sine respectu aut propriae infamiae aut patriae et popularium pudoris, circumforanei viles et pudendas merces in sinu aut collo gestantes omnibus intuentibus ludibrio sunt et ipsi omni fere turpitudini dediti raro ad frugem perveniunt, nullo prorsus modo tolerandi sunt : sed aut ad aliis inserviendum aut eo unde venerant redeundum cogendi sub poena amissionis bonorum quae habuerit et corporis severe castigandi.

42. Et ut hujusmodi incommodis in posterum commode occuratur nemini licebit libere negotiari aut merces venales ullibi exponere nisi bona possideat aut propria aut legitime concredita ad valorem 50 fl. aestimata, nisi ob virtutem et industriam alicui seniores libertatem indulserint, s. p. 5 fl.

43. Itidem in oppidis liberis, nulli alibi degenti licitum

erit nisi nundinarum tempore merces clam et aperte
divendere cum civium offensione, popularium damno et
gentis opprobrio, s. p. 20 fl.

44. Praeterea si quidem multi insolentes juvenes aleis,
ebrietati libidini, aliisque enormibus vitiis dediti bona
vel sua vel sibi ab aliis credita summo cum dedecore et
damno consumunt et ne illonum turpitudo palam fiat
locum subinde mutant; nemo cum illis conversabitur
neque ejus ore aut opere subserviat ut praecipites ad
interitum ruant; s. p. 2 fl.

45. Iidem quoque sic turpiter viventes et fraternitatis
sodalitio exterminabuntur donec agnita culpa misericordia
impulsi seniores arbitrio suo eosdem in gratiam receperint
neque quisque cum iis interea conversabitur.

46. Si quis vero furtum aut perjurium commiserit e
fraternitate absque ullo testimonio ejicietur. Et si quis
testimonium dederit damni inde sequentis merito con-
demnabitur.

Titulus Quintus.
De Pecuniis publicis.

47. Ad pauperum et afflictorum necessitatem sub-
levandam ad inopum defunctorum sepulturam et ad
omnium honestarum actionum quae publico auxilio
opus habent, patrocinium, sive in aula sive in urbibus
aut rure, pecunia singulis diebus Sabbathi et alias quovis
tempore opportuno colligetur et seniorum custodiae
tradetur. Eodem etiam mulctae omnes et bonorum
virorum voluntariae eleemosynae et testamentis legata
inferentur. Quas pecunias universas seniores ad usuras
publici boni causa provide exponent cum consensu fraternitatis; parique modo easdem, ut necessitas postulabit
ad indigentium et communes usus erogabunt.

48. Verum, si seniores suo privato arbitrio pecuniam publicam non necessario aut cum damno exponent, eandem restituere tenebuntur, una cum mulcta, quae offensae correspondebit ex arbitrio totius fraternitatis.

49. Si quis paupertate aut morbo laborans in patriam redire desiderat, seniores eidem e publica pecunia sumptus ad iter necessarios suppeditabunt atque is tum absque ulteriori mora ad proximum portum maritimum se conferet, ut inde commode prima occasione transvehatur.

50. Si quis obstinate impudens mendicus ad laborem corporis perferendum validus, cui semel abunde provisum est, discedere noluerit, sed ab unis nundinis ad alias oppidatim mendicare perseverabit, in eundem omni rigore animadvertetur.

51. Aegrotis vero, infirmis, coecis, surdis, mutilis et senio confectis aut in nosocomiis aut alibi pro fraternitatis facultatibus ex Christ. charitate providendum erit.

52. Si quis e morbo decesserit aut quovis modo occisus fuerit bona relinquens proximis haredibus longe absentibus; ejusdem servus aut socius bona ea tum possidens aut eisdem postea potitus, senioribus de ratione creditoribus et haeredibus legitimis reddenda sufficienter cavebit. Quod si nec servus nec socius ullus bona ulla possideat, seniores eorundem inventarium conficiendum curabunt, ne creditoribus aut haeredibus fraus ullu fiat: quoscunque vero sumptus seniores in hoc negotio fecerint, creditores et haeredes jure optimo eosdem refundent una cum convenienti eleemosyna pauperibus ex sententia seniorum distribuenda.

53. Servus autem aut socius defuncti, aut Seniores penes quoscunque bona ejusdem fuerint, eorum tantum modo quae in potestate sua habuerunt, rationem reddere tenebuntur. Salva omni modo ea, quae ad Serenissimi Principis Fiscum pertinet portione, eo inferenda.

Titulus Sextus.

De debitoribus.

54. Singuli debitores lubenter et gratanter creditoribus debita persolvere, aut iisdem saltem satisfacere jure tenentur. Quod si debitor die solutionis neglecto, dilatione dolo malo utatur seniores novum solutionis terminum longiorem aut breviorem pro natura debiti praecise debitori observandum assignabunt sub poena competenti.

55. Si quis publicae pecuniae debitor aliis etiam debeat; publicum debitum primo solvendum erit. Caeteris deinde Creditoribus secundum jus et aequitatem satis fiat, prout debitoris facultates suppetunt. Neque quisquam huic solutionis ordini contradicat aut resistat sub p. 3 fl.

Titulus Septimus.

De tabernis mercatoriis.

56. Nemo tabernam in nundinis eriget, nisi ex consuetudine et ordine illius oppidi ubi nundinae celebrantur 1 p. 1 fl.

57. Nemo alterius tabernam occupabit aut detinebit injuste s. p. 2.

58. Nemo tabernam aut stationen ab alio conductam aucto pretio denuo conducere praesumat s. p. 2½ fl.

59. Duo ejusdem negotiationis participes una tantum fruantur taberna, s. p. 10 fl.

60. Nullus duplicem negotiationem id est duobus in locis per diversas personas simul exercebit, s. p. 20 fl.

61. Nullus voce, nictu, nutu, manus extensione aut alio modo aut gestu emptores aut venditores a vicini taberna abducere tentabit, s. p. 2 fl.

Titulus Octavus.

De falsis aut corruptis mercibus et injusta mensura.

62. Quicunque fraudulenter falsas aut corruptas merces pro veris et sufficientibus vendiderit ad proximi damnum et fraternitatis infamiam, praeterquam quod emptorem indemnem praestabit pretio reddito merces quoque suas ad publicos et operum usus extradet una cum 2½ fl.

63. Quicunque illegitimas aut suspectas merces uti aurum argentumve integrum aut fractum, vestesque novas vel detritas et alias hujusmodi a suspectis personis emerit aut pignoris loco sumpserit aut ab ejusmodi personis quicquam mutuo sumpserit aut eis mutuo dederit aus cum illis familiariter vixerit praeter arbitrariam poenam ex seniorum decreto irrogandam propter publicam ignominiam mulctam etiam persolvet 2½ fl.

64. Quicunque mensura falsa sive ulnae sive ponderis usus fuerit aut falsam mensuram . . . primo sic deprehensus persolvet, 2 fl., secundo, 10 fl., tertio tanquam bonorum virorum societate indignus censebitur.

Titulus Nonus.

De Injuriis.

65. Nullus proximi aut amicorum aut domesticorum illius famam probrosis verbis laedet nec parentum aut propinquorum progeniem exproprabit nec quemque agnomine indecore compellabit aut deridebit, s. p. 2 fl.

66. Quicunque vero manu alteri alassam impegerit aut alias nocendi animo ullum manu percusserit persolvito, 2 fl. Sin utraque pars pari offensionis modo deliquerit parem mulctam pendat.

67. Nullus gladium aut pugionem evaginabit aut aliis armis minas ulli intentabit, s. p. 5 fl.

68. Nullus proximi merces secreto aut aperte ad venditionis impedimentum contemnet, s. p. 8 fl.

Titulus Decimus.

De hospitiis.

69. Singuli in honestis hospitiis diversentur, s. p. 3 fl.

70. Neque quisquam vicini hospitium ingrediatur ut rixas jurgia cieat, aut hospitibus molestus sit, 2 fl.

71. Si quis lupinaria aut famosas domos frequentaverit persolvito, 10 fl.

Titulus Undecimus.

De itineris periculis.

72. Si quis in itinere morbo correptus fuerit, aut laesionem damnumve corporis aut bonorum incurrerit, socii itineris unus aut plures, eundem solatio et auxilio destitutum nequaquam relinquent, sed ad hosp. aut locum tutum, ubi ipse curetur et consoletur et bona ejus conserventur ut Christianos decet, deducent. Quod si facere recusaverint aut neglexerint, damni inde sequentis participes erunt et mulctam persolvent, 5 fl.

73. Si quis in publicis viis in diversoriis aut alibi ubicunque publice vel secreto a latronibus, proditoribus aut praedatoribus obtruncatus, mutilatus aut spoliatus bonis fuerit, ad facinoris auctorem jure apprehendendum, persequendum et plectendum omnes fraternitatis socii sint obligati.

Titulus Duodecimus.

De Contributionibus.

74. Ad omnes honestas et licitas actiones veluti ob subsidiorum solutionem Serenissimo Principi pariter cum

indigenis ad defensionem honoris patriae, ad vindicandas
publicas et privatas odiosas injurias fratribus nostris illatas
et hujusmodi alias singuli pro modo census contribuent.
Ad quod debite efficiendum Seniores quatuor honestos
homines solemniter juratos deputabunt.

Titulus Decimus Tertius.

De appellationibus.

75. A seniorum sententia in actionibus, 20 fl. non
excedentibus nulla fiat appellatio, s. p. 3 fl.

76. Si quis ad totius societatis Seniores sive ad
ordinarium superiorem judicem inutile appellabit, mulctum
luet, 5 fl.

Titulus Decimus Quartus.

De sententiae executione.

77. Ubi ad omnium et singulorum articulorum observa-
tionem omnes et singuli fraternitatis collegae sunt obstricti
ita ad sententiam eatam jure exequendam Seniores tenentur.

78. Si quis vero sententiae legitime latae stare noluerit
aut honestae disciplinae se subjicere pervicariter recusaverit
Seniores Superioris judicis auxilium implorabunt. Ad quod
praestandum mandato Ser^{mi} Principis justitiae exequendae
et decentioris ordinis observandi causa est obligatus.

79. Si quis civitate donatus libertatem suam popularium
suorum contemptus praetexens praedictos articulos . . .
aspernatus fuerit, is veluti patriae ingratus, pristinae
conditioni oblitus, successu fortunae elatus, et divini
beneficii immemor omnibus fraternitatis sociis odiosus
habebitur et communi cum ipsis mensa et omni negotiatione excludetur. . . .

80. Postremo si qui alii articuli hujus generis ratione
contractuum Chirographorum . . . mutua negotiatione

JOHANNES VON LAMOND
Royal Bavarian Astronomer

necessarii hic praetermissi sunt, iidem omnino observandi erunt, acsi hic expressi forent.

V.

Letter of Croffts (Crofts), Regis Angliae Legatus, to the members of the Council Boards in Prussia.

ANNUNTIAVERAM non ita pridem Thorunis Generositatibus vestris subsidium Sacrae Regiae Majestati Anglicae in Comitiis Generalibus anno proxime praeterito laudatum; nunc vero in procinctu itineris mei promissam mihi hac in parte a Generositatibus vestris expecto resolutionem peramice rogando, ut latori praesentium Domino Seton, Sacrae Regiae Majestatis colonellum, cui hocce commisi negotium, plenariam in omnibus fidem adhibere suamque mentem Generositates vestrae aperire velint. Res enim moram pati nequit, cum Seren. Rex totalem a me exigat informationem quam dare non potero donec certum a Generositatibus vestris habuero responsum, quarum benevolentiae diligenter me commendo.

Gedani (Danzig), 31 July 1651.

VI.

Letter of the Magistrates of Danzig concerning the Letter of King Charles II. to his subjects in Poland.

UNIVERSIS et singulis cujuscunque status, gradus, conditionis seu dignitatis . . . praesentium notitiam habituris imprimis vero quibus id scire expedit, praemissa salute et officiorum nostrorum commendatione nolum testatumque facimus Nos Praeconsules et Consules Regiae civitatis Gedanensis exhibitas esse nobis literas papyreas infra scriptas authenticas Serenissimi M. Brit. et Hyb. Regis ejusdem sigillo munitas manusque Regiae super inscriptione roboratas ac idiomate Anglico ad Joannem Moleyson atque alios nationis Scoticae in Regno Polonico habitantes mercatores et factores directas, petitumque a nobis est, ut earum literarum in latinam linguam translatarum exemplar fide dignum . . . sub sigillo nostro ederemus. Quo circa iisdem literis visis et diligenter perspectis et cum aliis ejusdem Regiae Majestatis literis collatis ac undique quam in sigillo et scriptura salvis integris et ab omni suspicione alienis repertis aequis praedictorum Nationis Scoticae in Regno Poloniae incolarum petitis annuimus. Quarum literarum ex Anglico in Latinum idioma fideliter translatarum tenor talis est ut sequitur:

Carolus Rex.[1]

Vere fideles ac dilecti salutem. Expositum Nobis vestro subditorum nostrorum in Regno Poloniae habitantium atque negotiantium nomine, exactas fuisse a Vobis per Colonellum Cochram praetextu mandati cujusdam nostri magnas pecuniae summas eoque illum processisse ut pro eis facilius consequendis autoritatem interponendam sollicitaverit Serenissimi Polon. Regis, fratris nostri honorandi, qua de causa vos certiores facimus nihil tale a nobis unquam Colonello nostro demandatum fuisse. Praeterea audivimus Vos denuo urgeri per Baronem Croft pro tertia parte facultatum et bonorum . . . in subsidium nostrum exsolvenda. Et quamvis modo memoratum Baronem Croft ex Hollandia ad Ser. Polon. Regem, fratrem nostrum honorandum, ablegaverimus nullum tamen ipsi mandatum dedimus ut autoritate aliqua munitus quicquam a quopiam subdito nostro in praedicto Polon. regno aut aliis mundi locis degentibus. Et hanc voluntatem Nostram Regiam significandam duximus omnibus et

---

[1] As there are some slight verbal variations from the version given in the *Scots in Germany*, the letter is here reprinted from the Danzig MS.

singulis Scotis subditis nostris in Polonia versantibus, benigneque ipsis concedimus ut sive habitent sive negotiationes exerceant in praedicto Pol. regno aut aliis terrae locis praesentibus literis Nostris Regiis utantur ut coram Regibus Principibus, Statibus ac Judicibus quibusvis eas producant, contraque impositiones exactionesve quasvis ad instantiam praedicti Baronis Croft aut alterius cujusdam pro usu et commodo Nostro aliorumve flagitandas et imponendas iisdem sese defendant. Valete. Datum in Curia Nostra Perthensi 9 die Mensis Decembris 1650. Regn. nostr. secundo anno.

The accuracy of the translation is certified by the Secretary, Arnoldus van Holten, Danzig, April 4th, 1651.

VII.

Credentials of Richard Baillie issued by the Magistrates of Edinburgh, April 7th, 1665.

UNIVERSIS et singulis . . . notum testatumque facimus quod hodie coram nobis comparuit Joannes Howison, apothecarius Edinburgensis nominibus quibus infra Marionae Baillie sponsae Adami Baillie de Eastertoun, Margarethae Baillie sponsae Thomae Adair, Sartoris Edinburgensis, et Janetae Baillie sponsae Guildoni Thomson in Normigall, filiarum legitimarum defuncti Magistri Jacobi Baillie quondam ministri verbi Dei apud Lamington infra Vicecomitatum de Lanark cum speciali consensu dictorum eorum sponsorum, ac etiam coram nobis produxit quandam literam dispositionis factam datam et concessam per dictas Mareonem Margaretam et Janetam Baillie in favorem Ricardi Baillie filii legitimi secundogeniti dicti quondam T. Baillie, pistoris Edinburgensis in qua dispositione pro causis ibi insertis dictae personae superscriptae disposuerunt dicto Ricardo Baillie totas et integras terras, tenementa, legata, pecuniarum summas et alia accreta aut accrescentia per decessum dicti Roberti Baillie mercatoris Dantiscani.

RAMSEY, *Praefectus.*

CALDERWOOD
DAVIDSON
FULLERTON
DRUMMOND } *Bailies.*

VIII.

Birth-briefs and Legitimations.

THERE were two ways for the Scottish settler to prove his identity and his legitimacy. One was the birth-brief which was issued in the town of his birth, signed by one or more of the magistrates and duly sealed; another was the oral declaration of legitimate birth. It was accepted instead of a birth-brief. Two friends of the person concerned had to declare on oath before the magistrates of the German town, here Danzig, that they knew him (or her) to be the legitimate son (or daughter) of so-and-so, and his wife in Scotland.

Either of these proofs was needed for the acquisition of civil rights and in cases of succession.

The Royal State Archives at Danzig preserve a great number of these birth-briefs and birth-declarations; whilst the two Archives at Königsberg, the Royal State Archive and the Stadt Archiv or Town Record Office,[1] offer none or hardly any material.

In the following list birth-briefs have been marked by

[1] The Stadt Archiv of Königsberg has passed through a long period of shameful neglect. Owing chiefly to the energetic industry of Archivrath Doctor Joachim, the small remnant of records is now well arranged and secured from further spoliation. It is kept in the Kneiphöfische Rathhaus, whilst the State Records are kept in the Castle.

the letters "Bb." The bracketed numbers after the names refer to the age of the witnesses. D. = Danzig.

1. *Robert Ainslie*, father James Ainslie, late barber at Jedburgh. Witnesses: James Ainslie, glover and soldier, and Albert Ainslie, a burgess and silk merchant at Stolp in Pomerania. (1649.)

2. *A. Allant*, witness: Ernest Maxwel. (1627.)

3. *Alb. Anderson*, from Perth. Witnesses: Thamson and Andr. Anderson.

4. *David Anderson*, father Jacob Anderson; mother Margaret Oggelberg, at Danzig. Witnesses: A. Löbel and Ernest Maxwel, stocking-weaver. (16?)

5. *Fr. Anderson*, father Gilbert Anderson, late skipper and burgess of Aberdeen; mother Isab. Carnegie. Witnesses: Ths. Gordon and J. Swien (?), from Aberdeen.

6. *J. Bage* (?), pastry-cook, from Edinburgh. Witnesses: Ths. Tamson and Matthew Frisell, from Edinburgh. 1596.

7. *Jacob Balwray*, father, John Balwray, from St Johannis Stadt (Perth). Witnesses: Chs. Andrew and Ths. Dundy, a glover of Danzig. 1653.

8. *David Balfuhr*, father Patrick Balfour of St Andrews; mother Agnes Inglis. Witnesses: Robt. Morris, a tailor, "near the Dominican Abbey Danzig," and John Gourlay, skipper and burgess of Anstruther. 1652.

9. *Robert Baylie*, of Lamington, in Lanarkshire; his father a retired clergyman. Witnesses: W. Currie, of Barten in Prussia, and J. Ballentine from Edinburgh, now at Danzig. 1659.[1] Bbr.

10. *Andrew Bell*, of Bamoyll, near Cupar Angus; mother,

---

[1] Compare Part III., p. 174.

Catharina Blair. Witnesses: Captain A. Blair (65) and James Halyburton. 1637. Bbr.

11. *Elisabeth and Agneta Bell*, of Dundee. Bbr. 1603.

13. *Andrew Black*, from the village of Alreck (?), near Banff. Witnesses: Alb. Morrisson, an illuminator, and J. Robinson at Danzig. 1619.

15. *Jacob Black*, father James Black, in Hirschberg, later in Annaberg, Silesia. 1634.

16. *James Bruce*, son of Robert Bruce, in the town of Skellitoun (?), parish of Dunserf; grand-parents John Bruce and Grizel Hamilton, daughter of Gavin Hamilton. 1673. Bbr.

17. *Robert Bruce*, in the parish of Erroll.

18. *Mariot Bruce*, wife of Ths. Mar, in Kilspindie.

19. *Isabel Bruce*, wife of John Robertson, Kinnaird. Nos. 17-19 are certified to be brothers and sisters of the late John Bruce at Danzig. Bbr. Perth. 1654.

20. *Will. Brown*, father Henry Brown; mother Margaret Houston (or Hewiston), from Dundee. Witnesses: Robert Lesslie and Jacob Houston, burgesses of Dundee. Have been school-fellows. 1663.

21. *Jacob Burnet*, from Aberdeen, son of Thos. Burnet, "dominus a Campbell," and Margaret Keith. 1652. Bbr.

14. *Albr. Blackhall*, son of the late A. Blackhall at Aberdeen. His brother William having died at Frauenburg in Prussia, he and his sister Catharine, who married Hans Forquart (Farquhar), became heirs. 1655.

22. *H. Buchanan*, father Hans Buchanan, in Danzig. 1651.

23. *W. Chisholm*, father John Chisholm, in the town of Lamington; mother Christina Portiers (Porteous).

Witnesses: Robt. Baillie and Ja. Anderson, glover, neighbours' children. 1662.

24. *Geo. Cleghorn*, from Edinburgh, son of John Cleghorn of Quhitsome (Whitsome), Berwick; mother Helen Innerwick. Witnesses: Revd. Geo. Cleghorn, minister of Dornick (Dornock), Alex. Kinnair, minister of Quhitsome. Bbr.

24A. Jac. Jeffrey and W. Flockhart in Duns. Bbr. 1633.

25. *Will. Clerk*, parents John Clerk and Anne Porter, in Dunfermline. Birth-brief issued by the Consules *Fermelinodum* civitatis, Dunfermline. March 29, 1669. Bbr.

27. *Geo. Cuik*, from Glasgow, son of J. Cuik and Janet Neilson of Glasgow. Sept. 8, 1645. Bbr.

26. *A. Grockart.* Bbr. from Aberdeen, 1687. "Nos subscribentes Pastor et Seniores ecclesiae Fintriensis in Diocesi Abredonensi in regno Scotiae testamur praesentium laborem Alexandrum Crockart honestis apud nos parentibus defuncto Andrea Crockart agricola et Margareta Ray legitima ipsius conjuge natum esse. Alex. Taylor, senior; Robertus Smith, senior; Alex. Forbes, pastor; Georgius Melvine, senior; Alex. Sangster.

28. *Dan. Davidson*, "Patricius" of Zamosc in Poland. Witnesses: John and Andrew Davidson, cives et mercatores; Jacob Ventour, Secretary of the King; William Forbes, famatus cives. 1680.[1]

29. *Geo. Davidson*, father William Davidson of Aberdeen; mother, Elizabeth Menzies. 1668.

30. *John Davidson*, father, Alexander Davidson of Marienculter (Maryculter), "about a mile's walk from Aberdeen." Witnesses: Thos. Mengis from

---

[1] See about him Part I.

Collerlie, near Aberdeen; and Hans Brown, from Aberdeen, glover and indweller of Danzig. 1652.

31. *Andr. Dellor*, from the village of Alborti (?), ten miles off Aberdeen. Witnesses: Will. Anderson and Ths. King, from Aberdeen. 1592. Bbr.

32. *David Demster*, son of Geo. Demster and Isabella, from Brechin. 1631. Also written Dempster. Bbr.

33. *Thomas Demster*, son of the late Jas. Demster, "one of the nobility" (einer vom adell), domiciled in Engelsmead (Inglismaldie in Marykirk, Kincardineshire), near Brechin, and of Agneta Lyall, his mother. Witnesses: Alexander Demster, burgess and merchant of Danzig, and Alb. Demster, a braid maker. 1633.

34. *R. Dempstarton*, mother Christina Balfour, at Stirling. Witnesses at Stirling: Alex. Cousland, Geo. Norvel, Alex. Miller. Juli 3, 1610. Bbr.

35. *Gilbert Dennis*, father in Zamosc, Poland; mother Susanna Boyd, from St. Johannis Stadt = Perth. Witnesses: Gleghorn and Jacob Lyon, a glover. 1657.

36. *John Duget*, son of the "noble" John Duget, domiciled in Disblehr (Disblair in Fintray), "seven miles from Aberdeen"; mother, Margaret Siton (Seaton). 1655.

37. *H. Duncan*
38. *Jas. Duncan*
39. *Thos. Duncan*
} Sons of Thomas Duncan in Königsberg, 1652. Witnesses: Jacob Ruthven and Hans Short, of Königsberg.

43. *P. Forbes*, son of Robert Forbes of Mowney and Margareta Farquhar. Witnesses: Duncan

Forbes of Camphill, and Joannes Forbes, burgess of Aberdeen.

44. *William Forbes*, son of Geo. Forbes and Catharine Reedfurth of Baltingtuhr (?) in Aberdeenshire. Witnesses: William Forbes and Alex. Mitchell, burgesses of Aberdeen. Bbr. 1632.

40. *William Farquhar*
41. *Robert Farquhar* } Emigrated from Aberdeen in 1639. Sons of Arch. Farquhar, de Dillab infra parochiam de Monymusk et generosa femina, Marg. Ritchie. 1687. Bbr.[1]

42. *David Fermer*, son of William Fermer, Kirkcaldy. 1616. Bbr.

45. *William Fraser*, son of W. Fraser, "magistri de Phoppachi." (Fopachy on the Beauly Firth.) 1670. Bbr. Inverness.

46. *John Fyffe*, son of Jas. Fyffe in St Andrews. Witnesses: David Brodie and Robt. Morrisson, tailor at D. 1652.[2]

47. *Ths. Gall*, son of Ths. Gall in Montrose. Witnesses: W. Grub and W. Jeffrey at D., both from Montrose. 1632.

48. *Hans Gilmore*, father, burgess in Thorn. Witnesses: J. Ruthven and Jacob Lyon, burgesses and glovers at D. 1653.

49. *James Grun (Green.)* Witnesses: Hans Robertson and Gelletlie, burgesses of D. 1582.

50. *Robt. Guthrie*, son of the "noble" William Guthrie of Minus, not far from the town of Fervor (Forfar), and of Elis. Fenton. Witness: Henry Guthrie, merchant at D. 1662.

[1] In the *Kgl. St. Archiv*, Posen; adorned with coat-of-arms.
[2] "Robt. Morrisson has been growing up with J. Fyffe, the younger, and was a schoolfellow of his."

51. *W. Halyburton*, son of the "Magister" Andr. Halyburton of St Andrews and Cath. Lumsden.
Witnesses: Morrisson and Cassinus of D. (80).
1680. Bbr.

52. *Andr. Hervie*, son of William Hervie of Torreloyth
(?) near Aberdeen. Witnesses: W. Anderson
and Oswald Dirring, of Aberdeen, inhabitants
of D. 1598.

53*a*. *Al. Henderson*, son of John Henderson, burgess of
Perth, and Elis. Ellor. Witnesses: W. Anderson, Hans Snell, Alex. Salmon, natives of Perth,
now of D. Alex. Henderson died 1597 at D.

53*b* *William Henderson*, son of William Henderson, the
Earl of Orkney's late "Court Butcher" in
Kirkwall, and of Anne Spens. Witness: Elis.
Sinckler, widow of Peter Wilson. 1653.

54. *W. Hewison*, son of W. Hewison, Aberdeen. 1650.

55. *Dan Heij* (Hay). Witness: Alex. Karkettle. 1690.

56. *Hans Innes*, son of Alb. Innes, an "arrendator" at Park
in Banffshire and of Marg. Leitch. Witnesses:
Jacob Stewart, a lieutenant, and Ths. Mackie, a
tailor, both of D. 1660.

57. *Albrecht Jack*, son of Thomas Jack, merchant of D.
Witnesses: W. Wadrop and David Hogg,
burgesses of D. 1622.

58. *Thos. Jamieson*, son of John Jamieson, domiciled in
Sklete (or Sklote), "about a mile's walk from
Aberdeen," and of Barbara Simson. Witnesses: Alexander Simson, burgess of Krakaw,
and Will. Hewison, burgess of Posen. 1658.

59*a* *Andreas Kant*, a tanner, now a musketeer under
Sergeant-Major Goltz, son of And. Kant.
1661.

59*b* *W. Kant*, son of the late John Kant, a tailor.

Witnesses: Robt. Morisohn (80) and Alex. Stuhrt (73), in the Elizabeth Hospital, D. 1681.

60. *Hans Kilau* (?), son of the late I. Kilau, shoemaker and burgess of Aberdeen. Witnesses: Gilb. Tzamer (Czamer), and Will. Ellhus (Ellis) of Aberdeen, now at D. 1637.

61. *Jacob Kingawer* (?), son of Jas. Kingawer, late weaver at Wasserkarney (?), "three miles' walk from Aberdeen," and of M. Young. 1666.

62. *Jacob Leo (Lyon)*, son of David Lyon, burgess of Edinburgh, and of Cath. Patterson, a citizen of Danzig and a glover by trade. Died without male issue. One of the witnesses is Alb. Morris, a tailor of Danzig and son-in-law to David.

63. *Jacob Lermont*, father J. Lermont, late burgess and gunsmith of St Andrews; mother, Elis. Smith. Witnesses: S. Robertson, burgess of St Andrews, and Jacob Smith, burgess of Danzig. 1636.

64. *Walter Leslie*, from Aberdeen; father Patrick Leslie, Provost of Aberdeen; mother, Isab. Chien. Witnesses: Ths. Leslie, burgess of Danzig, an uncle, and J. Littgo (Lithgow), burgess and distiller, D. (73). 1683.

67. *John Littko*, son of Jas. Littkow, citizen and distiller of D. (formerly a "lieutenant" in Aberdeen), born in Aberdeen; mother Elis. Henderson. 1669.

68. *Will. Littgow*, from Sandwick (Shetlands). Witness: Jacob Lissko, stocking-weaver (48). 1657.

65. *Thos. Ledderdel* (Litherdale?), father, Jas. Lither-

dale, domiciled on St Mary's Isle, County
Galway (Galloway). 1649.

66. *Abr. Lindsay*, son of Will. Lindsay and of Euphemia,
from Edinburgh. 1598.

69. *John Macallen.* 1648. Bbr.

70. *John Mackie.* 1640. Bbr.

71. *A. Marshall*, Bbr. issued by the town of Aberdeen,
son of Robt. Marshall and Marg. Mollisson.
Witnesses: Alex. Davidson, "advocatus," John
Tullydaff, Hector Smith and Jas. Birnie.
Dec. 1, 1634.

72. *John Maxwell*, son of James Maxwell, peasant, in the
village of Auchtermuchty, "a two miles' walk"
from Facheln (Falkland), "a small town in the
Kingdom of Scotland." Witnesses: Alex. Ross
(75) and Hans Casin (90), labourers of D. 1682.

73. *J. Mill*, father burgess of D.; mother Anne
Robertson. Witnesses: Hans Morton and
Jas. Duncan (66), burgesses of D. 1675.

74. *Robt. Mill*, father Robert Mill, in Aberdeen; mother
Jane Burnett. 1674.

75. *Robt. Mitchell*, son of Robert "Dominus de Preston
Grange," and Janeta Wilson. 1697. Bbr.

76. *G. Moir*, from New Aberdeen. Mother Anna
Paip, daughter of Alex. Paip of Mickley Rany.
1738. Witnesses: And. Turner (76) and John
Marshall (56), burgesses of D.

77. *Alex. Moncrieff*, skipper, from Burntisland. Mother,
Marg. Brown. Witnesses: Andr. Alexander
and John Scott of Burntisland.
Hennerson, an interpreter, "verstabet" = repeated
and translated the oath to them. 1678.

78. *Hugh Mongall*, son of George Mongall, judge and
burgess of Fallkirch; mother, Marg. Hall. 1664

79. *R. Morrisson*, son of John Morrisson of St Andrews. Witness: David Brachy of St Andrews. 1655.

80. *Ths. Murray*, son of Al. Murray, late merchant in Aberdeen, and of Cath. Cullen. Witnesses: Robt. Chapman and J. Liddel. 1681.

81. *Hans Ogilvie* (boy), from Kopenhagen. 1685. Bbr.

82. *Peter Ogilvie*, father, the "noble" Thos. Ogilvie of Balgowen, near Gowrie (Perth); mother, Elis. Morton. Witnesses: Major Ths. Anderson and Hans Watson of D. 1649.

83. *Al. Paip* from the town of Tania (Tain) in Ross-shire, son of Gilbert Paip of Mickle Rainy and Anne Munro, daughter of John Munro of Pitonachy. Witnesses: Alex. Ross of Cockenzie and John Fergusson "de Allan." 1686.

84. *Al. Paip*, son of the above. Witnesses: Geo. Buchan (70) and John James Gorman, burgess of D. 1696.

85. *A. Patterson*, from Kiling (?), Aberdeenshire. 1619.

86. *David Patterson*, son of Hans Patterson in Erbraht (Arbroath). Witnesses: Jacob Smith, "a horse soldier," and David Patterson. "Went to school together." 1656.

87. *H. Pollock*, from Glasgow. Bbr.

88. *Archibald Rait*, son of A. Rait and Elis. Abercrombie, parish of Rayne, Aberdeenshire. Left Scotland 1651. Bbr. issued by J. Gordon, ballivus, Geo. Cruikshank de Berrihill, Ja. Basken de Orde et Robt. Cruikshank de Rainystone. 1677.[1]

88*a. Samuel Ramsay*, father and grandfather in Elbing.

---

[1] In the *Kgl. St. Archiv*, Posen. The Bbr. is adorned with the coat-of-arms of the Raits of Halgrein, Abercromby de Birkenbog, Cruikshank of Tullymorgan and Leith of Likliehide. See further on.

Witnesses : John Mallison, burgess and brewer, and Thos. Smeaton, burgess, both of Elbing. 1687.

89. *William Ramsay*, son of Patrick Ramsay, in the village of Wettray (?) Angus. Witnesses : Will. Ramsay and David Macrecht. " Scottish Krämers." Bbr. 1629.

90. *Jacob Ramsay*, father a small grocer at Praust near D. 1656.

91. *Alexander Ramsay*, son of No. 89. " Freyer deutscher art gezeuget."[1] 1689.

92. *Walter Ramsay*, ⎫ sons of Al. Ramsay of Galre (?)
93. *Gilbert Ramsay*, ⎭ near Coupar Angus, and of Marg. Halyburton. Walter is said to have died when journeying in Wallachia; Gilbert settled in Königsberg. 1652.

94. *Alex. Rennie*, son of Al. Rennie. 1637.

94a. *M. Riese* from Edinburgh. 1701.

95. *Jas. Robertson*, son of Geo. Robertson, burgess of D. 1591.

96. *David Robertson*, from Pomerania. 1638. Bbr.

97. *Thomas Robertson*, from Brandenburg. 1638. Bbr.

98. *Will. Robertson*, son of Jas. Robertson (95) in D. Born at D. 1662. Bbr.

99. *Jacob Ross*, son of John Ross at D. and of Margaret Essken (Erskine). Witnesses: Jas. Lyon and David Dempster (60), glovers and burgesses of D. 1657.

100. *Abr. Sinclair*, son of W. Sinclair of D. Witnesses: Hans Fergusson and Jacob Söto (Soutar), burgesses and shoemakers of D. 1669.

101. *David Skene*, from Bahelwick (Balhelvie), near

[1] " Of free German offspring."

Aberdeen. Mother Mabel Kennett. 1586. Bbr.

102. *Jacob Sinckler*, father Jas. Sinckler, a "seafaring man"; mother, Agneta Morton. Witnesses: Hans Morton, burgess of D., and David Brady of St Andrews. 1659.

103. *Thomas Smart*, from Dundee. Son of David Smart and Elizabeth Smith. Witnesses: Geo. Brown and Mallisson from Königsberg. 1639. Bbr.

104. *Jacob Smith*, son of James Smith at Dundee and of Marg. Gillin. Witnesses: Robert Lessli, burgess of Dundee, and John Cargill, clerk in D. 1664.

105. *John Strachan*, son of Al. Strachan, merchant at D., and of Barbara Schmidt (Smith). Witnesses: J. Smith, burgess and jeweller of D., and William Lumsdehl, burgess of D. 1680.

106. *Alb. Strehren*,[1] son of Matth. Strehren from Penketland (Pencaitland), "eight miles'" walk from Edinburgh. Witnesses: Hans Cumming, burgess of D. 1665.

107. *Jas. Steffen*, from Glaskaw, son of the late B. Steffen. Witnesses: B. Hall and Hans Donnell, burgesses of Glaskaw. 1612.

108. *Donald Sutherland*, from Caithness. Bbr. 1751.
109. *James Sutherland*, ,, ,, Bbr. 1752.
110. *John Thomson*, son of Math. Thomson of Glasgow. Witnesses: Matth. Macleish, glover, and Henry Simson, retail merchant, D., "neighbour's children." 1667.

111. *John Turner*,[2] son of John Turner and Marg.

---

[1] See *Scots in Germany*, p. 261.
[2] See about him above. The reader will do well to compare the lists above with those given in the Appendix of the *Scots in Germany*.

M

Keith, Aberdeen. Witnesses: William and Andr. Turner, merchants at Przemysl in Poland, the heirs. 1688.

112. *Richard Turner*, father in D. as clerk. 1684.

113. *Hans Walles* (Wallace), son of H. Walles in D., and Cath. Robertson. Witnesses: H. Morton and Geo. Cleghorn, burgesses of D. 1660.

114. *Will. Watson*, from Stolp in Pomerania, son of J. Watson, there. 1676. Bbr.

115. *Andr. Watson*, son of A. Watson in St Johnstown (Perth). Witnesses: P. Wadrup, a soldier, and William Puri (Pourie). 1649.

116. *Jacob Watson*, son of H. Watson, born in the village of O. (?), ten miles from D. 1686.

117. *Jacob Wright*, from Pomerania. Bbr. 1653.

IX.

Three Birth-briefs as Specimens.[1]

I.

Birth-brief of the Brothers Francis, Simon and Gilbert Johnston (1596).

UNIVERSIS et singulis ad quorum notitias praesentes litterae pervenerint . . . nos ballivi et consilii senatus burgi Lanercae in regno Scotiae salutem. Quatenus Franciscum Johnstoun, Simonem Johnnstoun et Gilbertum Johnnstoun filios fratresque germanos inter quondam nobilem Joannem Johnnstoun de Cragaburne et Mareotam Mure ejus legitimam conjugem rite et legitime procreatos fuisse notum facimus ac tenore praesentium attestamur. Quae quidem Mareota legitima fuit filia quondam Joannis

---

[1] I have purposely selected three birth-briefs very different in style.

Mure, nobilis domini de Annestona, nec non in ecclesia
parochiali de Spinemton (Symmington) infra vicecomitatum
de Lanark debite et secundum divini numinis ordinem dicti
quondam Joannes et Mareota ejus conjux in conjugali
nexu perimplerunt. Illa autem Mareota adhuc favente
Deo vitam agente. Nunc vero veritatis causa dictorum
Francisci, Simonis et Gilberti legitimae procreationis fide-
le testimonium perhibeamus perque has literas nostras
attestamur. Quapropter hoc nostrum testimonium serio
scribere mandavimus et vos procul dubio certiores reddimus
et ipsa veritate notum facimus [ac] dictos fratres germanos
minime nothos sed de legitimo thoro honestoqne conjugio
genitos per parentes praedictos procreatos esse : quorum
primores absque originis memoria nobiles ac honestos fuisse
attestamur [nobiles ad honestos fuisse usus scimus].[1]
Vobis itaque universis et singulis, quibus ipsa veritas et
pia bonorum generatio cordi est, hos fratres germanos et
de legitimo thoro natos commendamus eosque honesta
societate in omnibus rebus dignos obnixe rogamus,
quemadmodum, si quando par referendi facultas a vobis
dabitur qua possumus opera compensatum iri pollicemur.
In omne rei testimonium sigillum commune dicti nostri
burgi de Lanark ad causam praedictam testandum praesentibus appendi curavimus. Lanercae, decimo quinto die
mensis Maji anno Domini millesimo quingentesimo
nonagesimo sexto.

> DAVID BRENTOUN, notarius ac scriba ejusdem.
> ANTONIUS LOKHART, balivus dicti burgi.
> VILELMUS MONAT, communis clericus dicti burgi,
> manu mea propria.

[1] Thus the Vienna copy. There are two authenticated copies of the
lost original, one at Breslau from which the above text is taken, the other
at Vienna. See *Urkunden zur Geschichte der Familie von Johnston,*
Breslau, 1895.

2.

Birth-brief of John and Gabriel Spalding (1675).

Carolus Dei gratia Magnae Britanniae Franciae et Hyberniae Rex fideique defensor universis et singulis Regibus, Principibus . . . atque ceteris quibuscunque has patentes nostras literas inspecturis perpetuam felicitatem et salutem in domino nostro summo et magistro. Quandoquidem summa eorum quibus administratio rei publicae est commissa cura esse debet ut virtutis studiosis et bene merentibus debitus honos conferatur et vitiosorum scelera constitutis suppliciis coerceantur nos hactenus quidem ne in his negligentius providisse videremur obnixe quantum a re nata fieri potuit et sedulo dedimus operam semperque damus et quaecunque generosi sanguinis praeclarive facinoris a majoribus derivata sunt jura et encomia eadem apud posteros . . . qua longissima fieri possit serie sarta et tecta maneant quo et ipsi post geniti stemmatis sui memores nihil parentum amplitudine aut integra fama indignum committant sed ad parem accensi laudem aliquam propria virtute lucis accessionem claritudini majorum superaddant et sic pari conatu proavos aemulati fideles et probos regi et patriae se subditos et cives pro virili prestent, hinc factum est ut famam nobilis quondam viri domini Joannis Spalding virtutis splendore et prudentia inclytam hac commendationis et benevolentiae nostrae tessera exornare statuerimus . . . et nos idcirco notum et certum facimus . . . praedictum nostrum subditum et civem dominum Johannem Spalding legitimum et legitimo thoro et matrimonio et ex utroque parente nobili et generoso natum esse ; et ex illustribus et praeclaris familiis paternum et maternum genus jam multis retro seculis traxisse utpote ortum patre nobili viro domino Georgio Spalding, comarcha de Milhaugh avo domino Georgio Spalding Toparcha de Grange Airly gentis anti-

quissimae et nobilissimae Spaldingorum Phylarcha proavo
Jacobo Spalding Toparcha de Grange Airly et ex uxore sua
domina Joanna Gairnes filia domini Gairnes baronis de
Lantoun gentis sue etiam Phylarcha avia vero paterna
domina Isabella Ogilvia filia domini Gualteri Ogilvie
baronis de Clova et conjugis suae dominae Margarete
Creightoun filie domini Crightonii baronis de Ruthven, ex
stirpe vero materna genitum esse nobili matrona domina
Helena Ogilvia filia domini Guilelmi Ogilvie baronis de
Keiler nepte domini Roberti Ogilvie baronis de Keilor et
conjugis suae dominae Anna Lindsei filie domini Lindsei
baronis de Eagle et Gleneske pronepte domini Davidis
Ogilvie illustrissimae et fortissimae Ogilviorum Phylarcha
. . . et conjugis suae dominae Euphemiae Forbesiae filiae
illustris domini baronis de Forbes gentis suae preclarissimae
Phylarchae, avia vero materna domina Maria Collesia filia
domini Alexandri Colessii baronis de Bellinamoon gentis suae
antiquae Phylarchae et conjugis suae dominae Helenae Car-
negiae filiae illustrissimi domini baronis de Carnegie postea
vero comitis de Southesk gentis suae inclytae nobilissimae
et prudentissimae Phylarchae. Qui omnes legitimis nuptiis
copulati ex legitimis et ipsi thoris et ex illustribus et
nobilissimis familiis oriundi fuere, omnes generis et virtutis
splendore claruere et a Serenissimis Scotorum regibus de-
cessoribus nostris ob praeclara sua in hostes facinora et
probatam in patriam fidem magnis honoribus muniis et
muneribus ab omni ferme memoria jure merito omnes con-
decorati famam suam cum sanguine puram et integram sine
labe aut ullo contamine ad posteros etiam adhuc superstites
majorumque suorum virtutum aemulos transmisere. Quorum
tenore vos omnes amicos nostros . . . rogatos obtestatosque
cupimus ut modo laudatos cives nostros D. D. Joannem et
Gabrielem Spalding fratres praedictos in omni humanitate virtute et prudentia . . . omnibus humanitatis honoris

et dignitatis officiis persequamini . . . quae omnia sicut ex se vera sunt et firma itidem ut apud universos et singulos testatiora et certiora fiant . . . has patentes nostras literas praedictis D. D. Joanni et Gabrieli Spalding fratribus germanis concessimus . . . [1]

3.

Birth-brief of Archibald Rait.

Issued by the City of Aberdeen.

March 21, 1676.

We have chosen the following letter out of a vast number of birth-briefs, because it is a fair specimen of the grandiloquence and the turgid Latinity of letters of the sort. The family of the applicants is always " perantiqua " —very old—and often " nobilis "; coats-of-arms of grand-father and grandmother are more or less faithfully reproduced; all to impress the benighted Prussians and Poles with the idea that in Scotland every tradesman or small farmer was in the happy possession of a patent of nobilit;, hoary with old age, and that in one of the many daughters of Robert Bruce was to be seen the great-great-great-grandmother of every young Scot who found himself compelled to push his fortune by the poverty of his country and cast upon the " inhospitable shores " of the Baltic.

Universis et singulis in quacunque dignitate civili, ecclesiastica vel militari ubivis gentium constitutio ad

---

[1] The brother of old Johann Spalding in Gothenburg was Andreas, who settled at Plau in Mecklenburg, and became the ancestor of the many Spaldings now spread over the North of Germany. See : *Geschichtliches, Urkunden, Stammtafeln der Spaldin₀*. Privately printed *Gloedenhof, Kreis Greifswald,* by Eduard Spalding, 1898.

quorum notitiam praesentes literae pervenerint, Nos Praefectus, consules reliquusque senatus civitatis Abredoniensis in Scotia salutem in Domino sempiternam.

Cum veritati non adesse nostro deesse sit officio sine fuco aut fallaciis candide et ex animo testificamur, quod quo die datae sunt haec literae coram nobis pro tribunali ad jus dicendum causasque audiendas sedentibus apparuit generosus vir Jacobus Skenaeus Leoni regi armorum in Scotia substitutus, qui in gratiam generosi viri Archibaldi Rait, mercatoris Leisnensis (Lissa) qui viginti sese aut eo circiter abhinc annis e Scotia in exteras profectus est regiones, petiit et rogavit, ut nos qua pollemus auctoritate tam popularibus quam exteris testatum redderemus eum generoso stemmate et honesta prosapia oriundum et ex parentibus conjugali foedere sibi consociatis susceptum esse. Cujus petitioni tam aequae pro officii ratione deesse non potuimus. Itaque ut innotescat Nos non temere aut ex assentatione sed diligenti prius scrutinio hoc super negotio instituto praesens diploma indulsisse, in judicium vocavimus probatae fidei, spectatae probitatis provectaeque aetatis viros Johannem Gordon Ballivum, Bamfiensem Georgium Cruikshank de Berrihill, Jacobum Basken de Orde et Robertum Cruikshank de Rainystone qui solemni interposito jurejurando elatis dextris sanctissime confirmarunt dictum Archibaldum Rait filium fuisse legitimum generosi viri Archibaldi Rait de Lentuss infra parochiam de Rayne et vicecomitatum de Aberdene, ex generosa foemina Elizabetha Abercrombie legitima ipsius conjuge, dictum vero Archibaldum Rait praefati Archibaldi patrem filium fuisse legitimum generosi viri Gulielmi Rait de Lentuss praefati Archibaldi avi paterni ex generosa foemina Joanna Kruikshank legitima ipsius conjuge praefati

Archibaldi avia materna, filia legitima generosi viri
Roberti Cruikshank de Glenmaglen infra parochiam de
Forige (?) et vicecomitatum de Aberdeen ex antiqua familia
de Cruikshank de Tillimorgan oriundi; dictosque praefati
Archibaldi majores ex linea paterna ex antiqua familia
de Rait de Halgreine [1] legitime oriundos esse. Praefatam
vero Elizabetham Abercrombie dicti Archibaldi matrem
filiam fuisse legitimam generosi viri magistri Walteri
Abercrombie praefati Archibaldi avi materni, filii legitimi
Domini de Birkenboge, ex generosa foemina Margaretta
Leith legitima ipsius conjuge, praedicti Archibaldi avia
materna, filia legitima Domini de Liklieheide (or cheide);
Nominatosque omnes praefati Archibaldi majores ex
testibus supradictis constat nullo thalami probro aut
degeneris labis suspicione laborasse sed sub sacratissimo
matrimonii vinculo vitam suam transegisse illibatam.
Quae cum ita sint omnes et singulos apud quos praedictum Archibaldum versari contigerit rogatos percussimus,
ut illum generoso stemmate et honesta prosapia oriundum
et ex parentibus conjugali foedere sibi consociatis legitime
prognatum esse intelligant et pro innata sibi humanitate
ingenito virtutis studio cum omni (qua par est) benevolentia
acceptum in destinatum dirigere terminum non graventur.
Quam gratiam non minus quam in singulos hujus civitatis
collatam et cum foenore (si se dederit occasio) quantum
in nobis est, referendum medullitus apud nos perennaturam
unanimes spondemus. Et ut huic nostro testimonio sua
constet et maneat fides, secretarii nostro autographo
(nostro omnium nomine) signatum appenso civitatis
nostrae sigillo muniendum curavimus.

Datum Abredoniae vigesimo primo die mensis Martii
anno Domini millesimo sexcentesimo septuagesimo sexto
et regni serenissimi principis nostri Caroli secundi Dei

[1] In Kincardineshire.

gratia Magnae Brittanniae, Franciae et Hiberniae regis, fideique defensoris, anno vigesimo octavo.

L. S.   Magister Alexander Robertson.
Secretarius Abredonensis.[1]

X.

*List of Scotsmen
who became burgesses of Danzig.*[2]

1531. Thomas Gilzet from Dundee.
1536. Jacob Bruce.
1552. James Kilfauns.
1552. John Watson.
1552. James Brathinson (?).
1558. Andr. Robbertson from Aberdeen.
1559. Geo. Robbertson   ,,   ,,
1563.   Butchart from Dundee.
1564. James Somerfeld (ville).
1565. Robt. Hoddon (Hutton) from Dalkona.
1565. Andr. Dehlhoff (?) from Aberdeen.
1566. Hans Forbes   ,,   ,,
1566. Hans Kilfauns.
1567. Andr. Bruin from Dundee.
1573. John White (Witte) from Cupro (Cupar), a coppersmith.
1577. Andr. Moncreiff.
1578. Osias Kilfauns.
1578. Geo. Patterson.

[1] *Kgl. St. Archiv*, Posen. Dep. Lissa C 1 a. N. 1.
[2] *Kgl. St. Archiv*, Danzig, D. XXIII. XCVII. A. Bürgerbücher.

About 1580. William Forbes.

  1581. Geo. Kittrick (?) from Dumfries.

  1581. Alex. Mirhi (Murray) from Banff.

  1581. Geo. Smith from St Andrews, a goldsmith.

  1582. Hans Gelletlie from Dundee.[1]

  1587. Andr. Hardy   ,,   ,,

  1587. James Gelletlie ,,   ,,

  1592. Andr. Liddel.

  1592. James Kignet (?).

  1592. James Brun from Aberdeen.

  1592. John Watson ,,   ,,

  1593. Will. Roan (Rowan).

  1593. Andr. Thomson from Edinburgh.

  1593. Andr. Telliour (Taylor).   "Intercessione Dominae Reginae."

  1593. James King.

  1598. Andrew Steven from Aberdeen.

  1598. William Duncan ,,   ,,

  1598. Abr. Lindsay from Edinburgh.

  1598. Jas. Greger   ,,   ,,

  1598. Andr. Goring from Aberdeen.

  1598. Peter Blair from Dundee.

  1598. Thos. Blair ,,   ,,

  1598. Alex. Ramsay from Aberdeen.

  1599. Geo. Hebron (Hepburn).

  1606. John Stoddart.

  1606. Hans Kilfauns.

About 1610. Al. Rennie.

  1612. Arch. Williamson.

  1614. Alex. Newland from Edinburgh.

  1614. Jas. Smith from St Andrews.

  1616. Alex. Demster from Brechin.

---

[1] He has a house in the Frauengasse in 1655.

1621. W. Lamb from Sandwick.

1621. David Hogg from Stirling.

1621. Hans Kammer (Chambers) from Edinburgh.

1622. Hans Pratus from Dunfermline.

1623. Thos. Makkenssin (Mackenzie) from Dundee.

1624. J. Abernethy from Aberdeen.

1626. Thos. Stalker.

About 1630. Thos. Demster.

1631. Reinhold Portus from Douglas.

1631. Jas. Meldrum.

1632. Jas. Man from Dundee.

1633. Geo. Cleghorn from Quhitsome.

1634. W. Balfour from St Andrews.

1638. W. Kenrick from Culross.

1639. Thos. Smart from Dundee.

1639. Henckly (?).

1640. Alb. Agnus from Lochiedt (?).

1640. William Gordon.

1641. W. Ramsay from Rattray; a twiner.

1642. John Duncan from Dunblane.

1642. Alex. Bell from Bamoyll.

1643. Hans Morton from St Andrews, a twiner.

1647. Geo. Cuik from Glasgow.

1652. David Demster.

1652. J. Smith from Auchenthaw (?).

1653. John Tamson.

1658. Geo. Mitchell.

1659. Adrian Stoddart.[1]

1662. Robt. Guthrie from Minus, near Forfar.

1663. Thomas Fraser.

---

[1] An eminent man, who as " Syndic " took an active part in the politics and the government of the City. Cp. Part II.

1663. A. Guthry.

1664. Alex. Barclay.

1664. Robt. Baylie from Lamington.[1]

1664. W. Robbertson.

1666. Al. Hotchisson (Hutchison).

1668. Robt. Chalmer from Aberdeen.

1669. J. Litgow from Aberdeen.

1668. W. Brown from Dundee.

1674. Al. Karkettle.

1674. Jas. Bruce from Edinburgh.

1675. Robt. Mill.

1676. W. Clerk from Dunfermline, and two sons.

1676. W. Watson.

1677. Arch. Rait from Aberdeenshire.

1678. Al. Moncrieff from Burntisland.

1680. W. Halyburton from St Andrews.

1681. Dan. Davidson.

1682. Thos. Fraser from Aberdeen.

1682. Thos. Murray ,,   ,,

1682. Hans Ogelbey.

1682. Thos. Burnet.

1682. Dan G. Davidson.

1683. John Gerne from Zamosc.

1685. Peter Forbes from Aberdeen.

1687. William and Robert Farquharson.

1689. Al. Paip with two sons.[2]

1689. Thos. Leslie from Aberdeen.

1691. Andr. Turner from Wreatoun (Rathen ?).

1691. William Turner from Kininmond, Aberdeenshire.

1691. Thos. Davidson from Aberdeen.

[1] See Birth-briefs.

[2] For obtaining civil rights Paip had to pay 3000 gulden; Andr.
Turner for himself and his brother 5000.

1695. Francis Moncrieff.
1695. (?) Walter Leslie.[1]
1700. James Leitch.
1705. Al. Buchan.[2]
1705. Peter Stuart from Posen.
1705. Jas. Irving.
1705. A. Majoribanks.
1705. G. Malabar.
1710. Gilbert Moir.[3]
1710. John Farquhar.[3]

The following Scottish names are also mentioned in Danzig[4]: Mustard (1475); Seymour (1557); C. Lawson (1546); Dickson (1557); P. Law (1558); Melville, Stirling, Simson (1556); Andrew Cromforth (Crawford); W. and Al. Forbes (1556); Stein (1585); Middleton (1598); Murray (1599); Jac. Agilbey (Ogilvie), (1599); Al. Mitchell (1604); Andr. Keay (1611); Nisbet, Wolson (1611); Jacob Rennie (abt. 1640)[5]; Th. Duff († 1619); P. Masterton (1620); Wadrop (1622); Macallen (1621); D. Haig (1637); Norrie (1637); Hans Ingram (†1649)[6]; Patterson from Arbroath (1656); Jac. Ruthven (1653); Jac. Lyon (1653); A. Morton and Jas. Morton, his son (1660); G. Ochterlony († 1644); W. Konigem (Cunningham); H. Roy or Ruy († 1683);

[1] He paid 2000 gulden. See *Scots in Germany*, p. 268.
[2] See *Scots in Germany*, pp. 268, 269.
[3] After paying 1400 gulden.
[4] In the *Schöppenbücher* and elsewhere; most of these Scotsmen were also citizens.
[5] He was a cattle-dealer; in 1649 he is in great distress about 120 oxen, which he had ordered from Poland. Only a few of them arrived at Danzig on account of what he calls the "Kosackische Revolte." *Kgl. St. Archiv*, Danzig.
[6] He left a house in the "andere Damm" Street, Danzig.

Geo. Morton († 1665); A. Baylie († 1665); Robt. Tevendale (1689); John Brown,[1] Al. Coutts [2] (about 1720).

It will be seen from the above list how much more generous Danzig was in the admission of the Scots to the freedom of the city. A grateful remembrance of the military services of the Scots in times of war has, no doubt, to do with it. The town deserves the eulogy of some Scottish petitioners who write in 1594: "The Magistrates of Danzig enjoy the honour and glory with foreign nations, of not wholly avoiding good people for the sake of their difference of tongue and language to the exclusion and refusal of civil rights, but they make known their name far and wide above many other countries and towns by means of their humanity and friendliness."

XI.

List of thirty-seven

Scottish Krämers attending the Fair at Wehlau.

1644.

1. Will. Anderson.	9. Al. Nick (from Nordenburg).
2. Jacob Marshall.	
3. Al. Demster.	10. Ja. Mongall.
4. Andr. Daschach(?).	11. J. Lietschwett (?).
5. Alb. Nucastoll.	12. Ja. Grant.
6. W. Kinkett (Kincaid).	13. Will. Abernetti.
7. Th. Gregor.	14. Hans Lowry (from Königsberg).
8. J. Mitchell.	

[1] John Brown was made Burgess and Guild Brother of Edinburgh in 1684. He also received a baronetcy. His patent is still preserved in Danzig, and is signed by Sir George Drummond. In 1717 he possessed a fine house on the Langemarkt.

[2] Alex. Coutts and Company, merchants at Danzig, send a fine brass drum with the town's arms upon it, a present to the burgh of Banff (1730).

15. Andr. Hunt.
16. Thos. Schmidt.
17. Balzer Davidson.
18. W. Schott.
19. Robt. English.
20. Jac. Morra, burgess of Domnau.
21. Jac. Hamilton, ,, ,, Sensburg.
22. Geo. Kriegschank.
23. Ja. Ritterfart (Rutherford).
24. Hans Nielson (burgess of Königsberg).
25. Jac. Allison.
26. J. Ertzbell (Archibald).
27. Ch. Small.
29. Jac. Mohr (burgess of Nordenburg).
30. David Watson.
31. Thos. Strach (?).
32. E. Karr (from Ragnit).
33. W. Kurrie (from Barten).
34. Ths. Moir (burgess of Drengfurt).
35. Andr. Johnstone.
36. Ths. Hamilton (burgess of Augerburg).
27. H. Dornthon (Thornton).

XII.

List of Scottish Members of the Guild of Merchants at Königsberg (Kneiphof).

As the old burgesses' rolls have been lost at Königsberg, the following list of Guild members obtains an additional value.

Hans Greiff, 1602.
R. Mitchell, 1648.
Chr. Patton, 1659, entrance fee 2 Thaler.
H. Wolson, 1650.
Th. Penicuik, 1662, for 100 Thaler.
Gilb. Ramsay, 1669, ,, 100 Marks.
Andr. Ritch, 1669, ,, ,, ,,
M. Mickel, 1669, ,, ,, ,,
Geo. Gordon, 1677, ,, ,, ,,
Jac. Kuik, 1681.

Jac. Hervie, 1684, for 100 Thaler.
J. Krehl, 1684.
C. Ramsay, 1685.
W. Ritch, 1686,   ,,   4 Thaler.
Ths. Hervie, jun., 1691, for   30   ,,
C. Ramsay, Gilbert's son ,,   12 Gulden.
Dav. Hervie, 1692,   ,,   18   ,,
Andr. Marshall, 1693,   ,,   160   ,,
J. Morisson, 1699,   ,,   100   ,,
John Irwing, 1700,   ,,   18   ,,
W. Tevendale, 1700.
H. Hunter, 1701,   ,,   200   ,,
J. Rait, 1701.
D. Cramond, 1706,   ,,   200   ,,
J. Mitchelhill, 1706,   ,,   50   ,,
A. Gern, 1707,   ,,   50   ,,
W. Gordon, 1711,   ,,   30   ,,
L. Birrell, 1716.
Geo. Gray, 1716,   ,,   200   ,,
A. Karkettle, 1720,   ,,   30   ,,
Ths. Hervie, 1723,   ,,   5 Thaler.
Peter Kuik, 1726,   ,,   6   ,,
Dan. Hunter, 1740.
L. Crichton, 1742,   ,,   140 Gulden.
G. Fothergill, 1749.
Mackmüller (Macmillan).

Pennicuik soon obtained the eldership. Among the possessions of this Guild, there is or was a silver shield with the Coat of Arms of Scotland crowned, and two " Euchhörner " (squirrels?) [1] as supporters.

Amongst the Guild members of the Altstadt were: H. Wolson, Will. Hervie (1695), John Duglass (1720),

[1] The word may also read " Einhörner " = unicorns. *Stadt Archiv*, Königsberg. Cp. *Scots in Germany*, pp. 261, 262.

and Geo. Ross (1723). The last two also being "Grossbürger" = full burgesses.

XIII.

List of Scottish Settlers and Burgesses at Königsberg up till 1700.[1]

*A. Rutherford (1561).
D. Bewick (1586).
Gregor Kolborn (1562).
Two Ogilvies (1562).
W. Kinloch
P. Kinloch } 1584.
*J. Stein (1586).
*   (1622).
A. Wright (1620).
D. Lindsay (*1637).
*D. Grant (1622).
*H. Dennis (1642).
*H. Abernethy.
*G. Ramsay
*A. Ritch } 1656.
*M. Mickel
P. Leermonth.
*G. Weyer (Wier), 1661.
Calander.
*Ths. Pennicuik, 1664.
*J. Krehl (Crail), 1676.
Jackson.
*Wopster, 1660.
D. Barclay.
A. Fullert, 17th century.

*W. Buchan, 1616 (?).
*A. Dunbar, 1616 (?).
*G. Bayllie, 1660.
G. Murray
Rob. Walker } End of
Morrisson } 17th
R. Mill } century.
*Robt. Marshall
J. Gertner, 1690.
J. Wass.
*A. Dennis.
*J. Hervie, 1691.
*G. Hutcheson, abt. 1660.
H. Brown.
W. Ritch.
*D. Hervie.
W. Gray, 1694.
*A. Marshall, 1692.
J. King.
Th Taylor (*1692).
*Ths. Hervie
*Fr. Hay } 1699.
*Ch. Ramsay
H. Lowry
*H. Nelson } 1614.
J. Allison

[1] Compare the list given in *Scots in Germany*, p. 261, comprising the years 1700-1740. Those marked with an asterisk are burgesses.

*J. Hay
*Adrian Hay } 1650.

D. and J. Lawson, abt. 1690.

XIV.

*List of Scottish Burgesses and Settlers in other towns of
Eastern and Western Prussia.*[1]

Eastern Prussia.

In *Memel*: Hans Wricht (1650), D. Henderson (1589),
A. Adams, A. Murray (1657), Eliz. Ogilvie
(*1746).

In *Tilsit*: Jac. Koch (1611), Hans Butchart (1627),
Hans Philipp (died about 1626), Thos. Hay
(1637), Thos. Ritch (1637), Charles Ramsay
(1628), Geo. Johnston, Alex. and Bastian
Dennis (1679), James Murray (1680), M.
Hamilton (1687), Chr. Anderson (1697), Jacob
Lamb (1698), J. Napier (1605), Ths. Crichton
(1687), R. Kerr (1696), Irwing (1743).

In *Goldap*: *H. Dempster, *H. Anderson (1604), A
Fairweather (*1737).

In *Fischhausen*: J. Stein (1592).

In *Sensburg*: A. Meldrum (1594).

In *Tapiau*: Andr. Geddes.

In *Pr. Holland*: Albr. Kinkaid (1627), G. Porteous.

In *Rastenburg*: A. Robertzon, A. Schott, J. Andres,
D. Hunter.

In *Ragnit*: Scotowski (1604), Thos. Wilson (1604).

In *Ortelsburg*: Ths. Norrie (1601).

In *Insterburg*: A. Abernetti.

In *Braunsberg*: Al. Anderson (1607), H. Morra (1611),

---

[1] Cp. *Scots in Germany*, Appendix, pp. 262, 263.

W. Barclay (1682), Ths. Zander, Jacob Lafus
(Laws), A. Bennett, H. Midday.

In *Johannisburg*: A. Wright, A. Robertson, G. Meldrum
(1587), Mickel.

In *Bartenstein*: P. Ray (1589), G. Forster (1588), Z.
Wilson, Z. Koch, John Cochran, W. Patton,
P. Rehe (1590), G. Forster (1588), Miller.

In *Angerburg*: H. Andres (1602).

In *Barten*: Ths. Gordon, M. Ogston (1652).

Western Prussia.

In *Neuenburg*: *Jacob Bennett (1573), John and Alb.
Morrisson (1640), A. Law (1643), A. Anderson
(1590), A. Patton (1555), D. Alston, G. Fleck
(1555), G. Foster, Al. Linn, Hector Munro,
Will. Bruce.

In *Stuhm*: *Hans Drom and *Jacob Rennie (1595), *M.
Steinson.

In *Elbing*: Will. Lamb (1637), W. Ramsay (1620),
P. Ramsay, Patton (1648), Nisbet (1617).

In *Marienburg*: Rischyson Gilchrist (1509), H. Wricht
(1640), Jac. Kant, P. Ogilvie, A. Johnston, A.
and Will. Hay (1650), B. Königheim (Cunningham), (1622), J. Duncan (1657), Al. Seton
(1658), J. Steen (*1622).

In *Marienwerder*: Th. Smith, J. Mackarty, A. George
(1587), O. Hutcheson, A. Morriss, M. Stirling,
J. Lawson (*1657).

In *Thorn*: Gourlay (1637), A. Hewison, Ths. Ogilvie
(1720).

In *Konitz*: H. Wieland, A. Bernt, a jeweller, M. Davidson, H. Patrszin, *M. Reise, a hatter (1701).

In *D. Krone*: J. Malson (about 1600), J. Lawson, J.
Walson (about 1630).

In *Christburg*: J. Smith, G. and Th. Blackhall, D. Schott, B. Zander.

XV.

List of Scottish Burgesses at Posen. 1585-1713.

1585. *Alexander Reid* Scotus de Edenburg adscriptus in numerum civium feria quarta post festum Scti. Mathiae Apostoli proxima anno domini 1585 pro quo quidem Alexandro Rei[n]dt fideijusserunt famati Andreas Gencz et Casparus Hempell, cives Posnanienses, quod litteras testimonii de honesto et legitimo ortu suo et bona conservatione pro die festo Sancti Bartholomaei proxime venturo spectabili consulatui Posnaniensi authentice offeret et exhibebit. Actum ut supra.

1586. *David Skin* (Skene), Scotus, jus civile suscepit die et anno quibus supra [feria sexta post festum S. Bartholomaei apostoli].

1587. *Joannes Scotus Broun* [1] adscriptus juri civili feria quarta ante Dominicam Palmarum proximo anno quo supra.

1589. *Joannes Peterson* Scotus jus civile suscepit die et anno quibus supra [feria sexta ante festum S. Bartholomaei apostoli].

1593. *Jacobus Loson* (Lawson) ex Trimelendia Scotus patre Toma Lason adscriptus juri civili feria sexta ut supra . . . fidejusserunt famati Andreas Gencz et Joannes Peterson cives Posnanienses

---

[1] Very possibly this man's name was Brown, and Scotus should have been written after it.

quod literas ortus pro festo S. Bartholomaei Apostoli proximo adferet.

1595. *Jacobus Czap* de Berwig ex civitate Scotie adscriptus juri civili feria quarta ante festum nativitatis beatae Mariae Virginis anno quo supra, fidejusserunt pro eodem Michael Reichnaw auri faber et Caspar Hempell, locularius, cives Posnanienses, quod intra hinc et duos menses literas ortus adferet sub privatione juris civilis.

1597. *Ricardus Tonson* mercator Scotus statutis testibus jure legitimi sui ortus itidem Scotis recognoscentibus adscriptus juri civili.

1598. *Jacobus Gordon* Scotus Abredoniensis, ostensis literis ortus sui legitimi adscriptus juri civili feria quarta pridie festi visitationis gloriosissimae virginis Mariae anno quo supra.

1598. *Robertus Ramze,* Scotus Eideburgensis die et anno quibus supra juri civili est adscriptus pro eodem famati Martinus Schubert et Jacobus Czap, cives Posnanienses, quod literas legitimi ortus pro nundinis quadragesimalibus proxima futura adferet, fideijusserunt

1600. *Bernardus Bellenten* de Leswad nec non *Valterus Rob* e Dundi Scoti juri civili adscripti sunt die et anno quibus supra. Fideiussit pro eis Albertus Wocziechowski institor civis Posnaniensis quod abhinc pro festo S. Bartholomaei Apostoli literas ortus sui legitimi adferent.

1600. *Patricius Chalmer* Abredonensis Scotus ostensis literis legitimi ortus sui adscriptus juri civili feria sexta in crastino SS. Viti et Modesti martyrun anno quo supra.

1602. *Joannes Older* Dupertatensis Scotus adscriptus

juri civili feria sexta ante festum S. Michaelis
Archangeli proxima a. q. s.

1605. *Joannes Ondrom* de Edenburk in Scotia praestito
corporali juramento iuxta formam civium solitam
tum de non exercenda cum extraneis ratione
mercimoniorum campania iure civili donatus
feria quarta post dominicam Invocavit proxima
anno q. s. pro quo de afferendis literis ortus
ipsius legitimi pro festo natali S. Joannis
Baptistae venturo famati Jacobus Gordon et
Bernardus Bellendin fideiusserunt.

1606. *Georgius Lessel* Canaricensis (Carnach) Rossensis
Scotiae adscriptus iuri civili . . .

1608. *Gaspar Wass* Scotus Ouwernensis (?) iure civili
donatus . . . pro quo fideiusserunt famati
Jacobus Gordon et Joannis Ondron Scoti, cives
Posnanienses, de afferendis literis ortus ipsius
legitimi et officio praesentandis in praetorio pro
festo S. Joannis Baptistae proxime futuro sub
poena privationis eiusdem iuris civilis.

1608. *Archibald Kokker* Scotus de civitate Monte Roza
dicta adscriptus iuri civili feria quarta ante
festum exaltationis S. Crucis pro quo fideiusserunt famati Jacobus Gordon et Gaspar Wass
Scoti, cives Posnanienses, quod sit legitimus
literasque sui ortus pro festo Paschalis adferet.
Presentavit literas originis feria sexta ante
Invocavit anno millesimo sexcentesimo decimo.
Cassatur fideiussio.

1608. *Georgius Johnstowne* oriundus de civitate Abredoniae
regni Scotiae filius Georgii Johnstowne artium
liberalium magistri quondam eiusdem civitatis
consulis, prout literae legitimi ortus coram

spectabili consulatu Posnaniensi productae test-
antur, iure civili donatus. . . .

1608. *Jacobus Bran* (Brown?) de civitate Endeburg feria
quarta in vigilia S. Stanislai iure civili donatus
pro quo fideiusserunt famatus Jacobus Gordon
et Gaspar Wass Scoti, cives Posnanienses, de
afferendis literis ortus ipsius legittimi . . . pro
festo S. Michaelis proxime imminente sub poena
privationis eiusdem iuris civilis. . . .

1624. *Vilhelmus Brun* Scotus ad mandatum sacrae et serenissimae regiae Majestatis manu eiusdem propria
subscriptum ac sigillo regni minori communitum
quo Sacra Regia Majestas ipsius eximiam dexteri-
tatem, modestiam et fidem singularem per eundem
tam in aula suae serenissimae Majestatis quam
in variis expeditionibus praestitam et probatam
commendare utque ad privilegia et libertates
civitatis huius recipiatur ac in album civium
adscribatur mandare dignatur. Tum ad literas
itidem commendacitias serenissimi Domini domini
Wladislai Sigismundi principis Poloniae . . .
iuri civili est adscriptus. Literas vero legitimi
sui ortus quoniam ad praesens ob distantiam
loci transmarinalis praesto non habet, ideo de
afferendis et producendis intra quatuor menses
eisdem literis spectabilis Christopherus Arnoldt
scabinus pro eodem Vilhelmo spectabili consulatui fidem suam interposuit. Produxit literas
A.D. 1631.

1630. *Erasmus Lilitson* Abardiensis
Gilbertus alias Gasparus *Blenschel*,
 Abardiensis
Georgius Gibson, Curosiensis
 } Scoti

die hodierna literis reproductis sacrae regiae

Majestatis Domini domini nostri clementissimi
quarum contextus actis infertus habetur iuri
civili ut moris et iuris est adscripti. Literas
vero legitimi sui ortus quoniam ad praesens ob
distantiam . . . praesto non habent ideo de
afferendis et producendis intra annum et diem
. . . spectabilis et famatus Stephanus Gruszowicz
et Jacobus Broun cives Posnanienses pro eisdem
spectabili magistratui fidem suam interposuerunt
eidemque caverunt eundem ab omnibus im-
pedimentis ubivis locorum et contra quosvis
conditionisque cujusvis evincendi propriis sump-
tibus eliberandi ratione quorum omnium sese
successoresque suos prout et ipsimet superius
dicti nunc vero recenter facti cives conjunctim et
divisim super omnibus bonis tam mobilibus
quam immobilibus obligant etque inscribunt
ratione sibi collati iuris civilis promittentes,
desuper *omnibus Catholicis concionibus diebus
festivis adesse* et funera, si contigerit aliosque
actus expedire sub poena decem marcarum
toties quoties submissioni suae contravenerint
spectabili magistratui irremissibiliter luenda et
persolvenda. Sabbatho ipso die S. Margarethae
virginis et martyris anno millesimo sexcentesimo
trigesimo. Superius dicti Scoti dederunt ad
aerarium civitatis noningentos florenos Poloni-
cales pro mercede solvenda artificibus et operariis
pauperibus. . . .

1636. Feria quinta videlicet die quinta mensis Junii anno
domini 1636. In praesentia totius spectabilis
magistratus famatus *Jacobus Watson*[1] de civitate
Dondi in Scotia oriundus in ius civitatis adscitus

---

[1] Cp. *Scots in Germany*, p. 249.

et ad praerogativas praevio juramento tum et libertates adscriptus. Literas genealogiae suae commonstrabit in festo S. Michaeli Archangeli pro quo fideiusserunt famati Jacobus Brun et Caspar Blenzel[1] Scoti itidem cives Posnanienses qui postea quietati sunt commonstratis literis ex Scotia feria sexta ante festum S. Andreae Apostoli A.D. 1636.

1636. Famatus *Gilbertus Blentsczel*[1] Abredoniensis ex regno Scotiae et *Georgius Gibsone* apud Culros itidem in regno Scotiae oriundi ortus sui legitimi literas pergameneas ex illis civitatibus emanatas exhibuerunt feria sexta ante Sanctorum Viti et Modesti in Junio anno currenti iuxta fideiussionem de afferendis pro se per famatas Stephanum Grussewitz et Jacobum Braun, cives Posnanienses, sabbatho ipso die S. Margarethae virginis et martyris anno 1630 factam et praestitam, quapropter fideiussores supradicti liberi pronunciati de sententia officii.

1640. Famatus *Jacobus Choijt* (?) Scotus de civitate Scotiae Dondij oriundus in ius civitatis Posnaniensis adscriptus est, juramentum super fidelitate praestitit. Literas legitimi ortus commonstrabit in decursu unius anni pro quo fideiussit famatus Jacobus Kenadei feria tertia ante festum S. Crucis proxima A.D. millesimo sexcentesimo quadragesimo.

1642. Honestus *Alexander Feinlosen* (Finlayson) de Edenburg Scotiae civitate oriundus ad fideiussionem famati Wilhelmi Braun de producendis literis ortus sui legitimi intra annum et sex

---

[1] The spelling seems to have given considerable trouble.

septimanas praestitoque fidelitatis iuramento per spectabiles dominos proconsulem et consules civitatis Posnaniae iuri civili adscitus est.

1642. Honestus *Albertus Smart* de Dundia Scotiae oriundus ad fideiussionem famati Wilhelmi Braun Scoti, civis Posnaniensis, pro illo officio praestitam, quod literas sufficientes legitimi ortus sui e patria sua authenticas intra dimidium anni procurabit et producet, praestito fidelitatis iuramento, iuri civili . . . per spectabiles dominos proconsules et consules est adscriptus feria quarta ante festum S. Valentini Presbyteri et Martyris . . .[1]

1645. Famatus *David Makili Roy* (Mackilroy) de civitate Kulross in regno Scotiae oriundus ad fideiussionem famatorum Adami Maturski et Jacobi Watson de producendis literis ortus sui legitimi intra annum et sex septimanas praestito fidelitatis et oboedientiae iuramento ad ius civile civitatis Posnaniae per spectabiles dominos proconsulem et consules est susceptus. . . . Exhibuit et commonstravit literas ortus legitimi authenticas et sufficientes quibus spectabilis . . . fideiussores eius a fideiuissione liberos prononciavit consulatus (1648).

1645. Ingenuus Joannes *Orrok* de Brattellen[2] civitate in regno Scotiae oriundas ad fideiussionem famati Jacobi Watson et honorati Stephani Lawnikowitz . . . ad ius civile civitatis Posnaniensis praestito iuramento per spectabiles dominos proconsulem et consules adscriptus est. . . .

1649. Famatus *Jacobus Ferguson* Edinburgensis ex regno

[1] Birth-brief produced in the same year. See *Scots in Germany*, p. 54, n.

[2] Burntisland (?).

Scotiae oriundus mercatoriae addictus, exhibitis literis ortus legitimi a civitate regia Edinburgo (?) praestitoque fidelitatis et oboedientiae juramento ad ius civile civitatis Posnaniensis per spectabiles dominos proconsulem et consules est admissus feria quinta ante dominicum Misericordia proxima. . . .

1649. Famatus *Wilhelmus Hayson*[1] Aberdoniae in regno Scotiae oriundus ad fideiussionem famatorum Jacobi Douni Scoti et Andreae Czochran (Cochran), de producendis literis ortus legitimi intra annum et sex septimanas . . . ad ius civile est admissus, feria secunda in vigilia festi S. Mathaei Apostoli et Evangelistae. . . .

1649. Famatus *Thomas Jamieson* de civitate Aberdoniae regni Scotiae oriundus ad fideiussionem famatorum Andreae Czochranik[2] et Jacobi Dounij institorum civium Posnaniensium . . . per spectabiles dominos proconsulem et consulas admissus anno die ut supra. Exhibuit literas authenticas Dantisco. Fideiussores liberi pronunciantur. . . A.D. 1650.

1649. Honestus *Jacobus Mora* (Murray), de civitate Edeburg regni Scotiae oriundus ad fideiussionem famatorum Andreae Czochranik et Jacobi Douny . . . ad ius civile est susceptus feria sexta post festum S. Matthaei Apostoli et Evangelistae. . . .

1650. Ingenuus *Jacobus Lindzay* de civitate Abredoniae in regno Scotiae oriundus exhibitis literis sufficientibus ratione ortus sui legitimi emanatis praestitoque . . . iuramento ad ius civile civitatis Posnaniae . . . admissus.

1650. Ingenuus *Andreas Watson* de Fano S. Joannis in

---

[1] Probably Hewison.   [2] Cochrane.

regno Scotiae oriundus exhibitis literis ortus
legitimi a civitate Gedanensi emanatis . . .
praestitoque . . . juramento ad jus civile . . .
admissus eodem die ut supra.

1667. Ingenui et honesti . . . *Jacobus* Joachimus *Watson*
Graboviensis, *Georgius Edislay* Neubattlensis in
Scotia. . . . *Wilhelmus Aberkrami* [1] Aberdonien-
sis in Scotia . . . . reproductis sufficientibus
ortus sui legitimi literis praestitisque more
aliorum civium iuramentis super oboedientiam
et fidelitatem ad ius civile civitatis Posnaniensis
per spectabiles dominos proconsulem et consules
*ea conditione quatenus conciones diebus dominicis
et festis in ecclesia parochiali* S. Mariae Mag-
dalenae *frequentent et audiant*, possessiones
immobiles quam primum poterint procurent *et
fidem Catholicam Romanam intra annum suscipi-
ant* et quidem Watson, Edislai, Aberkrami . . .
cum liberis iam procreatis suscepti ad omnes
praerogativas et immunitates civitati huic servi-
entes admissi sunt; sclopeta [2] vero ad aerarium
civile infra tres menses inferre tenebunter. . . .

1685. Ingenuus *Wilhelmus Watson* Dundinensis ex Scotia
ad fideiussionem famatorum Stanislai Piatkowic
et Alexandri Sztuard mercatorum . . . de producendis ortus legitimi literis intra annum et
sex septimanas post praestitum fidelitatis . . .
iuramentum ad ius civile civitatis Posnaniae
. . . admissum est, sclopetum autem intra
tempus suprascriptum ad aerarium civili inferet
. . . Reproduxit sufficientes ortus sui legitimi
literas et sclopetum ad aerarium civile reddidit
quapropter de fideiussione et satisfactione eidem

---

[1] Cp. *Scots in Germany*, p. 245.   [2] Sclopetum = a musket.

fideiussioni pro se factae una dum suis fideius-
soribus quietatus est per officium consulare
. . . A.D. 1688.

1687. Ingenuus *Joannes Ines* ex Scotia oriundus ad
fideiussionem spectabilis Jacobi Watson advo-
cati subdelegati et Thomae Ryt (Reid)
mercatoris de producendis ortus sui legitimi
literis intra annum et medium factam post
praestitum fidelitatis . . . iuramentum iuri
civili Posnaniensis per spectabiles dominos . . .
adscriptus est, sclopetum vero circa productionem
literarum ad aerarium civile inferet; actum Sabbatho ante festum S. Fabiani et Sebastiani
Martyrum . . . Reproduxit sufficientes . . .
literas ex Scotia emanatas . . . et sclopetum
ad aerarium publicum intulit[1] . . . A.D.
1691.

1696. Ingenuus *Albertus Watson* de civitate Dondia in
Scotia oriundus ad recommendationes ecorum-
dem quorum supra praestito . . . iuramento
ad ius civitatis Posnaniensis per spectabiles
dominos proconsulem et consules est susceptus,
literas legitimi ortus intra annum producere,
sclopetum, dictum "Flint,"[2] ad aerarium civitatis
intra tres menses importare tenebitur.

1696. Ingenuus *Albertus Rydt* (Reid) de civitate Clac-
manen in Scotia oriundus artis mercatoriae
socius ad recommendationem famatorum Vilhelmi
Watson et Alberti Farquhar,[3] mercatorium
civium Posnaniensium de producendis legitimi

[1] Here follow the same phrases as above.
[2] The word "flint" or "flinte" is German and means musket.
[3] See *Scots in Germany*, p. 247.

ortus sui literis . . . ad ius civitatis Posnaniensis . . . est susceptus. Literas legitimi
ortus intra annum producere, sclopetum dictum
flint ad aerarium civile intra tres menses importare tenebitur . . . Die 27 mensis Octobris
1700, sufficientes literas reproduxit.

1710. Honestam *Robertum Ryth* artis mercatoriae socium
de civitate Klakmanin oriundum in Scotia,
Calvinum, ad recommendationem famatorum
Vilhelmi Watson et Joannis Friderici Fogelsank
mercatorum civium Posnaniensium in consensu
suo debite factam et interpositam proconsul et
consules civitatis Sacra Regiae Majestatis
Poloniae ad ius civile . . . susceperunt
qui solitum fidelitatis ac oboedientiae corporale
iuramentum flexis genibus ad imaginem crucifixi
domini nostri Jesu Christi praestitit, in fundo
civili et non alias mansurus, sclopetum ad
aerarium civile in spatio mensis importaturus
et literas legitimi ortus in spatio unius anni
producturus est . . .

1713. Ingenuum *Guilhelmuni Ferguson* artis mercatoriae
socium de Eaverun (Irvine?) civitate in Scotia
oriundum calvinum ad recommendationem famatorum Guilhelmi Forbes et eiusdem nominis
Thausor, mercatorum civium Posnaniensium
recepto ab eo positis super sacra crucifixe
duobas dexterae manus digitis et flexis genibus
corporali iuramento iuxta articulos solitos
praestito, nobiles et spectabiles domini proconsul et consules . . . ad ius civile eiusque
praerogativas susceperunt, literas legitimi ortus
producturus et duo vasa coriacea[1] in spatio

---

[1] " Leather buckets."

medii anni ad aerarium civile importaturus.
. . . Vasa duo dedit civitati.[1]
This list contains forty-four names of Scotsmen, seven
of them hailing from Edinburgh, nine from Aberdeen,
six from Dundee, two from Culross, two from Clack-
manan, and one each from Newbattle, Carnack, Lasswade,
Montrose, Perth, Irvine and Berwick. The following
place names could not be identified: Trimelendia,
Dupertat, Ouwernensis, Brattellen (Burntisland?)

XVI.

Letter of Captain William Moncrieff to the Magistrates of Danzig. 1577.

GESTRENGE edle ehrveste erbare nahmhaffte grossgünstige Herren! Nach erbietung meiner allezeit gantz
willigen untertänigen dienste wirt sich E. G. günstiglich
wol zu erinnern haben, das ich zu kurtz verschienen (?)
wochen alle die Kriegsleute unter meinen Fahnen aus den
Niederlanden auff mein eigen Unkosten unnd Zehrung bis
anhero dieser gutten Stadt Danzigk zum besten kegens
ihren feind zu dienen gebracht. Nun hab ich meines
eigenen geldes der Unkosten, Zehrung und Fracht halber
mehr dan inn die 600 Thaler auszgegeben, wodurch ich
denn auch zu Holschenore zu Dennemarken meine besten
Kleider versetzen habe müssen. Und ob ich nun wol bei
E. G. umb erstadtung solcher Unkosten anngehalten unnd
gebetten, habe ich derhalben den Bescheidt bekommen,
das ich alle unnd jede Unkosten so auff gemelten Kriegs-
volk unter meinen Fahnen gewendet, schrifftlich auffsetzen
unnd übergeben soll. Darauff mir alsdann was billich
sein würde auch mir gegeben werden sollte. Dass ich

---

[1] Compare with this list *Scots in Germany*, p. 54 f.   *Kgl. St. Archiv*,
Posen.

aber alle und jede Persehlle (?) der gemelten ausgaben
unnd auffgewandten Unkosten so klarlich unnd schrifftlich
auffsetzen unnd übergeben sollte, wie dieselbe geschehen,
ist mir zu thuende unmöglich, den ich deshalb keine
Register gehalten. Derohalben stelle ich solches Allesz
der 600 Thaler halber E. G. unnd einem ehrbarn hoch-
weisen Rath zur rechtlichen Erkenntnusz verhoffende
E. G. werden mir was billig und recht seyn wirdt hierauff
zu erkennen geben unnd zustellen. Damit ich auch
alsdan wol zufrieden sein will. Hierauf E. G. günstige
Antwort erwarttende. . . .

Dienstwilligst,

WILHELM MONCRIEFF,

Captain, der geburt aus Schottland.

XVII

Letter from the Magistrates of Edinburgh to Danzig,
April 6th, 1605.

UNIVERSIS et singulis cujuscunque dignitatis gradus et
conditionis fuerint pertinentium literarum notitiam habituris Nos Praefectus Ballivi et Consules Regiae Civitatis
Edinburgensis in Regno Scocie Salutem in Domino sempiternam. Vestris Prudentiis notum testatumque facimus
hodierno die coram nobis comparuisse Nobilem Margaretam de Monro defuncti non ita pridem Generosi
Alexandri Ruthven militum Praefecti viduam et nobis
exposuisse quemadmodum praefectus Alexander Ruthven
quondam ejus maritus bona ejus omnia tum mobilia quam
immobilia in variis expeditionibus Polonicis et Sueticis
impenderit ita ut eo vita functo in militia Serenissimi
Regis Poloniae et Suetiae jam parum ei suppetat ad se

cum familia et orphanis liberis tuendam solamque spem
secundum Deum in liberalitate Serenissimi Sigismundi
Tertii, Poloniae Regis, positam habere cujus vices in
bello regeus Illustrissimus Dominus Johannes Zamoscius,
supremus Poloniae Cancellarius et Capitanus Generalis
mortem pro rege in oppugnatione Volmeriensi oppetenti
praefato Alexandro Ruthven ejus marito effecturum se
addixit si quid ei humanitus illo in bello contigerit ut
Regia Majestas Poloniae liberaliter uxori et liberis de
omnibus ad vivendum necessariis provideret ideoque cum
ipsa rei familiaris angustia aliisque urgentibus negotiis
impedita tantum viae conficere non posset ut Sacram
Majestatem Poloniae et ejus vicarium generalem Dominum Johannem Zamoscium appellet, omnibus melioribus
modo, via forma et jure quibus melius et efficacius potuit
et debuit, potestve aut debet, fecisse et constituisse solemniter ordinasse et in mandatis dedisse prout harum literarum nostrarum tenore facit constituit solemniter ordinat
et in mandatis dat Generoso Guilelmo Brussio, ut ejus
nomine tam Serenissimum Poloniae regem quam Illustris-
simum Cancellarium adeat et compellat ut ei juxta fidem
publice datam prospicere benigne dignentur atque eum
ejus mandatarium et plenipotentem tam in hoc negotio
quam in omnibus actionibus persecutionibus et petitionibus
ad defunctum quondam maritum spectantibus, ita tamen
ut transigere de bonis aut pensionibus quibuscunque non
possit nisi approbantibus et consentientibus vel Georgio
Smyth aurifice vel Georgio Hepburne mercatore, civibus
Gedanensibus vel utroque si utriusque copia fuerit, vel
eorum alterutro, ambos enim curatores deligit eisque cum
suo mandatario praefato Georgio Brussio commodum
potestatem quatenus de jure potest, concedit res quaslibet
ad se vel defunctum maritum spectantes administrare
debita exigere apochas dare omnia agere quae ipsa posset

si praesens adesset, tutrix liberorum defuncti saepe nomi-
nati mariti; ratum autem gratum firmum et stabile id
omne se habiturum quod a dictis suis mandatariis vel eorum
majore parte in premissis rite gestum fuerit Nobis stipu-
lantibus sancte et fideliter promisisse sub poena et obli-
gatione omnium bonorum suorum mobilium et immobilium
presentium et futurorum. In quorum omnium et singulorum fidem et testimonium praemissorum his literis nostris
per Alexandrum Guthrie primarium nostrum scribam
sigillum Civitatis appendi curavimus. Datum Edinb.
sexto Aprili millesimo sexcentesimo quinto.

XVIII.

*Letter of the Elector of Brandenburg and Duke of Prussia
to the Revd. Schlemüller in Königsberg.*

EHRWÜRDIGE wird es annoch im Gedächtnus vor-
schweben wie das ohngefähr vor zweien oder dreien Jahren
einige von der Schottländischen Nation allhier in ihren
Häusern Privatzusammenkunft mit Predigen gehalten,
darwider aber die von den Städten unter dem Namen
irriger und verbotener Lehre gar hart geredet und umb
Verbietung dergleichen verdächtigen conventiculn bei
der Churfürstlichen Regierung in Unterthänigkeit eifrigst
gebeten. Als wir nun hierauf in solche heimliche
Zusammenkunft inquiriren lassen und befunden, dass ein
Schottländischer Exulant von reiner Lehre und gutem
Wandel der reformirten Religion zugethan gute freunde
zu ersuchen anhero gekommen wäre und aber wegen des
entzwischen eingefallenen Seekrieges zwischen Engeland
und Holland in sein Vaterland nicht sicher zurückreisen
konnte, unterdess aber sein Brot allhier nicht gerne

müssig essen und demnachen die Gelegenheit hiesigen
seinen Landsleuten in ihrer Muttersprache Gottes Wort
predigen wollte, da haben wir den Argwohn und Klagen
zu benehmen und diesem in so christlichen Beginnen zu
willfahren ad tempus gnädigst verstattet, das nach verrich-
tetem Sonntäglichen Gottesdienst der Reformirten Gem-
einde sie in dem Churfürstlichen Kirchensaal im Schloss
vorerwähntes Exercitium öffentlich vortsetzen möchten.
Wann wir aber eben jetzund kurtz für unserer Abreise
nicht ohne Befrembden von widrigem Theil vernehmen
müssen, wie das dennoch gedachte Schottländer wider
unsern Zulass die privat Versammlung zu continuiren
sich unterstehen, und auch in der Lehre etwas vorlauffe
. . . das nicht allerdings richtig sei und das deswegen
auf vorstehendem Landtag ein gross Gravamen gemacht
werden soll, welches in Zeiten zu verhindern hochnötig,
als ist an Ew. Ehrwürden Unser gnädiges Begehren
hiemit diesen Leuten in unserm Nahmen auzudeuten das
weil nunmehr der Landtag herzunahet und zu Verlust
durch dieses von uns zugelassene Werk Anlass zu geben
wir billiges Bedenken tragen, Sie beide das publicum
und privatum religionis exercitium in Schottländischer
Sprache einstellen sollen; dafern sie aber hernachmals
neben den Churfürstlichen Hofpredigern einen dritten in
ihrer Sprache zu halten gedenken, können sie bei Seiner
Churfürstlichen Durchlaucht selben darumb in Unterthänigkeit auhalten wie wir dann nicht zweifeln Seine
Churfürstliche Durchlaucht werden ihnen dergleichen
petitio gnädigst deferiren.

Königsberg d. 3tten April 1668.[1]

[1] *Kgl. St. Archiv*, Königsberg.

XIX.

Letter of the General Assembly of the Church of Scotland to the Synod of the Reformed Church in Lithuania.

REVERENDISSIMI et carissimi Fratres,

Vir reverendus Boguslaus Kopyewicz Verbi Divini apud Vilnensis Minister cum hic esset anno Decimo octavo supra Millesimum septingentesimum a Reformatis ecclesiis Magni Ducatus Lithuaniae delegatus suis ipse oculis testatum habebat quanta miseratione fratrum suorum, puriorem in vestra gente religionem profitentium, res afflictae literis vestris ab eo coram traditis commemoratae Ecclesiam Scoticanam nationalem tum Synodum agentem affecerint, quantoque ea studio suis commendarit ut pecuniis corrogandis eorum inopia subveniretur. Eventus autem satis docuit populares nostros eodem plane modo erga vos quo Synodus nationalis animatos fuisse. Caeterum eam omnem pecuniam ad vos ex praescripto vestro praeferendam curavimus praeter novem libras duosque asses monetae Brittanicae quam quidem summulam nupera nostra Synodus nationalis tanti esse non rata quae ad vos mitteretur, juveni Polono Samueli Chien sacrae Theologiae in Academia Edinburgensi operam navanti donandam existimavit. Porro ut novo documento constaret eandem Synodi Nostrae Nationalis erga vos manere benevolentiam, animumque ad beatissimi nostri Redemptoris regnum promovendum et ad fratres nostros ejusdem Reformatae religionis communione nobis conjunctos, quantum in se est, ope sublevandos promptissimum, ea mihi negotium dedit ut vobis eorum nomine significarem se literis vestris morem gerentes, Decreto suo—cujus exemplar et una missum est, duobus studiosis vestroque testimonio sibi commendandis in Academia Edinburgensi alendis educandisque providisse.

Speramus autem hoc Synodi nostri propositum et vobis gratum novoque simul indicio futurum, quantopere Synodo vestrae Lithuaniensi ipsa studeat quamque sincero amore Ecclesia nostra fratres suos veram in vestra gente Christi doctrinam amplexos prosequatur.

Mihi vero gratissimum accidit quod Nostra Synodus per literas meas haec vobiscum communicari voluerit, unde et ampla datur occasio testandi quanta sim vobis animi propensione.

Reverendissimi et charissimi fratres
Summo obsequio et fraterna dilectione elevinctissimus
sic subscribitur

GULIELMUS MITCHELL, Moderator.

17th May, 1722.

(Verum exemplar Epist. ab Eccles. Scoticana ad Synod. Reform. Lithuaniensem.)

XX.

The Church Records of St Peter, and Paul, and of St Elisabeth at Danzig.

Marriage Register.

1573. Jacob Burgiss, marries Anne, Simon Lang's widow.
1574. Jacob Hardy.
1577. Simon Ritch.
   ,,   Hans Crockett.
1578. Hans Dunckel (Duncan).
   ,,   Al. Gray.
   ,,   C. Sinclair.
1579. Andr. Marshall.
   ,,   M. Nickell.
   ,,   Andr. Mutter.

1579. C. Alanth.
1582. U. Mitzell.
  ,,   P. Dennis.
  ,,   Jacob Ross.
1583. M. Burgiss.
1584. Th. Schotte.
1585. Simon, Generosi Domini Scoti, working man, and
      Helen of Copenhagen. The marriage took
      place in Heinrich Steffens' house in the large
      room of Mr Scott.
1586. Hans Stodertt
1593. Gregor Brun.
1595. Math. Black.
1600. Al. Steen.
1601. Thomas Schotte.[1]
1606. B. Rowell.
1608. A. Burnet.
  ,,   Hans Stewert.
1609. Andr. Anderson.
1615. Dan. Lofson (Lawson).
1620. Jacob Hamilton.
1624. M. Withorn and Joanna Baillie.
* ,,   Jacob Scot and Maria Nun.
  ,,   Jacob Morriss.
* ,,   W. Chalmer and Maria Leslie.
1629. Hans Morton and Maria Robertson.
  ,,   Jacob Meldrum and Christina Balfour.
1631. Wilhelm Balfour and Anna Pilgram.
  ,,   Dan. Ramsay and Sarah Nisbett.
1632. Nicl. Duget.
*1633. Jas. Law and Anne, widow of the late Hans Hay.
* ,,   Hans Kylow, a Scot, and Susanna, the widow of
      H. Dalen.

[1] Probably not the family name.

*1633 Will Simson, a soldier, and Elis. Moritz (Morriss).

* ,, Jac. Messun (Mason), from Edinburgh, and E. D. Warthurn (?).

* ,, Jac. Black and Anna Kamer (Chalmer) or (Chambers).

*1634. Peter Wilson and the widow of the late Robt. Olifant in Denmark.

* ,, Martin Dennis and Maria Matthis.

* ,, Will. Armack.

* ,, Will. Davis and Susan, widow of Glaser.

1634. Jacob Littlejohn, His Majesty's of Poland servant, and Barbara Edwards.

,, Francis Gordon, H.M. the King of Great Britain's Resident and Privy Councillor, and Anna Wegner, Apothecary to the King of Poland.

1635. Thos. Philipp and Hans Kant's daughter.

,, Alex. Stuart.

,, Alex. Donaltson.

,, Geo. Dempster and Elis. Stephen.

1636. Adam Law and Anna Nisbett.

,, Laurence Grohn and the "virtuous virgin Christina, legitimate daughter of the late Robt. Marshall, burgess of Aberdeen."

*1636. Alb. Kocherin (Cochrane) and the daughter of the late Griffith at Aberdeen.

* ,, Thos. Blackhall and Hans Morris's daughter.

1636. The Honourable W. Balfuhr and Maria von Hoffen.

,, Thos. Gellentin.

*1637. Hans Tuchal (Dougal).

1637. Jac. Gurley, burgess of Thorn, and Anna Norry.

* ,, Alb. Bartels, a glover, and El. Muttray, from Aberdeen.

,, Geo. Innes and Leonore Wicherling.

*1637. Jac. Kelly from Aberdeen.

*   „   Alex. Donaldson.

*   „   Robt. Wilson.

*   „   J. Withon.

*   „   A. Morris and Anna Leons (Lyon) from Edinburgh.

   1638. Andr. Law.

     „   Thos. Smart and Anne Wolson.

   1639. Bruin.

     „   Alex. Reilly and Abigail Thin.

   1640. Gilbt. Lonsdale and Barbara Schmidt.

*   „   Hans Karkettle and Anna Saunders.

*   „   Alex. Hamilton.

*   „   H. Robertson and the daughter of the late J. Horne in Aberdeen.

*   „   Alex. Cranston.

*   „   Will. Patton.

*   „   Hans Wricht and Anna, daughter of the late W. Lichthon.

*   „   J. Duncan.

     „   Gabriel Maxwell.

     „   Richard Lewis, the Honourable " Administrator " of the Royal Treasury and Governor of Marienburg.[1]

   1641. Andreas Peacock and Anna Maria Morrisson.

     „   John Collins.

     „   Geo. Sterling and Sara Thin.

     „   Anth. Bidney and Dan. Patterson's daughter.

     „   Will. Anderson and Mary Warden.

*1645. Jacob Crichton.

*   „   Andr. Bell.

[1] Possibly of the Lewis of Manor (Peeblesshire) family, members of which are known to have emigrated to Russia and Poland in the XVIth Century.

*1646. Will. Forbes and Widmann's widow.
   ,,   And. Skott.
*1647. Alex. Bernett.
* ,,   Alex. Nairn, a lieutenant, and J. Unwin's widow.
*1648. David Thomson from Leith.
* ,,   Robt. Brown.
*1651. W. Smith.
* ,,   R. Turner.
* ,,   H. Sander and J. Davidson's widow.
*1654. Jacob Ramsay, a Scottish captain, and Maria Gall.
* ,,   John Wood and Maria Robbertzon.
*1655. The Honourable Franciscus Gordon and Margaretha, daughter of the late James Porteous, minister in Scotland.[1]
*1662. Jacob Anderson.
*1667. John Dew.
*1668. Geo. Lawder.
*1669. G. Hutchinson.
*1670. W. Halyburton.
* ,,   D. Nichols and Anna Merivale.
*1672. W. Halyburton.[2]
*1673. Al. Karkettel.
*1676. J. Gourlay.
* ,,   J. Davidson.
*1677. Geo. Nisbett and Miss Littlejohn.
*1696. Peter Wobster.
*1697. Robt. Mill.
*1699. David Hervie.[3]

---

[1] His second wife.

[2] There seem to have been two W. Halyburtons, unless the first wife died very soon.

[3] Those marked * were married in St Elisabeth, the second Presbyterian Church at Danzig.

XXI.

List of Names in the Baptismal Register.[1]

*1573. M. Orem.
* „ A. Ross.
*1583. A. Brun.

1593-95.
{ Wolson.
Marlowe.
Law.
Tamson.

Rennie.
Fuller.
Hunter.
1599. Littlejohn.
Kock.
Stein.
Williamson.
Allan.
Schott.
Ballentine.
A. Malloy.
Th. Forbes.
Tamson.
Skoda.
Mitchell.
Fergus.
Klerk.
1614. Tsapman.
*1621. Patterson.
1622. Masterton.

[1] In most cases the name of the father only has been given. The records are careful to add the names of the godfathers and godmothers (compatres), as also the donations received for the Poor-Box.

*1624. Achterlony.

*   ,,   P. Wilson, mother Chr. Wadrup.

*   ,,   A. Dunbar.

*   ,,   Reinhold Porteous' son Reinholt.

*   ,,   H. Ingram.

*   ,,   W. Mubree (Mowbray).

*   ,,   Th. Morton.

*   ,,   D. Bell.

*   ,,   J. Crichton.

*1625. David Mauritz (Morriss).

       Patterson.

       Ray.

       Bally (Baillie).

       Hewell.

       Muttreich (Muttray).

       Gore.

       Allan.

       Pilgram.

       Prinsloe (?).

       Lamb.

       Morton.

       Jac. Meldrum.

       Duncan.

       B. Hamilton.

1631. H. Tamson.

1632. D. Biel.

1633. W. Balfuhr's son William.

       Adam Wood.

       J. Morris.

       Robertson.

       W. Ramsay.

       Hunt

       D. Dempster.

       Gillis.

Smart.

1637. W. Balfuhr's son Theodor.

Wallis.

Bishop.

A Barclay, a Colonel.

Henderson.

Al. Rennie.

H. Strachan.

David Mutro.

1639. W. Balfuhr's daughter Maria

1639. John Cochrom.

Walker.

1640. Dickson.

,,   A. Grieve.

,,   Al. Wobster.

,,   J. Dougal.

,,   Davis.

,,   Lonsdale.

1641. Woltzon.

,,   W. Balfour's son Jacob.

,,   D. Machomtosh.

,,   D. Moritz.

,,   A. Pilgram.

,,   P. Masterton.

XXII.

Extracts from the Burial Registers in the Records of St Peter and Paul's Church at Danzig (1631-1681).

BURIED in *St Mary's*, the principal Church of Danzig, called *Marienkirche* :—

George Pattersen (1602).

Thomas Demster, Aug. 5, 1631

Jacob Black, 1635.
Th. Burnett,
Adelgunda Wright, 1708.
Tho. Gellatlay (Gellentin), 1665.

Buried in *St Peter and Paul's* Church :—

Peter Dunbar(t), 1657.
Jacob Gourlay's wife, 1669.
G. Krukshank's wife, 1671.
Will. Clark, 1678.
Robt. Tevendale, 1686.
Thomas Wolworth, 1688.
David Wolworth, 1689.
Alex. Tamson, 1689.
Alex. Aidy and family, 1690.
Thos. Murray and family, 1690.
Peter Forbes and family, 1686.
Dan Davisson and family, 1685.
Jacob Carmichael and family, 1693.
Thos. Marshall and family, 1692.
Buchan and family, 1698.
John Clerk and family, 1700.
Jacob Gourlay and family, 1706.
Thos. Leslie and family, 1712.
W. Robertson and family, 1723.
G. Moir and family, 1715.
Jacob Boyd, 1726.
A. Paip and family, 1727.
John Farquhar and family, 1727.
Alex. Ramsay, 1731.
W. Forret and family, 1730.
Thos. Coutts and family, 1737.
A. Turner and family, 1736.
J. Gibson and family, 1746.

A. Kabrun and family, 1751.

A. Ross and family, 1765.

There are also Burnetts, Bennets, Elliots, Scotts, Setons and Thomsons buried there.

Buried in *St Elisabeth* :—

Alex. Collen, 1631.

Elis. Futthy (?), "eine schottische Hausmutter," 1631.

Hans Gieche (Geikie), from Glasgow, 1635.

Peter Metland, from Aberdeen, 1635.

Gilbert Edgear, from Aberdeen, 1635.

John Bailie, 1635.

Elis. Anne Constapple, 1635.

Peter Laudien, 1636.

Alex. Marschel.

George Mortimer.

Peter Irwing.

Chr. Sutton, a glover, 1638.

Elis. Robertson, 1639.

Hans Crafford, 1640.

Elis. Doncan, Alex. Cranston's wife, 1640.

Edward Kincaid, late Army Chaplain in the army of General Baner, 1641.

G. Hutcheson, 1641.

Alex. Rowy, 1642.

Jacob Ross, 1643.

Jacob Donaldson, 1643.

Alex. Watson, a Scottish youth, who received a shot wound on the walls of Schöneck, 1643.

Elis. Colvin, Ramsay's widow, 1643.

Jacob Ross, late Lieutenant and Innkeeper.

B. Wilson.

Nich. Morris.

J. Jack, a Scottish youth, 1644.

Adam Watt, 1645.

Chr. Muttreich, W. Law's wife, 1646.

Alb. Stevenson, 1646.

Andr. Wilson.

C. Merivale, 1648.

Hans Moll, 1650.

D. Robertson's wife, 1652.

W. Ramsay's wife, 1652.

Johann Cant, a Scottish Lieutenant, who died in passing through this town, 1652.

R. Meking (?) , 1653.

Jacob Crichton, 1653.

Agneta Donaldson, 1653.

Hans Allen, 1654.

Alex. Norry, ninety-three years old, 1656.

Jacob Norry, 1658.

Gretrud Uphagen, Lieutenant Jacob Stuart's wife.

Bl. Hamilton, 1659.

P. Stewart, 1660.

N. Lofson, 1661.

P. Ramsay, 1664.

Mary Dawson, 1664.

Anne Wadrup, 1665.

Barbara Gourlay, 1669.

W. Halyburton's wife, 1672.

W. Barclay, 1673.

H. Brun, 1680.

Buried in *St Johann's* :—

William Ramsay, 1612.

Thomas Bisset, 1643.

David Heggie, burgess and merchant.

Buried *elsewhere* :—

Daniel Beer, in the churchyard of St Barbara.

Alex. Vergiss, in the churchyard of Corpus Christi (Fronleichnam).

Cath. Watson, called the "Scotch Catherine," in the Hospital.

Maria MacLean, from Duart in Mull, 1806, in the churchyard of St Salvator.

Ramsay, St Salvator's churchyard.

Alex. Gibsone, in the churchyard of Corpus Christi, 1836.

Brothers Mackensen(zie), 1768, in the same place.

XXIII.

Schotte and Schottland.

BESIDES the name Schott or Schotte, which came to signify throughout the German Empire a pedlar, and its derivations as "Schottenkram," "Schottenhandel," "Schottenpfaffe," "Schottenfrau," we have quite a number of traces of the old immigrants in local topography. There is a village called "Schottland" in the district of Lauenburg, in Pomerania, with eighty-four inhabitants and ten houses; another Schottland in the Danzig lowlands in Western Prussia, numbering some 200 souls; a kirchdorf (village with a church), "Schottland," in the district of Bromberg in Posen, also numbering about 200 inhabitants. A so-called Schottenkolonie exists near Neuhausen, in the district of Königsberg, Eastern Prussia. There are besides three so-called "Schottenkrüge" = Scotch inns, one four miles distant from Marienburg, in the Danzig district, another in the district of Marienwerder, a third near the city of Culm, in Western Prussia. What the precise connection of these inns with the Scots was, whether they were at one time in possession of Scotsmen, or because they were placed in a district where many Scots lived, or finally, because they were much frequented by the Scots—and who would deny the latter eventuality? —it would be difficult to say. They are there, at any rate, witnesses of a dim past, when the county was flooded by Scottish traders.

There was also a "Schottengang" = "Scottish lane," at Danzig,[1] which already boasted of an Alt-and Neu-Schottland, as we have seen.

The small town of "Schotten," in Hesse, however, has nothing to do with the Caledonian Scot or the Scottish trader of the XVIth and XVIIth Centuries. It was originally called "Zu den Schotten" = "at the Scots," and owes its existence and church to the labours of Scoto-Irish missionaries. There were no less than nine such "Schottenkirchen" in Mayence and Upper Hessia, all of them founded in the ninth or tenth century, and dependent on Straszburg, where Florens, an Irish hermit, had been elected a bishop in the year 679.

The church at "Schotten" is traditionally connected with two Irish royal ladies, daughters of Brian Boru, whose names are variously given as Alcmudis and Dicmudis, or Rosamund and Dicmudis. After the disastrous battle of Clontarf in 1014 they fled and devoted themselves, like so many royal ladies at the time, to church and missionary work on the Continent.

This tradition receives a support from two very ancient gilt busts which are to this day preserved in the vestry of the church at Schotten. They represent two ladies with flowing hair; one of them has a crown on her head,

---

[1] *Duisburg, Versuch einer historisch topographischen Beschreibung Danzigs,* i. 362.

the other a wreath of flowers. The work is attributed by archæologists to the eleventh century. There was also a document found in the ball on the church spire, dating from the latter half of the fourteenth century. It says: "In the year of our Lord 1015, in the reign of the king called the Lame,[1] two sisters, natives of Scotland, one of whom was called Rosamunda, the other Dicmudis, commenced the building of this town and of our first Schotten kirche."[2] In connection with this question it must always be remembered that the Teutonic word Scot occurs in Germany as a man's name long before surnames derived from nationalities were thought of. At least so Foerstemann in his "Altdeutsche Namensbuch" assures us when speaking of the occurrence of that name in the Book of the Brotherhood of St Peter at Salzburg.[3]

SUPPLEMENT.

Scots at Ratisbon.

Whilst the present volume was in the press the following list of Scotsmen acquiring citizenship at Ratisbon in the fifteenth and sixteenth centuries reached us.

Considering it an important document, and one that raises the curious question of Scottish settlements in those cities of Middle and Southern Germany, where the famous Schottenklöster already existed and probably exercised an attraction for a large contingent of Scottish trading and lay immigrants as well, we had the choice of either burying it in some of the daily papers or in one of the antiquarian monthlies, which, formally speaking, would have been

---

[1] Henry II., Emperor of Germany, 1002-1024.

[2] See Ph. Heber, *Die neun vormaligen Schottenkirchen in Mainz und in Oberhessen.* Darmstadt, 1860, p. 137 f.

[3] See R. Ferguson, *Surnames as a Science*, p. 7.

J. ASLOAN

Lord Abbot of Würzburg, 1641

correct, or of tacking it on to a book from which the southern parts of Germany are excluded.

In preferring the latter irregular mode of proceeding, our excuse is the intimate connection of the two volumes on the Scots in Germany and the wish to let the reader have all available information on the subject up to the present date.

We therefore publish the list as it reaches us, asking the kind reader mentally to transfer it to its proper place, which would have been the Appendix of our first volume on the Scots in Germany.

One characteristic fact of the Scottish settlers in Ratisbon is, that none of them were vagrant Scots. The Scottish pedlar does either not occur at all or he is included in the general name of " Abenteurer " = adventurer, of whom there is mention on several occasions, for instance, in 1460, 1461, 1462, 1467, and frequently afterwards. Curious also is the admission of two Scotswomen to the citizenship of Ratisbon. The first on the list is Hannes Tung (John Young), 1484, with the addition of "a Scot swore the civil oath." Each of the following names occurs with the addition " Schott " = a Scot:—

    1493. Straichin (Strachan), Alexander.
    1495. Alexander (without family name).[1]
    1498. Flemyng, Wilhelm.
    1504. Guttler (?), Rubrecht.
      ,,   Strang, Reichart (Richard).
    1506. Königerm (Cunningham), Alexander.
    1508. Kochever (rer), (Cochrane), Jacob.
      ,,   Small, Andreas.
      ,,   Anndersi (Anderson), Reichart.
      ,,   Metland (Maitland), Hans.

[1] Or without Christian name, according to the word Alexander being taken as a surname or not.

1509. Lynndefeur (?), Alexander.

1510. Tampson, Wilhelm "der Klain" ("the small").

1511. Jung (Young), Simon.

  „ Rebischam (Robinson)?), Wilhelm "von Edenburg."

  „ Lynns, Wilhalm.

1512. Dubles (Douglas), Linhart (Leonard).

1513. Tumsen (Thomson), Hanns (maister = master of the craft).

1514. Wald, Thomas.

  „ Hubm (?), Ulrich.

1515. Abernit (Abernethy), Heinrich.

1516. Werckler (Farquhar?), Andreas.

  „ Goldstain, Jacob.

1518. Dewesen (Davison), Wilhalm.

  „ Strang, Thomas.

1520. Porthus (Porteous), Karl.

1522. Daxenpel (Dalrymple?), Alexander.

  „ Law, David.

1525. Huttung (Hutton), Andre.

1527. Maffen, Wilhalm.

1528. Ranol (Ranald), Hans.

  „ Bartleme, Brigitta, "a Scotswoman."

1530. Suderlandt (Sutherland), Alexander.

  „ Herwart, Albrecht.

  „ Lind, Agnes, "a Scotswoman."

1531. Currawr (Crafford), Hans.

  „ Eglinthon, Hans.

1532. Kochman, Jacob.

  „ Schwartza, Wilhalm (probably "Black").

1533. Praun (Brown), Andre.

  „ Pock or Pack (?), Hans.

1534. Mattissun, Hans.

1536. Kray (?), Wilhalm.
1538. Willison (Williamson), Albrecht.
  „   Schmidt (Smith), Wilhalm.
  „   Walker (?), Wilhalm.
1540. Demet (?), Wilhalm.
      Raberzon (Robertson), Thomas.
      Lorn, Davit.
1542. Wach (Waugh), Hans.
1543. Andersson, Hans.
1548. Englenthon, "a Scotswoman."
1559. Thene (Tain or Thin?), Wilhalm.

Among those that were married are :—

1548. Dirscham, Paulus (?).
1564. Pirckenson (Parkinson?), Jacob.
  „   Arta (?), Hans.
  „   Matisson, Hans.   (See above.)
1566. Gier (Grier?), Hans.
  „   Thene, Wilhalm.
1575. Niclason (Nicholson), David.
1576. Gudel (?), Thoman.
1577. Zarrer, Ott (?).[1]

[1] Cp. *Stadt Archiv*, Regensburg. Politica iii., 1, 117. **2**, 31, 37, 58.
3, 23, 27, 37, 46, 49, 53, 59, 65, 66, 71, 73, 77, 89, 93, 110 bis., 121.
4, 8, 12, 29, 43, 46 bis., 48, 55, 59, 69, 74, 82 bis., 91, 97, 105 bis.
106, 117, 119 bis., 129, 142.   **57**, 19, 111, 124, 126, 129 bis., 135,
160, 181, 189, 190.   **58**, 10 bis., 53 bis., 157.   **59**, 1, 14. Politica, i.,
7, 232 ff. ; i., 15, 17, 143, 185.

A SELECTION OF COATS-OF-ARMS OF SCOTTISH-GERMAN FAMILIES

GEO. BARCLAY   WILLIAM FORRET   DANIEL DAVIDSON

WILLIAM CLARCK   VON ROBERTSON   STODDART

VIRTUTIS · GLORIA · MERCES

Altera Merces.

G. BUCHAN   MACLEAN   KABRUHN (COCKBURN)

WILLIAM BROWN

GOURLAY

STODDERT

MACKENSIEN

VON JOHNSTON

P. DUNBAR

MOIR

CARMICHAELL

PETER FORBES

TURNER   BURNETT   MURRAY

GELLATLIE   SPALDING   RUPSOHN

GIBSONE   RAMSAY   YEFFERIES (JEFFREY)

WRICHT

ROSS

VON SIMPSON

V. DAVIDSON

BROWN

MACLEAN

LESLIE

INDEX.

TURNBULL AND SPEARS, PRINTERS, EDINBURGH.

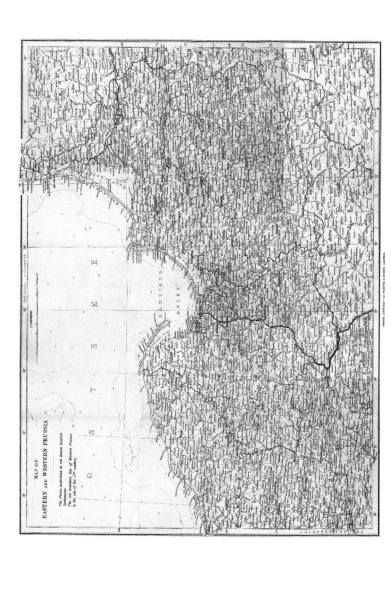

MAP OF
EASTERN AND WESTERN PRUSSIA

The Places underlined in red denote Scottish
Settlements.
The red boundary line of Western Prussia
is the one of the 17th century.

GEOGR. ANSTALT VON WAGNER & DEBES, LEIPZIG

Printed in Great Britain
by Amazon

66310709R00159